CHRISTOPHER MORLEY'S NEW YORK

I had a queer thought the other day, that the two subjects most worth thinking about, for me, are Shakespeare and New York City.

Internal Revenue

CHRISTOPHER MORLEY'S NEW YORK

ILLUSTRATED

BY

WALTER JACK DUNCAN

FORDHAM UNIVERSITY PRESS

NEW YORK

LC 88-81015
ISBN 0-8232-1214-9

Printed in the United States of America

But who will write me the book about New York that I desire? The more I think about it, the more astonished I am that no one attempts it. I don't mean a novel. I would not admit any plot or woven tissue of story to come between the reader and my royal heroine, the City herself. Not to be a coward, should I try to write it myself? It is my secret dream; but, better, it should be written by some sturdy rogue of a bachelor, footfree, living in the very heart of the uproar. Some fellow with a taste and nuance for the vulgar and vivid; a consort of both parsons and bootleggers; a *Beggar's Opera* kind of rascal. . . . Who is the man who will write me the book I crave—that vulgar, jocund, carnal, beautiful, rueful book!

"A Call for the Author,"
The Powder of Sympathy

A NOTE ON SOURCES

Each of the essays concludes with a bracketed code, showing the book from which the essay has been taken. These codes are as follows:

CMB	*Christopher Morley's Briefcase* (1936)
IB	*The Ironing Board* (1949)
IR	*Internal Revenue* (1933)
ODE	*Off the Deep End* (1928)
P	*Pipefuls* (1921)
PP	*Plum Pudding* (1923)
PS	*The Powder of Sympathy* (1923)
RS	*The Romany Stain* (1926)
Sg	*Shandygaff* (1921)
Sl	*Streamlines* (1936)

CONTENTS

THE THREE HOURS FOR LUNCH CLUB

SUBURBAN LIFE IN ROSLYN

NEW YORK

FLAMMANTIA MOENIA DEMIMUNDI

(To A. P. Herbert)

You saw Manhattan rising from the sea
And on the clear transparence of her sky
That spiring profile glitter to the sun.
Perhaps I can imagine what you thought:
Why, no one told me it would be like this,
So beautiful, so proud!

One cannot learn about a foreign land
Except by seeing her. So go your ways
Watching and harking in her tall, tall streets,
Alternately aghast, amused, amazed.
See how the bright, thin light that is her own
Shifts daylong on her terraces and cliffs
In opal tints; at dusk the fallen sun
A bonfire at the foot of crosstown streets.
Panelling night with wainscotry of gold,
She ends each day in gusts of phœnix fire—
The flaming ramparts of her demi-world!

Mark all these things: her generous reckless moods,
Proud, spendthrift, swift, assured, and terrible;
And make interpretation of your own.
But just one *caveat*:
She is not always merely what she seems:
I'd like to have you see her as I do—
The greatest unwrit poem in the world.

Parsons' Pleasure (1923)

O RARE CHRIS MORLEY

William S. Hall

One evening in June 1930 the phone rang in my apartment on Lexington Avenue and at the other end was the voice of John R. Fraser, book publisher. Fraser, who had managed to boss me around ever since our teen-age days, said, "Don't go out, I'm bringing over a friend." That meant I didn't go out, and I'm glad I didn't, for in a short while the bell rang and up the stairs trudged Fraser with a well-built chap after him.

"Meet Christopher Morley."

For some time I had collected Morley first editions, and he lost no time in spotting them; neither did he lose any time in signing his name, with comments, in some of them. And from that time on we were close friends.

Christopher Morley was born on May 5, 1890 at Haverford, Pennsylvania. He was graduated in 1910 from Haverford College, where his father was Professor of Mathematics, and spent the next three years studying at Oxford University on a Rhodes Scholarship. His first book, a collection of verse entitled *The Eighth Sin*, was published by Blackwell's while he was still at Oxford, and thereafter hardly a year went by without the publication of another of his works—a total of some fifty books embracing poetry, drama, essays, and fiction.

Not only was Morley the "onlie begetter" of The Baker Street Irregulars, as we all very well know; he was also the founder of the Three-Hours-for-Lunch Club and its immediate successor, the Grillparzer Club. His idea also was that of the emigration of the theatre to the shores of Hoboken for the staging of lusty, antique melodrama and the lowering of box office prices for seats. He was one of the founders of *The Saturday Review of Literature* (now *The Saturday Review*), and for almost thirty years, from 1926 to 1954, he served as one of the judges of the Book-of-the-Month Club. To all these enterprises, if we may call them that, he contributed his unbounded enthusiasm, his wit, and his never-ending all-round good humor. In the meantime, for many of these years, he conducted "The Bowling Green" column in *The Saturday Review* and later in the same paper his column entitled "Trade Winds," and it was through "The Bowling Green" that the world first became aware of the existence of a curious organization called The Baker Street Irregulars.

No man ever loved literature and authors, dead and living, more than Chris Morley did. His oft-quoted favorites were Chaucer, Shakespeare, Boswell and Sam Johnson, Lamb, Stevenson, Hazlitt, Saki (H. H. Munro), Conrad, Max Beerbohm, Winston Churchill, and, perhaps most quoted of all,

Arthur Conan Doyle, through the tart observations of Sherlock Holmes. Close author–friends of his whom he saw on every possible occasion were Don Marquis, Felix Riesenberg, and Capt. David Bone. To name only a few of his warm friends and admirers in other fields would take more space than has been accorded me; but their names and appropriate comments are recorded in a battered and wine-stained volume entitled *The Plays of Franz Grillparzer* which served as a sort of guest book of the Grillparzer Club.

Morley loved lunches with his friends, and the longer they lasted the better he liked them. He was one of that fast-vanishing breed, a delightful table-talker, and I well remember many of his sallies, particularly those aimed at me: "Bill, don't look so glum; actually, things are much worse than they seem!"

For many years Chris had a workroom up four flights of stairs on the top floor of a building on West 47th Street. To this studio he journeyed about twice a week from his home in Roslyn, Long Island, and the place was pure Morley—books, magazines, newspapers, maps and charts, oil paintings, water-colors, cartoons, unanswered mail and unopened packages—and a bottle, with drinking glasses. As time went on his trips to 47th Street became less frequent, and it was in 1954 that he suffered the first of a series of increasingly shattering apoplectic strokes. These were mercifully ended when death took him away on March 28, 1957 at the age of sixty-six years.

The tributes to Chris in the press were many, and most of them were written with a full sense of what we all had lost. I quote the closing paragraph of one, by Clifton Fadiman, in a memorial pamphlet issued by the Book-of-the-Month Club:

> In Westminster Abbey the small square of marble marking the remains of Shakespeare's great contemporary bears the inscription, "O Rare Ben Jonson." Those who knew Chris Morley can substitute his name for old Ben's and, with a full heart, find the beautiful adjective no less appropriate.

In 1932 Chris wrote a novel which he called *Human Being*. He was that.

[A Guest Editorial, *The Baker Street Journal* (N.S.), 11 No. 3 (September 1961), 131–33; copyright 1961 by The Baker Street Irregulars.]

PUBLISHER'S FOREWORD

CHRISTOPHER DARLINGTON MORLEY (1890–1957) was, for countless readers, *the* American man of letters of his generation. Whether they appeared as newspaper and magazine columns, literary essays, novels, or plays, his writings were eagerly awaited and avidly read. Born in Haverford, Pennsylvania, and raised in Baltimore, he was educated at Haverford College and then, as a Rhodes Scholar, at Oxford. But he spent virtually all the remaining years of his life in the journalistic and literary milieux of New York, with a brief stint as a journalist in Philadelphia.

His salad days were spent as a Doubleday employee in Garden City and in Manhattan, followed by the newspaper years in Manhattan, then in Philadelphia, and back again in Manhattan. Even in those days he seems to have been viewed as something of an anachronism, praising a New York on ground level when the city was manifestly rocketing upward. If he seems now to be quintessentially nostalgic, so be it, and good for him. Good for us, too. He was spoken of in reviews as an Elizabethan, probably in allusion to his gusto in food, drink (even if on occasion it *was* the apple cider of Prohibition), companionship, conversation, and general bonhomie. He was certainly a master of the essay, an art form fallen upon evil days.

What may be little realized is that his journalistic, and therefore in large part his essay-writing, days were over by the mid-1920s. After this, he pursued the precarious existence of the playwright, novelist, and freelance author. He tried his hand at the old skills on occasion in later years, and evidence of these resurgences will be found here, too. But the age of New York captured in all its youthful vigor in most of these essays is that heady time after the doughboys returned, the Twenties got roaring, the Volstead Act found itself deservedly thwarted, and a lot of progressive life got on with its business before running into the wall of the Great Depression. One of the delights of these essays is that, in their own unpretentious way, they capture the fresh spirit of the age. We now know only too well how ostensibly romantic it was to be in one's twenties in Paris in the 'twenties. But those expatriate Americans were largely self-causes of their achievements: they brought their American enthusiasm to their work and play. Their cousins who stayed at home may have done as well for themselves—at least those who directly or indirectly inspired and found their way into these essays.

Much of the New York captured in these essays has been wildly changed, but surprisingly much of it can still be found. It is relatively easy to do so: the urban archaeologist is quickly rewarded. The old prices for meals, alas, are gone without a trace, and those wonderful old restaurants, chop houses, saloons, and the like are mostly gone or changed beyond recognition, but several old book stores still offer great atmosphere and great bargains. You will wait in vain to hear the long gasp of steam whistles on the harbor, but the Staten Island ferry goes on forever. You can readily find, on a sunny day, the play of light and shade beneath the lacework of the elevated tracks ("the sun-and-shadow chequer under the L," in Morley's phrase), and you can still ride in the front car of the El, even if you have to go to one of the outer boroughs to do so. This is surely just as well: the best effect must be offered by the old Broadway local, nowadays the No. 1 train, on its northern stretch in the Bronx. That is also where the most rewarding old stations can be found—gingerbread houses on stilts, largely preserved in all their original splendor. Some even show traces of pot-bellied stoves and fireplaces in waiting rooms set aside for men and women separately. The subways are generally as packed during certain times of the day as Chris could wish for you, and as he claims he preferred. The commuter-train trips to and from the suburbs—especially Roslyn and points east—are just as tedious and uncertain as ever.

The Hudson River railroad ferries vanished with the late '60s, but you can recapture some of the flavor. The last of them, the octogenarian *Bing-*

hampton, is a restaurant on the New Jersey side, and well worth the trip. You can still explore what Chris called his Seacoast of Bohemia. Take a train over to Hoboken, scene of many a gathering of the Three Hours for Lunch Club. Stop in at the eccentric Clam Broth House. Visit the railroad station and wander in the quiet ferry terminal. You can find a fairly cheap lunch, and how long you spend at it is up to you. You will have a superb view of Manhattan as you walk up toward Stevens Institute, and you will easily find the spot from which Johnny sailed over there. After he came marching home, and the confiscated German liners rusted at their piers, this was the locale of Chris's stage career.

You will have to forgive the intrusive gentility. Hoboken is rapidly shooting up-scale, so let us go back to Manhattan. Chris often mentions the sunlight flashing off the lightning-bolts on the statue atop the Telephone and Telegraph Building on Broadway. He could look out in those days from his *Evening Post* office, across Vesey Street and St. Paul's churchyard, to Evelyn Longman Batchelder's "Electricity," high above Fulton Street. Now you will have to travel from the financial district to the fashionable East Side in midtown to repeat the thrill. You will find the gilded gentleman in residence on Madison and Fifty-fifth, safely indoors since 1984 in the lobby of Philip Johnson and John Burgee's A T & T Building. And you will have to travel all the way to Philadelphia—a train trip often recommended by Chris—to visit Diana of the Manhattans, at the top of the stairs of the Museum of Art.

But you really ought to be reading Christopher Morley's essays: they have captured what seems now to have been a golden age. As you read, will you hear the opening passages of Gershwin's *An American in Paris*—the hectic pace, the frenzy, the honk of taxi horns?

HGF

BALLAD OF NEW AMSTERDAM

There are no bowls on Bowling Green,
No maids in Maiden Lane;
The river path to Greenwich
No longer doth remain.
No longer in the Bouwerie
Stands Peter Stuyvesant his tree!

And yet the Dutchmen built their dorp
With sturdy wit and will;
In Nassau Street their spectral feet
Are heard to echo still.
In many places sure I am
New York is still Nieuw Amsterdam.

Sometimes at night in Bowling Green
There comes a rumbling sound,
Which literal minds are wont to think
The Subway. But I found
That still the Dutchmen ease their souls
By playing ghostly games of bowls!

Songs for a Little House (1917)

EAST SIDE, WEST SIDE, ALL AROUND THE TOWN

UNHEALTHY

ON SATURDAY afternoons Titania and I always have an adventure. On Sundays we stay at home and dutifully read manuscripts (I am the obscure creature known as a "publisher's reader") but Saturday post meridiem is a golden tract of time wherein we wander as we list.

The 35th Street entrance to McQueery's has long been hallowed as our *stell-dich-ein*. We meet there at one o'clock. That is to say, I arrive at 12:59 and spend fifteen minutes in most animated reflection. There is plenty to think about. One may stand between the outer and inner lines of glass doors and watch the queer little creatures that come tumbling out of the cloak and suit factory across the street. Or one may stand inside the store, on a kind of terrace, beneath pineapple shaped arc lights, looking down upon the bustle of women on the main floor. Best of all, one may stroll along the ornate gallery to one side where all sorts and conditions of ladies wait for other ladies who have promised to meet them at one o'clock. They divide their time between examining the mahogany victrolae and deciding what kind of sundae they will have for lunch. A very genteel old gentleman with white hair and a long morning coat and an air of perpetual irritation is in charge of this social gallery. He wears the queer, soft, flat-soled boots that are suggestive of corns. There is an information bureau there, where one may learn everything except the time one may expect one's wife to arrive. But I have learned a valuable subterfuge. If I am waiting for Titania, and beginning to despair of her arrival, I have only to go to a telephone to call her up. As soon as I have put the nickel in, she is sure to appear. Nowadays I save the nickel by going into a booth and *pretending* to telephone. Sure enough, at 1:14, Ingergersoll time, in she trots.

We have a jargon of our own.

"Eye-polishers?" say I.

"Yes," says Titania, "but there was a block at 42nd Street. I'm *so* sorry, Grump."

"Eye-polishers" is our term for the Fifth Avenue busses, because riding on them makes Titania's eyes so bright. More widely, the word connotes anything that produces that desirable result, such as bunches of violets, lavender peddlers, tea at Mary Elizabeth's, spring millinery, or finding sixpence in her shoe. This last is a rite suggested by the old song:

> And though maids sweep their hearths no less
> Than they were wont to do,
> Yet who doth now for cleanliness
> Find sixpence in her shoe?

A bright dime does very well as a sixpenny piece.

We always lunch at Moretti's on Saturday: it is

the recognized beginning of an adventure. The Moretti lunch has advanced from a quarter to thirty cents, I am sorry to say, but this is readily compensated by the Grump buying Sweet Caporals instead of something Turkish. A packet of cigarettes is another curtain-raiser for an adventure. On other days publishers' readers smoke pipes, but on Saturdays cigarettes are possible.

"Antipasto?"

"No, thanks."

"Minestrone or consommé?"

"Two minestrone, two prime ribs, ice cream and coffee. Red wine, please." That is the formula. We have eaten the "old reliable Moretti lunch" so often that the routine has become a ritual. Oh, excellent savor of the Moretti basement! Compounded of warmth, a pungent pourri of smells, and the jangle of thick china, how diverting it is! The franc-tireur in charge of the wine-bin watches us complaisantly from his counter where he sits flanked by flasks of Hoboken chianti and a case of brittle cigars.

How good Moretti's *minestrone* tastes to the unsophisticated tongue. What though it be only an azoic extract of intense potato, dimly tinct with sargasso and macaroni—it has a pleasing warmth and bulk. Is it not the prelude to an Adventure?

Well, where shall we go to-day? No two explorers dickering over azimuth and dead reckoning could discuss latitude and longitude more earnestly than Titania and I argue our possible courses. Generally, however, she leaves it to me to chart the journey. That gives me the pride of conductor and her the pleasure of being surprised.

According to our Mercator's projection (which, duly wrapped in a waterproof envelope, we always carry on our adventures) there was a little known region lying nor' nor'west of Blackwell's Island and plotted on the map of East River Park. I had heard of this as a picturesque and old-fashioned territory, comparatively free from footpads and lying near such places as Astoria and Hell Gate. We laid a romantic course due east along 35th Street, Titania humming a little snatch from an English music-hall song that once amused us:

"My old man's a fireman
Now what do you think of that?
He wears goblimey breeches
And a little goblimey hat."

She always quotes this to me when (she says) I wear my hat too far on the back of my head.

The cross slope of Murray Hill drops steeply downward after one leaves Madison Avenue. We dipped into a region that has always been very fascinating to me. Under the roaring L, past dingy saloons, animal shops, tinsmiths, and painless dentists, past the old dismantled Manhattan hospital. The taste of spring was in the air: one of the dentists was having his sign regilded, a huge four-pronged grinder as big as McTeague's in Frank

Norris's story. Oysters going out, the new brew of Bock beer coming in: so do the saloons mark the vernal equinox.

A huge green chalet built on stilts, with two tiers of trains rumbling by, is the L station at 34th Street and Second Avenue. A cutting wind blew from the East River, only two blocks away. I paid two nickels and we got into the front car of the northbound train.

Until Titania and I attain the final glory of riding in an aeroplane, or ascend Jacob's ladder, there never will be anything so thrilling as soaring over the housetops in the Second Avenue L. Rocking, racketing, roaring over those crazy trestles, now a glimpse of the leaden river to the east, now a peep of church spires and skyscrapers on the west, and the dingy imitation lace curtains of the third-story windows flashing by like a recurring pattern—it is a voyage of romance! Did you ever stand at the front door of an Elevated train, watching the track stretch far ahead toward the Bronx, and the little green stations slipping nearer and nearer? The Subway is a black, bellowing horror; the bus a swaying, jolty start-and-stop, bruising your knees against the seat in front; but the L swings you up and over the housetops, smooth and sheer and swift.

We descended at 86th Street and found ourselves in a new world. A broad, dingy street, lined by shabby brown houses and pushbutton apartments, led in a gentle descent toward the river. The neighbourhood was noisy, quarrelsome, and dirty. After a long, bitter March the thaw had come at last: the street was viscous with slime, the melting snow lay in grayish piles along the curbs. Small boys on each side of the street were pelting sodden snowballs which spattered around us as we walked down the pavement.

But after two blocks things changed suddenly. The trolley swung round at a right angle (up Avenue A) and the last block of 86th Street showed the benefit of this manœuvre. The houses grew neat and respectable. A little side street branching off to the left (not recorded by Mercator) revealed some quaint cottages with gables and shuttered windows so mid-Victorian that my literary heart leaped and I dreamed at once of locating a novel in this fascinating spot. And then we rounded the corner and saw the little park.

It was a bit of old Chelsea, nothing less. Titania clapped her hands, and I lit my pipe in gratification. Beside us was a row of little houses of warm red brick with peaked mansard roofs and cozy bay windows and polished door knockers. In front of them was the lumpy little park, cut up into irregular hills, where children were flying kites. And beyond that, an embankment and the river in a dim wet mist. There was Blackwell's Island, and a sailing barge slipping by. In the distance we could see the colossal span of the new Hell Gate bridge. With the journalist's instinct for superlatives I told Titania it was the largest single span in the world. I wonder if it is?

As to that I know not. But it was the river that lured us. On the embankment we found benches and sat down to admire the scene. It was as picturesque as Battersea in Whistler's mistiest days. A ferryboat, crossing to Astoria, hooted musically through the haze. Tugs, puffing up past Blackwell's Island into the Harlem River, replied with mellow blasts. The pungent tang of the East River tickled our nostrils, and all my old ambition to be a tugboat captain returned.

And then trouble began. Just as I was planning how we might bilk our landlord on Long Island and move all our belongings to this delicious spot, gradually draw our friends around us, and make East End Avenue the Cheyne Walk of New York—we might even import an English imagist poet to lend cachet to the coterie—I saw by Titania's face that something was wrong.

I pressed her for the reason of her frown.

She thought the region was unhealthy.

Now when Titania thinks that a place is unhealthy no further argument is possible. Just on what data she bases these deductions I have never been able to learn. I think she can tell by the shape of the houses, or the lush quality of the foliage, or the fact that the garbage men collect from the front instead of from the back. But however she arrives at the conclusion, it is immutable.

Any place that I think is peculiarly amusing, or quaint, or picturesque, Titania thinks is unhealthy.

Sometimes I can see it coming. We are on our way to Mulberry Bend, or the Bowery, or Farrish's Chop House. I see her brow begin to pucker. "Do you feel as though it is going to be unhealthy?" I ask anxiously. If she does, there is nothing for it but to clutch at the nearest subway station and hurry up to Grant's Tomb. In that bracing ether her spirits revive.

So it was on this afternoon. My utopian vision of a Chelsea in New York, outdoing the grimy salons of Greenwich Village, fell in splinters at the bottom of my mind. Sadly I looked upon the old Carl Schurz mansion on the hill, and we departed for the airy plateaus of Central Park. Desperately I pointed to the fading charms of East River Park—the convent round the corner, the hokey pokey cart by the curbstone.

I shall never be a tugboat captain. It isn't healthy.

[Sg]

THE ANATOMY OF MANHATTAN

SHE IS the only city whose lovers live always in a mood of wonder and expectancy. There are others where one may sink peacefully, contentedly into the life of the town, affectionate and understanding of its ways. But she, the woman city, who is bold enough to say he understands her? The secret of her thrilling and inscrutable appeal has never been told. How could it be? She has always been so much greater than any one who has lived with her. (Shall we mention Walt Whitman as the only possible exception? O. Henry came very near to her, but did he not melodramatize her a little, sometimes cheapen her by his epigrammatic appraisal, fit her too neatly into his plot? Kipling seemed to see her only as the brutal, heedless wanton.) Truly the magic of her spell can never be exacted. She changes too rapidly, day by day. Realism, as they call it, can never catch the boundaries of her pearly beauty. She needs a mystic.

No city so challenges and debilitates the imagination. Here, where wonder is a daily companion, desire to tell her our ecstasy becomes at last only a faint pain in the mind. If you would mute a poet's lyre, put him on a ferry from Jersey City some silver April morning; or send him aboard at Liberty Street in an October dusk. Poor soul, his mind will buzz (for years to come) after adequate speech to tell those cliffs and scarps, amethyst and lilac in the mingled light; the clear topaz chequer of window panes; the dull bluish olive of the river, streaked and crinkled with the churn of the screw! Many a poet has come to her in the wooing passion. Give him six months, he is merely her Platonist. He lives content with placid companionship. Where are his adjectives, his verbs? That inward knot of amazement, what speech can unravel it?

Her air, when it is typical, is light, dry, cool. It is pale, it is faintly tinctured with pearl and opal. Heaven is unbelievably remote; the city itself daring so high, heaven lifts in a cautious remove. Light and shadow are fantastically banded, striped, and patchworked among her cavern streets; a cool, deep gloom is cut across with fierce jags and blinks of brightness. She smiles upon man who takes his ease in her colossal companionship. Her clean soaring perpendiculars call the eye upward. One wanders as a botanist in a tropical forest. That great smooth groinery of the Pennsylvania Station train shed: is it not the arching fronds of iron palm trees? Oh, to be a botanist of this vivid jungle, spread all about one, anatomist of the ribs and veins that run from the great backbone of Broadway!

To love her, one thinks, is to love one's fellows; each of them having some unknown share in her loveliness. Any one of her streets would be the study and delight of a lifetime. To speak at random, we think of that little world of brightness and sound bourgeois cheer that spreads around the homely Verdi statue at Seventy-third Street. We have a faithful affection for that neighbourhood, for reasons of our own. Within a radius, thereabouts, of a quarter-mile each way, we could live a year and learn new matters every day. They call us a hustling folk. Observe the tranquil afternoon light in those brownstone byways. Pass along leisurely Amsterdam Avenue, the region of small and genial shops, Amsterdam Avenue of the many laundries. See the children trooping upstairs to their own room at the St. Agnes branch of the Public Library. See the taxi drivers, sitting in their cars alongside the Verdi grass plot (a rural breath of new-mown turf sweetening the warm, crisp air) and smoking pipes. Every one of them is to us as fascinating as a detective story. What a hand they have had in ten thousand romances. At this very moment, what quaint and many-stranded destinies may hail them and drive off? But there they sit, placid enough, with a pipe and the afternoon paper. The light, fluttering dresses of enigmatic fair ones pass gayly on the pavement. Traffic flows, divides, and flows on, a sparkling river. Here is that mystery, a human being, buying a cigar. Here is another mystery asking for a glass of frosted chocolate. Why is it that we cannot accost that tempting riddle and ask him to give us an accurate précis of his life to date? And that red-haired burly sage, he who used to bake the bran muffins in the little lunchroom near by, and who lent us his Robby Burns one night—what has become of him?

So she teases us, so she allures. Sometimes, on the L, as one passes along that winding channel where the walls and windows come so close, there is a felicitous sense of being immersed, surrounded, drowned in a great, generous ocean of humanity. It is a fine feeling. All life presses around one, the throb and the problem are close, are close. Who could be weary, who could be at odds with life, in such an embrace of destiny? The great tall sides of buildings fly open, the human hive is there, beautiful and arduous beyond belief. Here is our worship and here our lasting joy, here is our immortality of encouragement. Yes, perhaps O. Henry did say the secret after all: "He saw no longer a rabble, but his brothers seeking the ideal."

[P]

VESEY STREET

THE FIRST DUTY of the conscientious explorer is to study his own neighbourhood, so we set off to familiarize ourself with Vesey Street. This amiable byway (perhaps on account of the proximity of Washington Market) bases its culture on a solid appreciation of the virtue of good food, an admirable trait in any street. Upon this firm foundation it erects a seemly interest in letters. The wanderer who passes up the short channel of our street, from the docks to St. Paul's churchyard, must not be misled by the character of the books the bibliothecaries display in their windows. Outwardly they lure the public by Bob Ingersoll's lectures, Napoleon's Dream Book, efficiency encyclopædias and those odd and highly coloured small brochures of smoking-car tales of the Slow Train Through Arkansaw type. But once you penetrate, you may find quarry of a more stimulating kind. For fifteen cents we eloped with a first edition of Bunner's "Love in Old Cloathes," which we were glad to have in memory of the "old red box on Vesey Street" which Bunner immortalized in rhyme, and which still stands (is it the same box?) by the railing of St. Paul's. Also, even nobler treasure to our way of thinking, did we not just now find (for fifteen cents) Hilaire Belloc's *Hills and the Sea*, that enchanting little volume of essays, which we are almost afraid to read again. Belloc, the rogue—the devil is in him. Such a lusty beguilery moves in his nimble prose that after reading him it is hard not to fall into a clumsy imitation of his lively and frolic manner. There is at least one essayist in this city who fell subject to the hilarious Hilaire years ago. It is an old jape but not such a bad one: our friend Murray Hill will never return to the status quo ante Belloc.

But we were speaking of Vesey Street. It looks down to the water, and the soft music of steamship whistles comes tuning on a cold, gusty air. Thoroughly mundane little street, yet not unmindful of matters spiritual, bounded as it is by divine Providence at one end (St. Paul's) and by Providence, R. I. (the Providence Line pier) at the other. Perhaps it is the presence of the graveyard that has startled Vesey Street into a curious reversal of custom. On most other streets, we think, the numbers of the houses run even on the south side, odd on the north. But just the opposite on Vesey. You will find all even numbers on the north, odd on the south. Still, Wall Street errs in the same way.

If marooned or quarantined on Vesey Street a man might lead a life of gayety and sound nourishment for a considerable while, without having recourse to more exalted thoroughfares. There are lodging houses in that row of old buildings down toward the docks; from the garret windows he could see masts moving on the river. For food he would live high indeed. Where will one see such huge glossy blueblack grapes; such enormous Indian River grapefruit; such noble display of fish—scallops, herrings, smelts, and the larger kind with their dead and desolate eyes? There are pathetic rows of rabbits, frozen stiff in the bitter cold wind; huge white hares hanging in rows; a tray of pigeons with their iridescent throat feathers catching gleams of the pale sunlight. There are great sacks of nuts, barrels of cranberries, kegs of olive oil, thick slabs of yellow cheese. On such a cold day it was pleasant to see a sign "Peanut Roasters and Warmers."

Passing the gloomy vista of Greenwich Street—under the "L" is one of those mysterious little vents in the floor of the street from which issues a continual spout of steam—our Vesey grows more intellectual. The first thing one sees, going easterly, is a sign: THE TRUTH SEEKER, *One flight Up*. The temptation is almost irresistible, but then Truth is always one flight higher up, so one reflects, what's the use? In this block, while there is still much doing in the way of food—and even food in the live state, a window full of entertaining chicks and ducklings clustered round a colony brooder—another of Vesey Street's interests begins to show itself. Tools. Every kind of tool that gladdens the heart of man is displayed in various shops. One realizes more and more that this is a man's street, and indeed (except at the meat market) few of the gayer sex are to be seen along its pavements. One of the tool shops has open-air boxes with all manner of miscellaneous oddments, from mouse traps to oil cans, and you may see delighted enthusiasts poring over the assortment with the same professional delight that ladies show at a notion counter. One of the tool merchants, however, seems to have weakened in his love of city existence, for he has put up a placard:

WANTED TO RENT
Small Farm
Must Have Fruit and Spring Water

How many years of repressed yearning may speak behind that modest ambition!

Our own taste for amusement leads us (once luncheon dispatched; you should taste Vesey Street's lentil soup) to the second-hand bookshops. Our imagined castaway, condemned to live on Vesey Street for a term of months, would never need to languish for mental stimulation. Were he devout, there is always St. Paul's, as we have said; and were he atheist, what a collection of Bob Ingersoll's essays greets the faring eye! There is the customary number of copies of *The Pentecost of Calamity*; it seems to the frequenter of second-hand bazaars as though almost everybody who bought that lively booklet in the early days of the war must have sold it again since the armistice. Much rarer, we saw a copy of *Hopkins's Pond*, that little volume of agreeable sketches written so long ago by Dr. Robert T. Morris, the well-known surgeon, and if we had not already a copy which the doctor inscribed for us we would certainly have rescued it from this strange exile.

There are only two of the really necessary delights of life that the Vesey Street maroon would miss. There is no movie, there are no doughnuts. We are wondering whether in any part of this city there has sprung up the great doughnut craze that has ravaged Philadelphia in the past months. As soon as prohibition became a certainty, certain astute merchants of the Quaker City devoted themselves to inoculating the public with a taste for these humble fritters, and now they bubble gayly in the windows of Philadelphia's most aristocratic thoroughfare. It is really a startling sight to see Philadelphia lining up for its noonday quota of doughnuts, and the merchants over there have devised an ingenious method of tempting the crowd. A funnel, erected over the frying sinkers, carries the fragrant fumes out through a transom and gushes it into the open air, so that the sniff of doughnuts is perceptible all down the block. There is a fortune waiting on Vesey Street for the man who will establish a dough-nut foundry, and we solemnly pledge our own appetite and that of all our friends toward his success.*

At its upper end, perhaps in memory of the vanished Astor House, Vesey Street stirs itself into a certain magnificence, devoting its window space to jewellery and silver-mounted books of prayer. At this window one may regulate his watch at a clock warranted by Charles Frodsham of 84, Strand, to whose solid British accuracy we hereby pay decent tribute. Over all this varied scene lifts the shining javelinhead of the Woolworth Building, seen now and then in an almost disbelieved glimpse of sublimity; and the golden Lightning of the Telephone and Telegraph pinnacle, waving his zigzag brands in the sun.

[P]

* Since this was written, the lack has been supplied—on Park Row, just above the top of Vesey Street; probably the most luxurious doughnut shop ever conceived.

BROOKLYN BRIDGE

A WINDY DAY, one would have said in the dark channels of downtown ways. In the chop house on John Street, lunch-time patrons came blustering in, wrapped in overcoats and mufflers, with something of that air of ostentatious hardiness that men always assume on coming into a warm room from a cold street. Thick chops were hissing on the rosy grill at the foot of the stairs. In one of the little crowded stalls a man sat with a glass of milk. It was the first time we had been in that chop house for several years . . . it doesn't seem the same. As Mr. Wordsworth said, it is not now as it hath been of yore. But still,

> The homely Nurse doth all she can
> To make her foster-child, her Inn-mate Man,
> Forget the glories he hath known.

It's a queer thing that all these imitation beers taste to us exactly as real beer did the first time we tasted it (we were seven years old) and shuddered. "Two glasses of cider," we said to the comely serving maid. Alas

> That nature yet remembers
> What was so fugitive.

There is a nice point of etiquette involved in lunching in a crowded chop house. Does the fact of having bought and eaten a moderate meal entitle one to sit with one's companion for a placid talk and smoke afterward? Or is one compelled to relinquish the table as soon as one is finished, to make place for later comers? These last are standing menacingly near by, gazing bitterly upon us as we look over the card and debate the desirability of having some tapioca pudding. But our presiding Juno has already settled the matter, and made courtesy a matter of necessity. "These gentlemen will be through in a moment," she says to the new candidates. Our companion, the amiable G—— W——, was just then telling us of a brand of synthetic whiskey now being distilled by a famous tavern of the underworld. The superlative charm of this beverage seems to be the extreme rigidity it imparts to the persevering communicant. "What does it taste like?" we asked. "Rather like gnawing furniture," said G—— W——. "It's like a long, healthy draught of shellac. It seems to me that it would be less trouble if you offered the barkeep fifty cents to hit you over the head with a hammer. The general effect would be about the same, and you wouldn't feel nearly so bad in the morning."

A windy day, and perishing chill, we thought as we strolled through the gloomy caverns and crypts underneath the Brooklyn Bridge. Those twisted vistas seen through the archways give an impression of wrecked Louvain. A great bonfire was burning in the middle of the street. Under the Pearl Street elevated the sunlight drifted through the girders in a lively chequer, patterning piles of gray-black snow with a criss-cross of brightness. We had wanted to show our visitor Franklin Square, which he, as a man of letters, had always thought of as a trimly gardened plot surrounded by quiet little old-fashioned houses with brass knockers, and famous authors tripping in and out. As we stood examining the façade of Harper and Brothers, our friend grew nervous. He was carrying under his arm the dummy of an "export catalogue" for a big brass foundry, that being his line of work. "They'll think we're free verse poets trying to get up courage enough to go in and submit a manuscript," he said, and dragged us away.

A windy day, we had said in the grimy recesses of Cliff and Dover streets. (Approaching this sentiment for the third time, perhaps we may be permitted to accomplish our thought and say what we had in mind.) But up on the airy decking of the

Brooklyn Bridge, where we repaired with G—— W—— for a brief stroll, the afternoon seemed mild and tranquil. It is a mistake to assume that the open spaces are the windier. The subway is New York's home of Æolus, and most of the gusts that buffet us on the streets are merely hastening round a corner in search of the nearest subway entrance so that they can get down there where they feel they belong. Up on the bridge it was plain to perceive that the March sunshine had elements of strength. The air was crisp but genial. A few pedestrians were walking resolutely toward the transpontine borough; the cop on duty stood outside his little cabin with the air of one ungrieved by care. Behind us stood the high profiles of the lower city, sharpened against the splendidly clear blue sky which is New York's special blessing. On the water moved a large tug, towing barges. Smoke trailed behind it in the same easy and comfortable way that tobacco reek gushes over a man's shoulder when he walks across a room puffing his pipe.

The bridge is a curiously delightful place to watch the city from. Walking toward the central towers seems like entering a vast spider's web. The footway between the criss-cross cables draws one inward with a queer fascination, the perspective diminishing the network to the eye so that it seems to tighten round you as you advance. Even when there is but little traffic the bridge is never still. It is alive, trembling, vibrant, the foot moves with a springy recoil. One feels the lift and strain of gigantic forces, and looks in amazement on the huge sagging hawsers that carry the load. The bars and rods quiver, the whole lively fabric is full of a tremor, but one that conveys no sense of insecureness. It trembles as a tree whispers in a light air.

And of the view from the bridge, it is too sweeping to carry wholly in mind. Best, one thinks, it is seen in a winter dusk, when the panes of Manhattan's mountains are still blazing against a crystal blue-green sky, and the last flush of an orange sunset lingers in the west. Such we saw it once, coming over from Brooklyn, very hungry after walking in most of the way from Jamaica, and pledged in our own resolve not to break fast until reaching a certain inn on Pearl Street where they used to serve banana omelets. Dusk simplifies the prospect, washes away the lesser units, fills in the foreground with obliterating shadow, leaves only the monstrous sierras of Broadway jagged against the vault. It deepens this incredible panorama into broad sweeps of gold and black and peacock blue which one may file away in memory, tangled eyries of shining windows swimming in empty air. As seen in the full brilliance of noonday the bristle of detail is too bewildering to carry in one clutch of the senses. The eye is distracted by the abysses between buildings, by the uneven elevation of the summits, by the jumbled compression of the streets. In the vastness of the scene one looks in vain for some guiding principle of arrangement by which vision can focus itself. It is better not to study this strange and disturbing outlook too minutely, lest one lose what knowledge of it one has. Let one do as the veteran prowlers of the bridge: stroll pensively to and fro in the sun, taking man's miracles for granted, exhilarated and content.

[P]

PASSAGE FROM SOME MEMOIRS

HOW LONG AGO it seems, that spring noonshine when two young men (we will call them Dactyl and Spondee) set off to plunder the golden bag of Time. These creatures had an oppressive sense that first Youth was already fled. For one of them, in fact, it was positively his thirtieth birthday; poor soul, how decrepitly he flitted in front of motor trucks. As for the other, he was far decumbent in years, quite of a previous generation, a perfect Rameses, whose senile face was wont to crack into wrinklish mirth when his palsied cronies called him the greatest poet born on February 2, 1886.

It was a day—well, it is fortunate that some things do not have to be described. Suppose one had to explain to the pallid people of the thither moon what a noonday sunshine is like in New York about the Nones of May? It could not be done to carry credence. Let it be said it was a Day, and leave it so. You have all known that gilded envelopment of sunshine and dainty air.

These pitiful creatures arose from the subway at Fourteenth Street and took the world in their right hands. From this revolving orb, said they, they would squeeze a luncheon hour of exquisite satisfactions. They gazed sombrely at Union Square, and uttered curious reminiscences of the venerable days when one of them had worked, actually toiled for a living, upon the shores of that expanse. Ten years had passed (yes, at least ten—*O edax rerum*!). Upon a wall these observant strollers saw a tablet to the memory of William Lloyd Garrison. Strange, said they, we never noticed this before. Ah, said one, this is hallowed ground. It was near here that I used to borrow a quarter, the day before pay-day, to buy my lunch. The other contributed similar recollections. And now, quoth he, I am grown so prosperous that when I need money I can't afford to borrow less than two hundred dollars.

They lunched (one brushes away the mist of time to recall the details) where the bright sunlight fell athwart a tablecloth of excellent whiteness. They ate (may one be precise at so great a distance?)—yes, they ate broiled mackerel to begin with; the kind of mackerel called (but why?) Spanish. Whereupon succeeded a course of honeycomb tripe, which moved Dactyl to quoting Rabelais, something that Grangousier had said about tripes. Only by these tripes is memory supported and made positive, for it was the first time either had tackled this dish. Concurrent with the tripes, one inducted the other into the true mystery of blending shandygaff, explaining the first doctrine of that worthy draught, which is that the beer must be poured into the beaker before the ginger ale, for so arises a fatter and lustier bubblement of foam. The reason whereof they leave no testament. While this portion of the meal was under discussion their minds moved free, unpinioned, with airy lightness, over all manner of topics. It seemed no effort at all to talk. Ripe, mellow with long experience of men and matters, their comments were notable for wisdom and sagacity. The waiter, overhearing shreds of their discourse, made a private notation to the effect that these were Men of Large Affairs. Then they embarked upon some salty crackers, enlivened with Camembert cheese and green-gage jam. By this time they were touching upon religion, from which they moved lightly to the poems of Louise Imogen Guiney. It is all quite distinct as one looks back upon it.

Issuing upon the street, Dactyl said something about going back to the office, but the air and sunlight said him nay. Rather, remarked Spondee, let us fare forward upon this street and see what happens. This is ever a comely doctrine, adds the chronicler. They moved gently, not without a lilac trailing of tobacco fume, across quiet stretches of pavement. In the blue upwardness stood the tower of the Metropolitan Life Building, a reminder that humanity as a whole pays its premiums with decent regularity. They conned the nice gradations of tint in the spring foliage of Gramercy Park. They talked, a little soberly, of thrift, and of their misspent years.

Lexington Avenue lay guileless beneath their rambling footfalls. At the corner of Twenty-second Street was a crowd gathered, and a man with the customary reverted cap in charge of a moving picture machine. A swift car drew up before the large house at the southeast corner. Thrill upon thrill: something being filmed for the movies! In the car, a handsome young rogue at the wheel, and who was this blithe creature in shiny leather coat and leather cap, with crumpling dark curls cascading beneath it? A suspicion tinkled in the breast of Spondee, in those days a valiant movie fan. Up got the young man, and hopped out of the car. Up stood the blithe creature—how neatly breeched, indeed, a heavenly forked radish—and those shining riding boots! She dismounted—lifted down (so unnecessarily it seemed) by the rogue. She stood there a moment and Spondee was convinced. DOROTHY GISH, said he to Dactyl. Miss Gish and her escort darted into the house, the camera man reeling busily. At an upper window of the dwelling a white-haired lady was looking out, between lace curtains, with a sort of horror. Query, was she part of the picture, or only the aristocratic owner of the house, dismayed at finding her home suddenly become part of a celluloid drama? Spondee had always had a soft spot in his heart for Miss Dorothy, esteeming her a highly entertaining creature. He was disappointed in the tranquil outcome of the scene. He had hoped to see leaping from windows and all manner of hot stuff. Near by stood a coloured groom with a horse. The observers concluded that Miss Gish was to do a little galloping shortly. Dactyl and Spondee moved away. Spondee quoted a poem he had once written about Miss Dorothy. He recollected only two lines:

> She makes all the rest seem a shoal of poor fish
> So *we* cast *our* ballot for Dorothy Gish.

Peering again into the dark backward and abysm, it seems that the two rejuvenated gossips trundled up on Lexington Avenue to Alfred Goldsmith's cheerful bookshop. Here they were startled to hear Mr. Goldsmith cry: "Well, Chris, here are some nice bones for you." One of these visitors assumed this friendly greeting was for him, but then it was explained that Mr. Goldsmith's dog, named Christmas, was feeling seedy, and was to be pampered. At this moment in came the postman with a package of books, arrived all the way from Canada. One of these books was *Salt of the Sea*, a volume of tales by Morley Roberts, and upon this Spondee fell with a loud cry, for it contained "The Promotion of the Admiral," being to his mind a tale of great virtue which he had not seen in several years. Dactyl, meanwhile, was digging out some volumes of Gissing, and on the faces of both these creatures might have been seen a pleasant radiation of innocent cheer. Mr. Goldsmith also exhibited (it is still remembered) a beautiful photo of Walt Whitman, which entertained the visitors, for it showed old Walt with his coatsleeve full of pins, which was ever Walt's way.

How long ago it all seems. Does Miss Dorothy still act for the pictures? Does Chris, the amiable Scots terrier, still enjoy his bones? Does old Dactyl still totter about his daily tasks? Queer to think that it happened only yesterday. Well, time runs swift in New York.

[P]

ROUND COLUMBUS CIRCLE

THE OTHER EVENING as I was walking along Fifty-ninth Street I noticed a man buying a copy of *Variety* at a newsstand. Obedient to my theory that life deserves all possible scrutiny, I thought it would be interesting to follow him and see exactly what he did.

I chose my quarry not merely at random. People who read *Variety* are likely to be interesting because they are pretty sure to be connected, no matter how remotely, with that odd, unpredictable, and high-spirited race who call themselves "artists," or "professionals." He might be in vaudeville, or in burlesque, or in the world of "outdoor shows." He might be a "carnival man," or a cabaret performer, a dancer, an "equilibrist," a marimba bandsman, a "sensational perch artist," a "lightning change artist," a "jass baby," a saxophonist. He might be the manager of a picture house; he might be in the legitimate. He might even be one of my favourite pair of artists (of whom I think with affection: I have never seen them, but their professional card appears now and then in *Variety*—"Null and Void, The Dippy Daffy Duo").

So I followed him discreetly, to see what might happen.

At Columbus Circle he paused and looked about him rather as though he felt himself in a congenial element. The blue mildness of the night was bright with exciting signs, the ancient one of the full moon seeming rather pallid compared to the electric picture of Socony Oil pouring from a can into a funnel. There was a constant curving flow of skittering taxis, especially the kind that have slatted black panels abaft the windows: these look like little closed shutters and give a sense of secrecy, mystery, and vivid romance. Upon all this my fugitive gazed with a sort of affection; then he turned and stood a minute before the window of Childs' where small gas flames were as blue as violets under the griddle. I supposed that perhaps he was hungry, for he gazed pensively but perhaps he was also thinking that the restaurant had quaintly changed its sex since afternoon; for now it was bustling with white-clad men instead of the laundered ladies of a few hours ago. He went on to an adjoining florist's window, and here he studied the lilacs, orchids (in their little individual test tubes), lilies of the valley, forsythia, narcissus, daffodils, pussy-willows, sweet peas. It was a very springlike window. I saw his eye fall upon the deftly wrapped sheaves of paper inside the shop, where bright colours glimmered through swatches of pale green tissue. These parcels were all addressed; ready to go out, I supposed, to very beautiful ladies.

He passed on (he had lit a pipe, by the way) by the Park Theatre, and he cast an observant eye upon that, noting that it was dark. Perhaps he pondered the vicissitudes of the show business. The windows of several haberdashers, all announcing their proximate retirement from traffic, won declensions from his eye: there were some quite lively shirts at $1.85 that seemed nearly to obtain his suffrage. But again I saw him lured by food. A very minute, narrow doggery, intensely masculine in aspect, but with its courteous legend LADIES INVITED glossed upon the pane, exhibited a tray of hamburger steak, liberally besprinkled with onion slivers. These he gravely considered. But still he proceeded; and still, in the phrase of Mr. Montague, I "committed myself to his vestiges."

It was the automobile business, next, that drew his attention. Those astonishing windows just south of the Circle plainly afforded him material for thought—places where, in great halls of baronial aspect, on Oriental rugs and marble floors, under little whispering galleries where the salesmen retire to their orisons, America's most shining triumphs are displayed. He was fascinated by the window of U. S. Rubber—where a single tire, mounted on a canary-coloured wheel, and an array of galoshes and arctics, are gravely displayed under tall blue hangings and festoons of artificial flowers. Or the Goodrich window, where a huge flattened circlet has the space to itself on a crinkled wealth of purple-green shot silk. Amethystine lights shine through glazed screens behind this monstrous tire: drapes of imitation Spanish moss and enormous vases give the effect of a vaudeville stage set for some juggling act. The automobile business has learned all the tricks of Victorian stage *decor*; perhaps that was why my *Variety* reader was so thrilled. Another window, where the car comes bravely to the aid of the hard-pressed Church ("To Church in Their Chevrolet"—have you seen it?), is even more dramatic. Here the department store lends a hand also, for the modes worn by the figures are from Fifth Avenue. I was rather thrilled when I saw my fugitive halt also in front of the Dame Quickly showroom: a much more businesslike display, where the latest models of the Quickly family exhibit their modest and competent elegance.

But it was most interesting of all to find him striking off Broadway and entering the lobby of the Grenoble Hotel. He peered about the lobby as though he were expecting to meet someone; but

I couldn't help suspecting that this was chiefly for the benefit of the clerk at the desk; what he really wanted was a quiet place to sit down and read his *Variety*. At any rate, he occupied the resilient corner of a couch for some time, studiously conning the magazine. I should have liked to tell the clerk behind the counter the reason why the Grenoble is always a special place to me—it was there, I believe, that Rudyard Kipling lay dangerously ill twenty-five years ago. I wonder if the hotel register holds any record of that momentous incident.

Presently—after carefully scanning the columns which tell how much each play took in at the box-office last week: perhaps the only positively accurate gauge of New York theatrical tastes; you will learn with surprise, for instance, that one of the leading moneymakers is a show called *Abie's Irish Rose*—my subject folded up *Variety* and set forth again. Following, I was pleased to see him stop at Mr. Keyte's bookshop on Fifty-seventh Street; and even more surprised to note that the thing that seemed most to catch his eye was a fine photo of Henry James. He complimented the saleslady upon it, and he bought a book. It was a copy of Sherwood Anderson's *Winesburg, Ohio*, in the Modern Library.

But it was plain that all this time the idea of food had been loitering agreeably in the back of his mind. I trailed him back to Columbus Circle, and there, to my amusement, he returned straight to the little hash-alley where he had admired the meat patties with onions. He went in and sat down at the tiny counter. "Hamburg steak," he said, "and put plenty of onions on it." And then, after a moment, "Coffee with plenty," he added.

"It's plenty of everything with you to-night," said the whitecoat, genially.

"Sure, everything but money," remarked this mysterious creature. He propped up his *Winesburg* against the sugar basin and read while he ate.

At this point, fearing that my sleuthing might cause him to become self-conscious, I went thoughtfully away.

(*March, 1923*)
[RS]

ON BEING IN A HURRY

NEW YORK is a perplexing city to loaf in. (Walt Whitman if he came back to Mannahatta would soon get brain fever.) During the middle hours of the day, at any rate, it is almost impossible to idle with the proper spirit and completeness. There is a prevailing bustle and skirmish that "exerts a compulsion," as President Wilson would say. The air is electric and nervous. We have often tried to dawdle gently about the neighbourhood of the City Hall in the lunch hour, to let the general form and spirit of that clearing among the cliffs sink into our mind, so that we could get some picture of it. We have sat under a big brown umbrella, to have our shoes shined, when we had nothing more important to do than go to the doughnut foundry on Park Row and try some of those delectable combinations of foods they have there, such as sponge cake with whipped cream and chocolate fudge. And in a few seconds we have found ourself getting all stirred up and crying loudly to the artist that we only wanted a once-over, as we had an important appointment. You have to put a very heavy brake on your spirit in downtown New York or you find yourself dashing about in a prickle of excitement, gloriously happy just to be in a hurry, without particularly caring whither you are hastening, or why.

One of the odd things about being in a hurry is that it seems so fiercely important when you yourself are the hurrier and so comically ludicrous when it is someone else. We see our friend Artaxerxes scorching up Church Street and we scream with laughter at him, because we know perfectly well that there is absolutely not one of his affairs important enough to cause him to buzz along like that. We look after him with a sort of mild and affectionate pity for a deluded creature who thinks that his concerns are of such glorious magnitude. And then, a few hours later, we find ourself on a subway car with only ten minutes to catch the train for Salamis at Atlantic Avenue. And what is our state of mind? We stand, gritting our teeth (we are too excited to sit, even if there were a seat) and holding our watch. The whole train, it seems to us, is occupied by invalids, tottering souls and lumbago cripples, who creep off at the stations as though five seconds made not the slightest difference. We glare and fume and could gladly see them all maced in sunder with battleaxes. Nothing, it seems to us, could soothe our bitter hunger for haste but

to have a brilliant Lexington Avenue express draw up at the platform with not a soul in it. Out would step a polite guard, looking at his watch. "You want to catch a train at 5:27?" he asks. "Yes, sir, yes, sir; step aboard." All the other competitors are beaten back with knotted thongs and we are ushered to a seat. The bells go chiming in quick sequence up the length of the train and we are off at top speed, flying wildly past massed platforms of indignant people. We draw up at Atlantic Avenue, and the solitary passenger, somewhat appeased, steps off. "Compliments of the Interborough, sir," says the guard.

The commuter, urgently posting toward the 5:27, misses the finest flavour of the city's life, for it is in the two or three hours after office work is over that the town is at her best. What a spry and smiling mood is shown along the pavements, particularly on these clear, warm evenings when the dropping sun pours a glowing tide of soft rosy light along the crosstown streets. There is a cool lightness in the air; restaurants are not yet crowded (it is, let us say, a little after six) and beside snowy tablecloths the waiters stand indulgently with folded arms. Everybody seems in a blithe and spirited humour. Work is over for the day, and now what shall we do for amusement? This is the very peak of living, it seems to us, as we sally cheerily along the street. It is like the beginning of an O. Henry story. The streets are fluttering with beautiful women; light summer frocks are twinkling in the busy frolic air. Oh, to be turned loose at the corner of Broadway and Thirty-second Street at 6:15 o'clock of a June evening, with nothing to do but follow the smile of adventure to the utmost! Thirty-second, we might add, is our favorite street in New York. It saddens us to think that the old boarding house on the corner of Madison Avenue is vanished now and all those quaint and humorous persons dispersed. We can still remember the creak of the long stairs and the clink of a broken slab in the tiled flooring of the hall as one walked down to the dining room.

Affection for any particular street largely depends on the associations it has accumulated in one's mind. For several years most of our adventures in New York centred round Thirty-second Street; but its physique has changed so much lately that it has lost some of its appeal. We remember an old stoneyard that used to stand where the Pennsylvania Hotel is now, a queer jumbled collection of odd carvings and relics. At the front door there was a bust of Pan on a tall pedestal, which used to face us with a queer crooked grin twice a day, morning and evening. We had a great affection for that effigy, and even wrote a little piece about him in one of the papers, for which we got about $4 at a time when it was considerably needed. We used to say to ourself that some day when we had a home in the country we would buy Pan and set him in a Long Island garden where he would feel more at home than in the dusty winds of Thirty-second Street. Time went on and we disappeared from our old haunts, and when we came back Pan had vanished, too. You may imagine our pleasure when we found him again the other day standing in front of a chop house on Forty-fourth Street.

But one great addition to the delights of the Thirty-second Street region is the new and shining white tunnel that leads one from the Penn Station subway platform right into the heart of what used (we think) to be called Greeley Square. It is so dazzling and candid in its new tiling that it seems rather like a vast hospital corridor. One emerges through the Hudson Tube station and perhaps sets one's course for a little restaurant on Thirty-fifth Street which always holds first place in our affection. It is somewhat declined from its former estate, for the upper floors, where the violent orchestra was and the smiling little dandruffian used to sing solos when the evening grew glorious, are now rented to a feather and ostrich plume factory. But the old basement is still there, much the same in essentials, by which we mean the pickled beet appetizers, the minestrone soup, the delicious soft bread with its brittle crust, and the thick slices of rather pale roast beef swimming in thin, pinkish gravy. And the three old French waiters, hardened in long experience of the frailties of mortality, smile to see a former friend. One, grinning upon us rather bashfully, recalls the time when there was a hilarious Oriental wedding celebrating in a private room upstairs and two young men insisted on going in to dance with the bride. He has forgiven various pranks, we can see, though he was wont to be outraged at the time. "Getting very stout," he says, beaming down at us. "You weigh a hundred pounds more than you used to." This is not merely cruel; it is untrue. We refrain from retorting on the growth of his bald spot.

[P]

CONFESSIONS OF A HUMAN GLOBULE

As a matter of fact, we find the evening subway jam very restful. Being neatly rounded in contour, with just a gentle bulge around the equatorial transit, we have devised a very satisfactory system. We make for the most crowded car we can find, and having buffeted our way in, we are perfectly serene. Once properly wedged, and provided no one in the immediate neighbourhood is doing anything with any garlic (it is well to avoid the vestibules if one is squeamish in that particular) we lift our feet off the floor, tuck them into the tail of our overcoat, and remain blissfully suspended in midair from Chambers Street to Ninety-sixth. The pressure of our fellow-passengers, powerfully impinging upon the globular perimeter we spoke of, keeps us safely elevated above the floor. We have had some leather stirrups sewed into the bottom of our overcoat, in which we slip our feet to keep them from dangling uncomfortably. Another feature of our technique is that we always go into the car with our arms raised and crossed neatly on our chest, so that they will not be caught and pinioned to our flanks. In that position, once we are gently nested among the elastic mass of genial humanity, it is easy to draw out from our waistcoat pocket our copy of Boethius's *Consolation of Philosophy* and we really get in a little mental improvement. Or, if we have forgotten the book, we gently droop our head into our overcoat collar, lay it softly against the shoulder of the tall man who is always handy, and pass into a tranquil nescience.

The subway is a great consolation to the philosopher if he knows how to make the most of it. Think how many people one encounters and never sees again.

[P]

NOTES ON A FIFTH AVENUE BUS

FAR DOWN the valley of the Avenue the traffic lights wink in unison, green, yellow, red, changing their colours with well-drilled promptness. It is cold: a great wind flaps and tangles the flags; the tops of the buses are almost empty. That brisk April air seems somehow in key with the mood of the Avenue—hard, plangent, glittering, intensely material. It is a proud, exultant, exhilarating street; it fills the mind with strange liveliness. A magnificent pomp of humanity—what a flux of lacquered motors, what a twinkling of spats along the pavements! On what other of the world's great highways would one find churches named for the material of which they are built?—the *Brick Church*, the *Marble Church*! It is not a street for loitering—there is an eager, ambitious humour in its blood; one walks fast, revolving schemes of worldly dominion. Only on the terrace in front of the Public Library is there any temptation for tarrying and consideration. There one may pause and study the inscription—*But Above All Things Truth Beareth*

Away the Victory . . . of course the true eloquence of the words lies in the *But*. Much reason for that *But*, implying a previous contradiction—on the Avenue's part? Sometimes, pacing vigorously in that river of lovely pride and fascination, one might have suspected that other things bore away the victory—spats, diamond necklaces, smoky blue furs nestling under lovely chins. . . . Hullo! here is a sign, "Headquarters of the Save New York Committee." Hum! Save from what? There was a time when the great charm of New York lay in the fact that it didn't want to be saved. Who is it that the lions in front of the Public Library remind us of? We have so often pondered. Let's see: the long slanting brow, the head thrown back, the haughty and yet genial abstraction—to be sure, it's Vachel Lindsay!

We defy the most resolute philosopher to pass along the giddy, enticing, brilliant vanity of that superb promenade and not be just a little moved by worldly temptation.

[P]

SUNDAY MORNING

IT WAS a soft, calm morning of sunshine and placid air. Clear and cool, it was "a Herbert Spencer of a day," as H. G. Wells once remarked. The vista of West Ninety-eighth Street, that engaging alcove in the city's enormous life, was all freshness and kempt tranquillity, from the gray roof of the old training ship at the river side up to the tall red spire near Columbus Avenue. This pinnacle, which ripens to a fine claret colour when suffused with sunset, we had presumed to be a church tower, but were surprised, on exploration, to find it a standpipe of some sort connected with the Croton water system.

Sunday morning in this neighbourhood has its own distinct character. There is a certain air of luxurious ease in the picture. One has a feeling that in those tall apartment houses there are a great many ladies taking breakfast in negligée. They are wearing (if one may trust the shop windows along Broadway) boudoir caps and mules. Mules, like their namesakes in the animal world, are hybrid things, the offspring of a dancing pump and a bedroom slipper. They are distinctly futile, but no matter, no matter. Wearing mules, however, is not a mere vanity; it is a form of physical culture, for these skimpish little things are always disappearing under the bed, and crawling after them keeps one slender. Again we say, no matter. This is no concern of ours.

Near Broadway a prosperous and opulently tailored costume emerges from an apartment house: cutaway coat, striped trousers, very long pointed patent leather shoes with lilac cloth tops. Within this gear, we presently see, is a human being, in the highest spirits. "All set!" he says, joining a group of similars waiting by a shining limousine. Among these, one lady of magnificently millinered aspect, and a smallish man in very new and shiny riding boots, of which he is grandly conscious. There are introductions. "Mr. Goldstone, meet Mrs. Silverware." They are met. There is a flashing of eyes. Three or four silk hats simultaneously leap into the shining air, are flourished and replaced. The observer is aware of the prodigious gayety and excitement of life. All climb into the car and roll away down Broadway. All save the little man in riding boots. He is left on the sidewalk, gallantly waving his hand. Come, we think, he is going riding. A satiny charger waits somewhere round the corner. We will follow and see. He slaps his hunting crop against his glorious boots, which are the hue of quebracho wood. No; to our chagrin, he descends into the subway.

We sit on the shoestring stand on Ninety-sixth Street, looking over the Sunday papers. Very odd, in the adjoining chairs men are busily engaged polishing shoes that have nobody in them, not visibly, at any rate. Perhaps Sir Oliver is right after all. While we are not watching, the beaming Italian has inserted a new pair of laces for us. Long afterward, at bedtime, we find that he has threaded them in that unique way known only to shoe merchants and polishers, by which every time they are tied and untied one end of the lace gets longer and the other shorter. Life is full of needless complexities. We descend the hill. Already (it is 9:45 A.M.) men are playing tennis on the courts at the corner of West End Avenue. A great wagon crammed with scarlet sides of beef comes stumbling up the hill, drawn, with difficulty, by five horses.

When we get down to the Ninety-Sixth Street pier we see the barque *Windrush* lying near by with the airy triangles of her rigging pencilled against the sky, and look amorously on the gentle curve of her strakes (if that is what they are). We feel that it would be a fine thing to be off soundings, greeting the bounding billow, not to say the barroom steward; and yet, being a cautious soul of reservations all compact, we must admit that about the time we got abreast of New Dorp we would be homesick for our favourite subway station.

The pier, despite its deposit of filth, bales of old shoes, reeking barrels, scows of rubbish, sodden papers, boxes of broken bottles and a thick paste of dust and ash-powder everywhere, is a happy lounging ground for a few idlers on Sunday morning. A large cargo steamer, the *Eclipse*, lay at the wharf, standing very high out of the water. Three small boys were watching a peevish old man tending his fishing lines, fastened to wires with little bells on them. "What do you catch here?" we said. Just then one of the little bells gave a cracked tinkle and the angler pulled up a small fish, wriggling briskly, about three inches long. This seemed to anger him. He seemed to consider himself in some way humiliated by the incident. He grunted. One of the small boys was tactful. "Oh, gee!" he said. "Sometimes you catch fish that long," indicating a length which began at about a yard and diminished to about eighteen inches as he meditated. "I don't know what kind they are," he said. "They're not trouts, but some other kind of fish."

This started the topic of relative sizes, always fascinating to small boys. "That's a pretty big boat," said one, craning up at the tall stem of the *Eclipse*. "Oh, gee, that ain't big!" said another. "You ought to see some of the Cunard boats, the *Olympic* or the *Baltic*."

On Riverside Drive horseback riders were cantering down the bridlepath, returning from early outings. The squirrels, already grossly overfed, were brooding languidly that another day of excessive peanuts was at hand. Behind a rapidly spinning limousine pedalled a grotesquely humped bicyclist, using the car as a pacemaker. He throbbed fiercely just behind the spare tire, with his face bent down into a rich travelling cloud of gasoline exhaust. An odd way of enjoying one's self! Children were coming out in troops, with their nurses, for the morning air. Here was a little boy with a sailor hat, and on the band a gilt legend that was new to us. Instead of the usual naval slogan, it simply said *Democracy*. This interested us, as later in the day we saw another, near the goldfish pond in Central Park. Behind the cashier's grill of a Broadway drug store the good-tempered young lady was reading Zane Grey. "I love his books," she said, "but they make me want to break loose and go out West."

[P]

UPPER BROADWAY

ABOUT 11 O'CLOCK—it's a cool autumn evening—Upper Broadway begins to get ready for bed. The atheist orator, who talks outside the Baptist Church at the corner of 79th Street, has finished his spiel—his 173rd lecture in this year's campaign, he remarks. If it has been a vehement evening, the meeting has broken up into little knots of argument. The lecturer himself, a sharp assured fellow in a rakish soft hat, is skilfully slipping away through the throng. I imagine he's thirsty. "You can't prove there's a Supreme Being," he remarks to an indignant loyalist. "Well, prove there isn't one," is the retort. "Every time science takes a step forward, God takes a step back," says the lecturer. The name of Eddington is mentioned. A lady wedged in the midst of the group is repeating dolefully, "Well, then, who made the world?" A sombre young man says to his companion, "What I'm wondering, since we drifted away from religion are we any happier?"

The fruit vendor on that pitch benefits excellently. Theology and argument always leads to the apple, with which they began.

This particular pitch is considered more intellectual than the rival camp on the N.E. corner, where you will find chalked on the paving:

HOBO GROUP
TONIGHT

GOD
ATHEISM
POLITICS
THE HUMAN RACE

Or perhaps this has been Astrology night. (I believe Atheism and Astrology have some working arrangement by which they take turns.) The Astrology Lady used to chalk her zodiac signs on the pavement, but now she has a cardboard chart and a little folding easel. By 11:30, when you go out for your bedtime stroll—to see if the early *Herald Tribune* is up yet and to wrestle with the temptation of cashew nuts—the broad sidewalk beside Dr. Haldeman's church is empty. Cassandra is folding her easel and rolling up the American flag that every street showman uses for safety. The apple vendor is tacking up his crates; they confer together in a cheerful colleague spirit.

There are only a few lights in the great flank of the Apthorp—a dozen lighted windows, to be exact. This is a dull year for the special policemen in Confederate uniforms that guard the austere inner courtyard. Not nearly so many big cars rolling in and out.—The dark-browed law student at the Broadway Star Market is getting in some good licks at his notes on Contracts and Torts as he sits in the cashier's cage. A few minutes past twelve the lights are snapped off at Schulte's and in the Nauheim drugstores. Cassandra, joined by another lady who looks like her sister, has trudged off down Broadway toward 72nd Street. The big procession of midnight trucks has begun, headed by the huge vans of Sheffield Farms, bringing the morning milk. On the curb, in a dim stretch of pavement below the famous old Belleclaire, I discover two empty bottles standing, probably discarded from a smart roadster that was parked there a few minutes ago. One ginger ale, one rye.

Upper Broadway lives on rich food, I surmise, and pays its penalties cheerfully. To a delicatessen dealer slicing some turkey sandwiches I remarked that this was a little early for the Thanksgiving fowl. "Oh, this is a turkey neighbourhood," he said; "they eat it all the year round." Such ecumenical variety of meats and sweets and spices in the windows must account for the tall canisters of Bicarbonate of Soda, 5 lbs. for 24¢, and the packages of Abnehm Tea—"herbs imported from Germany to reduce overweight." In the Crystal Market they are fixing up the display for Friday—Jumbo Shrimps and flounders tucked in delicate curls among cracked ice, surrounded by sprays of fern. In another window I see the horrific allure "Waffles Buried in Crushed Fruit." Further to stimulate the gastric zone are the Port and Sherry Tonics from Egg Harbor City, "Not to be used as a beverage." Bravely the Diabetic Grocer tries to antidote these gluttonies with jars of Fatless Spread, Meatless Soup, Dietetic Grape Jelly, Dietetic Mayonnaise, and that elastic gluten bread.—It is a difficult region for the hungry.

This competitive civilization, if that's what it is being called nowadays, offers plenty of awkward paradoxes. It is disturbing, on a raw night, to see the little shacks of the Bonus Camp down along the riverside, and then just round the corner on 72nd Street the great abandoned hospital building which could easily shelter them all. There's one chap, near the 79th Street pier, living in a battered old sail-boat cast up in a gully. Another, in gay spirits, has propped up one of those profile cut-outs of a bungalow and shrubbery, such as florists and realtors use for signs in the country. By one theory, which I sometimes hear argued on bus-tops, the Bonus Campers are having a good time and don't need to live there if they don't want to. I don't pretend to know the truth. Even the most talented civilizations—bees, ants, beavers—have occasionally failed to solve some of their problems. What reason is there to suppose that man can do so much better?

But I often say to myself that in spite of its paradoxes and errors the Capitalist System has shown a great deal of flexibility and capacity for absorbing shocks. If the poison of nationalism can be medicined (it ought to be possible to take out swollen patriotisms as you take out tonsils), I still think the present system is a hopeful basis to work on. I can forgive it much for creating an institution like Woolworth's—which is good art, good fun, and good merchandise.

[IR]

A BIBLIOPHILE IN A BIG HOUSE

An Author Is Taken Unawares by His Least Conscientious Collector

ONE RAINY AUTUMN NIGHT, when we were living in an apartment in the city, I had a queer adventure. My wife and I were going to the theater, and I found that before starting downtown there was just time to walk round to the neighborhood cigar store, at Broadway and 80th, for a pack of cigarettes.

I came up the dark side street and into the light of the shop windows, pulling some coins from my pocket to see if I had the exact change. Just as I did so a young man came round the corner from Broadway. Both our heads were down against the rain and we almost collided. He was tall, neatly dressed and unusually alert looking. To my surprise he said politely "I wonder if you could spare me something? I'm crazy for a smoke."

I was partly surprised, and partly annoyed, for he was distinctly better dressed than I; particularly I noticed his smart loose-cut overcoat. But it's hard to refuse a touch when you are caught with money actually in your hand. And there's a kind of fellow-feeling among smokers.

"I'll blow you a smoke," I said. "What do you want. Chesties?"

"As a matter of fact I'd rather have a pipe," he said. "*Serene* is my mixture."

I was still a bit wary, for I felt in some way that I was being taken for a ride. But I was interested, because Serene is a tobacco that has never been advertised and is only smoked by experienced fumigators. "Step in the doorway out of the rain," I said. As we stood there I took out my package of tobacco and he filled his pipe. It was a handsome brier; and like his overcoat a better one than mine.

"I'm surprised to see a fellow like you come down to panhandling," I said.

He said he was looking for a job but there was only one kind of thing he was really good at. Of course I asked what.

"I'd like a job in the book business," he said.

Now I really was interested. I asked him some questions and found that he knew what he was talking about. "Maybe I can help," I said. "I'm in the book business myself, in a way. I'll give you a note to a friend of mine."

From his vest pocket he pulled out a sheaf of little paper slips, neatly cut to the exact size of calling cards. Each one had his name and address written on it in pencil. On the back of one of these I scribbled a message to a certain publisher. I bought him a package of Serene and we were about to part. We shook hands, and since he had given me his name I felt it only decent courtesy to mention my own.

"For pete's sake," he said, "you're just the man I want. Say, is that misprint on page 74 absolutely essential in a first issue of *The Haunted Bookshop*?"

"I'm sorry," I said; "they tell me it is, but I don't know much about those first editions."

"Well I'm certainly glad to see you," he went on. "I've rather specialized on your stuff. I had the copy of *Songs for a Little House* with the quotation opposite the title-page, and the 1918 *Shandygaff* with that blurb you wrote yourself for the wrapper; and say, that first little book of poems you wrote at Oxford. *The Eighth Sin.* Boy, that item's a honey. I got my copy from the University Library."

"What do you mean?" I asked.

"You've been a sportsman," he said. "I won't lie to you. I'm a Book Thief. A damned good one, too; I don't just steal stuff at random, I make it my business to know what's worth while. I've got a big respect for your stuff, it has resale value. There's some of your books I'll bet I've made more money out of than you have yourself."

I was rather speechless by this time.

"There's nothing in it in the long run," he said. "They get you, sooner or later. I've just come back from two years up at the Big House. I'm going straight now. This street-work is just to see me through till I can land a job."

He told me some of the details of his profession;

how he had the town mapped into certain routes; this evening just happened to be his night for upper Broadway. "A bad night for it," I suggested.

"Not a bit," he said, "I got *you*, didn't I? Of course you're easy, it sticks out all over you. Wet nights people feel sympathetic. Why don't you follow me down the street and watch me work."

I was sorry I couldn't; I explained I had an engagement. He was just leaving, and turned back. "I almost forgot," he said. "In case you don't believe me, have a look at this overcoat. These leather pockets inside the lining, all fixed up to slip books in. This big one, that's where I put the Rackham illustrated edition of *Where the Blue Begins*. I guess they won't forget that at the Hartford Public Library."

We said good-bye and although there was some subsequent correspondence I haven't seen him again. I've often wondered what has become of my most methodical collector.

[CMB]

WEST END AVENUE

YOU HEAR little about West End Avenue. It is too genteel to have much taste for publicity. But like all very decorous personalities it has its secret ligatures with grim fact. It begins at 106th Street, spliced into the western bend of Broadway, with a memory of the *Titanic* disaster (the Straus Memorial Fountain). It ends at 59th Street in Dead Storage and Loans on Cars, and in the gigantic Interborough Power House. Below that, though its uniformed hallboys do not like to admit it, it becomes Eleventh Avenue. 59th Street was the latitude where all those baseborn avenues of the old Tenderloin decided to go respectable by changing their names. Eighth became Central Park West, Ninth became Columbus, Tenth became Amsterdam, and Eleventh (or Death Avenue) became West End. But reform is as difficult for streets as for persons. Broadway, careering diagonally across (trollops follow the Trade), drew ever upward its witch-fires and its sulphurous glow. Good old strongholds of middle-class manners were swamped. Apartments once gravid with refinement were given over to the dentist and the private detective (who cries *Confidentially Yours* in the window). When the MacFadden Publications burst into that part of town, reticences tottered. Even as far up as the 70's the West Side struggles to disengage from sombre origins or too gaudy companionship. Then a Childs restaurant—unquestionable banner of fair repute—stems the tide on Broadway. Childs is too shrewd to step in on Doubtful Street. The church also comes to the rescue: a place of worship is combined with an apartment house. "The Cross on top of this building," says a notice, "Guarantees Safety, Security, and Enjoyment."

Of all this shifting struggle—so characteristic of New York and repeated in scores of regions all over town—West End Avenue is perfect symbol. The Interborough Power House, I dare say, gives it vitality to struggle successfully with the New York Central freight yards. It is humble enough here: it eats in Gibbs Diner and smokes its cob pipe in the switchman's little house. It sees lines of milk cans on the sidings and is aware of the solid realities of provender and communication on which citizens depend. (Much of West End Avenue's milk comes from Grand Gorge, N. Y., which is an encouraging name to find printed on the cardboard bottle-top when you rummage the ice-box late at night.) Then the Dodge and other automobile warehouses put ambition into it. It rises to a belt of garages and groceries. At 70th Street it makes as sudden a transformation as any street ever did—except perhaps that social abyss where Tudor City looks over the parapet onto First Avenue. "Here in A.D. 1877," says the tablet in difficult Tudor script, as hen-track as Shakespeare's, "was Paddy Corcoran's Roost." Who was Paddy? They have him in stone with an inverted Irish pipe. One day I walked through Tudor City with W. S. H., a heraldic expert, pursuivant of the various shields, emblems, armorial bearings and stained glaziery of that architect's heyday. Cockle-shells, pelicans, griffons, lymphiads, bars and bends most sinister, nearly made an imbecile of my poor friend. Rouge Dragon himself could never unscramble that débris of the College of Arms. "They intended a boar, but it turned to a talbot," cried W. S. H., examining one fierce escutcheon.

But West End Avenue, when it goes residential at 70th Street, does so in solid fashion, without freak or fantasy. For thirty-five blocks it has probably the most uniform skyline of any avenue in New York. It indulges little in terraces or penthouses; just even bulks of masonry. What other street can show me a run of thirty-five blocks without a shop-window? Few of its apartments have individual names. The Esplanade and the Windermere are two rare exceptions, as also the grand old Apthorp, the Gibraltar of our uptown conservatism. Inside its awful courtyard I have never dared to tread. We leave to the crosstown streets the need to hyperbolize their apartments with pretentious names.

West End is incomparably the most agreeable and convenient of large residential streets, second only to Riverside Drive—whose decline in prestige is mysterious. For that famous old glue-pot stench that used to come drifting across from Jersey has vanished altogether. West End is well churched and doctored. The abandoned hospital at the 72nd Street corner is something of a shock, but the Avenue hurries on uptown, consoling itself with Mr. Schwab's château, its proudest architectural surprise. I wander past Mr. Schwab's railings at night, noting the caretaker's light in the attic and regretting that Charley seems to get so little use of his braw mansion. I like to see the homes of our great barons gay with lights and wassail: I have a thoroughly feudal view of society and believe that we small gentry acquiesce gladly in our restricted orbit provided the nabobs are kicking up a dust at the top of the scale. Sometimes I fear that our rich men have been intimidated by modern doctrines and do not like to be seen at frolic. Nonsense! They owe it to us. When a man builds a French château he should live in it like a French seigneur. For the gayety of West End Avenue I desire to see more lights in that castle, and hear the organ shaking the tall panes.

Certainly with so many doctors (their names provide the only sociological data West End Avenue offers to the student) the street must be healthy. In older days many expectant couples used to come in from the country to West End Avenue to patronize its private maternity hospitals. I knew one fortunate pair to whom the avenue always meant just that. Years later they revisited it, merely to hibernate, and the wife looked around the comfortable sitting-room of the apartment. "I feel as if I ought to be having a baby," she said.

Exceptionally discreet and undemonstrative, West End Avenue offers little drama to the eye. It makes no cajolery to the various arts and Bohemianisms: the modest signs of a Harp Teacher and Hungarian Table Board in one of its few remaining rows of old private domiciles come with a pleasant surprise. It is mainly the battle-ground of the great apartment brokers, Slawson & Hobbs *versus* Bing & Bing, or Sharp & Nassoit *versus* Wood Dolson. Occasionally appears the mysterious ensign of the Rebus Corporation. Bing, Bing, as Penrod used to say, and another monthly payment bit the dust. SUPT. ON PREMISES is the motto of West End Avenue. If your necessity is an apartment with 12 rooms and 3 or 4 baths I think you will have no difficulty in finding one. At certain times of day you will see ladies urging their small dogs for an airing. It is a highway of both leases and leashes.

Behind those regular parallels of stone is plenty of tumultuous life. There are not only doctors and churches but schools also. The avenue is at its prettiest when the children come pouring out of Number 9 at lunch time. In apartment windows you can see the bright eyes of mothers looking down to see that the youngsters are safely on the way. In the afternoons games are chalked on pavements and the youthful bicyclist undulates among pedestrians. Riverside Park and the keen Hudson breeze are only a block away. It is the same breeze and the same river that Edgar Allan Poe knew when he was writing *The Raven* at Broadway and 84th Street. It seems unlikely, and yet perhaps somewhere in those honeycombed cubes of building is a forehead as full of heat and music as his. They cannot spend all their lives with Amos 'n' Andy or Mickey Mouse? When something thrilling comes along good Mr. Levy, the bookseller near Poe's corner, will be quick to welcome it.

It would come from one of the side streets perhaps, rather than from West End Avenue itself. The side streets are more frank with life. There the little notice *Vacancies* is frequent. Not that West End does not have its moments of relaxation. Above 90th Street there are still a few genial old brownstones with curbed bays and alluring circular windows in the attics. At 87th a kindergarten pastes on the window-panes facsimile autumn leaves, cut from paper and crayon-colored, to remind its small prisoners what November is really like. At 95th and 96th are the open tennis courts that have been there many years, and against the western end of the settlement called Pomander Walk old ladies come out, when the sun is warm, and sit in chairs on the pavement. High overhead on clear days you will observe sea-gulls swinging and soaring in the sky.

But in the main West End Avenue must remain an enigma. I have often walked it at night, scanning the rectangles of lighted panes and wondering. Between the dark stream on one side, the bright slices of Broadway on the other, what does it think about? It is too wise to be fashionable, yet it has a certain unostentatious dignity of its own, the more impressive because it has not thought much about it. Those massive portals of glass and iron have doormen with starched neck-cloths and white gloves and braided trousers: I see them off duty sometimes at Bickford's sitting to a cup of coffee. I know they are human, and perhaps profoundly bored; but speculation, a tender plant, abashes before such splendor. Alas, can it be that West End Avenue, like so many other things, has only the meanings we ourselves bring to it? It remains one of my favorite mysteries, and one of the few citadels (in this random city) of the most powerful order in the world: the not easily shakable Medium Class. It has its feet on a Power House.

[IR]

VENISON PASTY

THE GOOD OLD DAYS are gone, we have been frequently and authoritatively assured; and yet, sitting in an agreeable public on William Street where the bright eye of our friend Harold Phillips discerned *venison pasty* on the menu, and listening to a seafaring man describe a recent "blow" off Hatteras during which he stood four hours up to his waist in the bilges, and watching our five jocund companions dismiss no less than twenty-one beakers of cider, we felt no envy whatever for the ancients of the Mermaid Tavern. After venison pasty, and feeling somewhat in the mood of Robin Hood and Friar Tuck, we set off with our friend Endymion for a stroll through the wilderness. The first adventure of note that we encountered was the curb market on Broad Street, where we stood entranced at the merry antics of the brokers. This, however, is a spectacle that no layman can long contemplate and still deem himself sane. That sea of flickering fingers, the hubbub of hoarse cries, and the enigmatic gestures of youths framed in the open windows gave an impression of something fierce and perilous happening. Endymion, still deeming himself in Sherwood Forest, insisted that this was the abode of the Sheriff of Nottingham. "Stout deeds are toward!" he cried. "These villain wights have a damsel imprisoned in yonder keep!" With difficulty we restrained him from pressing to the rescue of the lady (for indeed we could see her, comely enough, appearing now and then at one of the windows; and anon disappearing, abashed at the wild throng). But gradually we realized that no such dire matter was being transacted, for the knights, despite occasional spasms of hot gesticulating fury, were mild and meant her no ill. One, after a sudden flux of business concerning (it seemed) 85 shares of Arizona Copper, fell suddenly placid, and was eating chocolate ice cream from a small paper plate. Young gallants, wearing hats trimmed with variegated brightly coloured stuffs (the favours of their ladies, we doubted not), were conferring together, but without passion or rancour.

We have a compact with our friend Endymion that as soon as either of us spends money for anything not strictly necessary he must straightway return to the office. After leaving the curb market, we found ourselves in a basement bookshop on Broadway, and here Endymion fell afoul of a copy of Thomas Hardy's *Wessex Poems*, illustrated by the author. Piteously he tried to persuade us that it was a matter of professional advancement to him to have this book; moreover, he said, he had just won five dollars at faro (or some such hazard) so that he was not really spending money at all; but we countered all his sophisms with slogging rhetoric. He bought the book, and so had to return to the office in disgrace.

We fared further, having a mind to revisit the old Eastern Hotel, down by the South Ferry, of whose cool and dusky bar-room we had pleasant memories in times gone by; but we found to our distress that this also, like many more of our familiar landmarks, is a prey to the house-wrecker, and is on its way to become an office building. On our way back up Broadway it occurred to us to revisit what we have long considered one of the most impressive temples in our acquaintance, the lobby of the Telephone and Telegraph Building, on Dey Street. Here, passing by the enticing little terrace with brocaded chairs and soft lights where two gracious ladies sit to interview aspiring telephone débutantes, one stands in a dim golden glow, among great fluted pillars and bowls of softly burning radiance swung (like censers) by long chains. Occasionally there is an airy flutter, a bell clangs, bronze doors slide apart, and an elevator appears, in charge of a chastely uniformed priestess. Lights flash up over this dark little cave which stands invitingly open: UP, they say, LOCAL 1–13. The door-sill of the cave shines with a row of golden beads (small lights, to guide the foot)—it is irresistible. There is an upward impulse about the whole place: the light blossoms upward from the hanging translucent shells: people step gently in, the doors close, they are not seen again. It is the temple of the great American religion, *Going Up*. The shining gold stars in the ceiling draw the eye aloft. The temptation is too great. We step into the little bronze crypt, say "Thirteen" at a venture, and are borne softly and fluently up. Then, of course, we have to come down again, past the wagons of spring onions on Fulton Street, and back to the office.

[P]

WEST BROADWAY

DID YOU ever hear of Finn Square? No? Very well, then, we shall have to inflict upon you some paragraphs from our unpublished work: "A Scenic Guidebook to the Sixth Avenue L." The itinerary is a frugal one: you do not have to take the L, but walk along under it.

Streets where an L runs have a fascination of their own. They have a shadowy gloom, speckled and striped with the sunlight that slips through the trestles. West Broadway, which along most of its length is straddled by the L, is a channel of odd humours. Its real name, you know, is South Fifth Avenue; but the Avenue got so snobbish it insisted on its humbler brother changing its name. Let us take it from Spring Street southward.

Ribbons, purple, red, and green, were the first thing to catch our eye. Not the ribbons of the milliner, however, but the carbon tapes of the typewriter, big cans of them being loaded on a junk wagon. "Purple Ribbons," we have often thought, would be a neat title for a volume of verses written on a typewriter. What happens to the used ribbons of modern poets? Mr. Hilaire Belloc, or Mr. Chesterton, for instance. Give me but what these ribbons type and all the rest is merely tripe, as Edmund Waller might have said. Near the ribbons we saw a paper-box factory, where a number of high-spirited young women were busy at their machines. A broad strip of thick green paint was laid across the lower half of the windows so that these immured damsels might not waste their employers' time in watching goings on along the pavement.

Broome and Watts streets diverge from West Broadway in a V. At the corner of Watts is one of West Broadway's many saloons, which by courageous readjustments still manage to play their useful part. What used to be called the "Business Men's Lunch" now has a tendency to name itself "Luncheonette" or "Milk Bar." But the old decorations remain. In this one you will see the electric fixtures wrapped in heavy lead foil, the kind of sheeting that is used in packages of tea. At the corner of Grand Street is the Sapphire Café, and what could be a more appealing name than that? "Delicious Chocolate with Whipped Cream," says a sign outside the Sapphire. And some way farther down (at the corner of White Street) is a jolly old tavern which looked so antique and inviting that we went inside. Little tables piled high with hunks of bread betokened the approaching lunch hour. A shimmering black cat winked a drowsy topaz eye from her lounge in the corner. We asked for cider. There was none, but our gaze fell upon a bottle marked "Irish Moss." We asked for some, and the barkeep pushed the bottle forward with a tiny glass. Irish Moss, it seems, is the kind of drink which the customer pours out for himself, so we decanted a generous slug. It proved to be a kind of essence of horehound, of notable tartness and pungency, very like a powerful cough syrup. We wrote it off on our ledger as experience. Beside us stood a sturdy citizen with a freight hook round his neck, deducing a foaming crock of the legitimate percentage.

The chief landmark of that stretch of West Broadway is the tall spire of St. Alphonsus' Church, near Canal Street. Up the steps and through plain brown doors we went into the church, which was cool, quiet, and empty, save for a busy charwoman with humorous Irish face. Under the altar canopy wavered a small candle spark, and high overhead, in the dimness, were orange and scarlet gleams from a stained window. A crystal chandelier hanging in the aisle caught pale yellow tinctures of light. No Catholic church, wherever you find it, is long empty;

a man and a girl entered just as we went out. At each side of the front steps the words *Copiosa apud eum redemtio* are carved in the stone. The mason must have forgotten the *p* in the last word. A silver plate on the brick house next door says *Redemptorist Fathers.*

York Street, running off to the west, gives a glimpse of the old Hudson River Railroad freight depot. St. John's Lane, running across York Street, skirts the ruins of old St. John's Church, demolished when the Seventh Avenue subway was built. On the old brown house at the corner some urchin has chalked the word CRAZY. Perhaps this is an indictment of adult civilization as a whole. If one strolls thoughtfully about some of these streets—say Thompson Street—on a hot day, and sees the children struggling to grow up, he feels like going back to that word CRAZY and italicizing it. The tiny triangle of park at Beach Street is carefully locked up, you will notice—the only plot of grass in that neighbourhood—so that bare feet cannot get at it. Superb irony of circumstance: on the near corner stands the Castoria factory, Castoria being (if we remember the ads) what Mr. Fletcher gave baby when she was sick.

Where Varick Street runs in there is a wide triangular spread, and this, gentle friends, is Finn Park, named for a New York boy who was killed in France. The name reminded us also of Elfin Finn, the somewhat complacent stage child who poses for chic costumes in *Vogue*. We were wondering which was a more hazardous bringing up for a small girl, living on Thompson Street or posing for a fashion magazine. From Finn Square there is a stirring view of the Woolworth Tower. Also of Claflin's packing cases on their way off to Selma, Ala., and Kalamazoo, Mich., and to Nathan Povich, Bath, Me. That conjunction of Finn and Bath, Me., suggested to us that the empty space there would be a good place to put in a municipal swimming pool for the urchins of the district.

Drawn from the wood, which legend still stands on the pub at the corner of Duane Street, sounds a bit ominous these wood alcohol days. John Barleycorn may be down, but he's never out, as someone has remarked. For near Murray Street you will find one of those malt-and-hops places which are getting numerous. They contain all the necessary equipment for—well, as the signs suggest, for making malt bread and coffee cake—bottle-capping apparatus and rubber tubing and densimeters, and all such things used in breadmaking. As the signs say: "Malt syrup for making malt bread, coffee, cake, and medicinal purposes."

To conclude the scenic pleasures of the Sixth Avenue L route, we walk through the cool, dark, low-roofed tunnel of Church Street in those interesting blocks just north of Vesey. We hark to the merry crowing of the roosters in the Barclay Street poultry stores; and we look past the tall gray pillars of St. Peter's Church at the flicker of scarlet and gold lights near the altar. The black-robed nuns one often sees along Church Street, with their pale, austere, hooded faces, bring a curious touch of medievalism into the roaring tide that flows under the Hudson Terminal Building. They always walk in twos, which seems to indicate an even greater apprehension of the World. And we always notice, as we go by the pipe shop at the corner of Barclay Street, that this worthy merchant has painted some inducements on one side of his shop; which reminds us of the same device used by the famous tobacconist Bacon, in Cambridge, England. Why, we wonder, doesn't our friend fill the remaining blank panel on his side wall by painting there some stanzas from Calverley's "Ode to Tobacco"? We will gladly give him the text to copy if he wants it.

[PP]

1100 WORDS

THE MANAGING EDITOR, the city editor, the production manager, the foreman of the composing room, and the leading editorial writer having all said to us with a great deal of sternness, "Your copy for Saturday has got to be upstairs by such and such a time, because we are going to make up the page at so and so A.M.," we got rather nervous.

If we may say so, we did not like the way they said it. They spoke—and we are thinking particularly of the production manager—with a kind of paternal severity that was deeply distressing to our spirit. They are all, in off hours, men of delightfully easy disposition. They are men with whom it would be a pleasure and a privilege to be cast away on a desert island or in a crowded subway train. It is only just to say that they are men whom we admire greatly. When we meet them in the elevator, or see them at Frank's having lunch, how full of jolly intercourse they are. But in the conduct of their passionate and perilous business, that is, of getting the paper out on time, a holy anguish shines upon their brows. The stern daughter of the voice of God has whispered to them, and they pass on the whisper to us through a megaphone.

That means to say that within the hour we have got to show up something in the neighbourhood of 1100 words to these magistrates and overseers. With these keys—typewriter keys, of course—we have got to unlock our heart. Milton, thou shouldst be living at this hour. Speaking of Milton, the damp that fell round his path (in Wordsworth's sonnet) was nothing to the damp that fell round our alert vestiges as we hastened to the Salamis station in that drench this morning. (We ask you to observe our self-restraint. We might have said "drenching downpour of silver Long Island rain," or something of that sort, and thus got several words nearer our necessary total of 1100. But we scorn, even when writing against time, to take petty advantages. Let us be brief, crisp, packed with thought. Let it stand as drench, while you admire our proud conscience.)

Eleven hundred words—what a lot could be said in 1100 words! We stood at the front door of the baggage car (there is an odd irony in this: the leading editorial writer, one of the most implacable of our taskmasters, is spending the summer at Sea Cliff, and he gets the last empty seat left in the smoker. So we, getting on at Salamis, have to stand in the baggage car) watching the engine rock and roar along the rails, while the rain sheeted the level green fields. It is very agreeable to ride on a train in the rain. We have never known just why, but it conduces to thought. The clear trickles of water are drawn slantwise across the window panes, and one watches, absently, the curious behaviour of the drops. They hang bulging and pendulous, in one spot for some seconds. Then, as they swell, suddenly they break loose and zigzag swiftly down the pane, following the slippery pathway that previous drops have made. It is like a little puzzle game where you manœuvre a weighted capsule among pegs toward a narrow opening. "Pigs in clover," they sometimes call it, but who knows why? The conduct of raindrops on a smoking-car window is capricious and odd, but we must pass on. That topic alone would serve for several hundred words, but we will not be opportunist.

We stood at the front door of the baggage car, and in a pleasant haze of the faculties we thought of a number of things. We thought of some books we had seen up on East Fifty-ninth Street, in that admirable row of old bookshops, particularly Mowry Saben's volume of essays, *The Spirit of*

Life, which we are going back to buy one of these days; so please let it alone. We then got out a small note-book in which we kept memoranda of books we intend to read and pored over it zealously. Just for fun, we will tell you three of the titles we have noted there:

The Voyage of the Hoppergrass, by E. L. Pearson.
People and Problems, by Fabian Franklin.
Broken Stowage, by David W. Bone.

But most of all we thought, in a vague sentimental way, about that pleasant Long Island country through which the engine was haling and hallooing all those carloads of audacious commuters.

Only the other day we heard a wise man say that he did not care for Long Island, because one has to travel through a number of half-built suburbs before getting into real country. We felt, when he said it, that it would be impossible for us to tell him how much some of those growing suburbs mean to us, for we have lived in them. There is not one of those little frame dwellings that doesn't give us a thrill as we buzz past them. If you voyage from Brooklyn, as we do, you will have noticed two stations (near Jamaica) called Clarenceville and Morris Park. Now we have never got off at those stations, though we intend to some day. But in those rows of small houses and in sudden glimpses of modest tree-lined streets and corner drug stores we can see something that we are not subtle enough to express. We see it again in the scrap of green park by the station at Queens, and in the brave little public library near the same station—which we cannot see from the train, though we often try to; but we know it is there, and probably the same kindly lady librarian and the children borrowing books. We see it again—or we did the other day—in a field at Mineola where a number of small boys were flying kites in the warm, clean, softly perfumed air of a July afternoon. We see it in the vivid rows of colour in the florist's meadow at Floral Park. We don't know just what it is, but over all that broad tract of hardworking suburbs there is a secret spirit of practical and persevering decency that we somehow associate with the soul of America.

We see it with the eye of a lover, and we know that it is good.

Having got as far as this, we took the trouble to count all the words up to this point. The total is exactly 1100.

[PP]

A CITY NOTE-BOOK

WELL, now let us see in what respect we are richer to-day than we were yesterday.

Coming down Fifth Avenue on top of a bus, we saw a man absorbed in a book. Ha, we thought, here is our chance to see how bus reading compares to subway reading! After some manœuvering, we managed to get the seat behind the victim. The volume was *Every Man a King*, by Orison Swett Marden, and the uncrowned monarch reading it was busy with the thirteenth chapter, to wit: "Thoughts Radiate as Influence." We did a little radiating of our own, and it seemed to reach him, for presently he grew uneasy, put the volume carefully away in a brief-case, and (as far as we could see) struck out toward his kingdom, which apparently lay on the north shore of Forty-second Street.

We felt then that we would recuperate by glancing at a little literature. So we made our way toward the newly enlarged shrine of James F. Drake on Fortieth Street. Here we encountered our friends the two Messrs. Drake, junior, and complimented them on their thews and sinews, these two gentlemen having recently, unaided, succeeded in moving a half-ton safe, filled with the treasures of Elizabethan literature, into the new sanctum. Here, where formerly sped the nimble fingers of M. Tappe's young ladies, busy with the compilation of engaging bonnets for the fair, now stand upon wine-dark shelves the rich gold and amber of fine bindings. We were moved by this sight. We said in our heart, we will erect a small madrigal upon this theme, entitled: "Song Upon Certain Songbirds of the Elizabethan Age Now Garnishing the Chamber Erstwhile Bright With the Stuffed Plumage of the Milliner." To the Messrs. Drake we mentioned the interesting letter of Mr. J. Acton Lomax in yesterday's *Tribune*, which called attention to the fact that the poem at the end of *Through the Looking Glass* is an acrostic giving the name of the original Alice—viz., Alice Pleasance Liddell. In return for which we were shown a copy of the first edition of *Alice in Wonderland*. Here, too, we dallied for some time over a first edition of Dr. Johnson's *Dictionary*, and were pleased to learn that the great doctor was no more infallible in proofreading than the rest of us, one of our hosts pointing out to us a curious error by which some words beginning in COV had slipped in ahead of words beginning in COU.

AT NOON to-day we climbed on a Riverside Drive bus at Seventy-ninth Street and rode in the mellow gold of autumn up to Broadway and 168th. Serene, gilded weather; sunshine as soft and tawny as candlelight, genial at midday as the glow of an open fire in spite of the sharpness of the early morning. Battleships lay in the river with rippling flags. Men in flannels were playing tennis on the courts below Grant's Tomb; everywhere was a convincing appearance of comfort and prosperity. The beauty of the children, the good clothing of everybody, canes swinging on the pavements, cheerful faces untroubled by thought, the warm benevolence of sunlight, bronzing trees along Riverside Park, a man reading a book on the summit of that rounded knoll of rock near Eighty-fourth Street which childen call "Mount Tom"—everything was so bright in life and vigour that the sentence seems to need no verb. Joan of Arc, poised on horseback against her screen of dark cedars, held her sword clearly against the pale sky. Amazingly sure and strong and established seem the rich façades of Riverside Drive apartment houses, and the landlords were rolling in limousines up to Claremont to have lunch. One small apartment house, near Eighty-third or thereabouts, has been renamed the Château-Thierry.

After crossing the long bridge above Claremont and the deep ravine where ships and ferryboats and coal stations abound, the bus crosses on 135th Street to Broadway. At 153d, the beautiful cemetery of Trinity Parish, leafy paths lying peaceful in the strong glow. At 166th Street is an open area now called Mitchel Square, with an outcrop of rock polished by the rearward breeks of many sliding urchins. Some children were playing on that small summit with a toy parachute made of light paper and a pebble attached by threads.

On 168th Street alongside the big armoury of the Twenty-second Engineers boys were playing baseball, with a rubber ball, pitching it so that the batter received it on the bounce and struck it with his fist. According to the score chalked on the pavement the "Bronx Browns" and the "Haven Athletics" were just finishing a rousing contest, in which the former were victors, 1–0. Haven Avenue, near by, is a happy little street perched high above the river. A small terraced garden with fading flowers looks across the Hudson to the woody Palisades. Modest apartment houses are built high on enormous buttresses, over the steep scarp of the hillside. Through cellar windows coal was visible, piled high in the bins; children were trooping home for dinner; a fine taint of frying onions hung in the shining air. Everywhere in that open, half-suburban, comfortable region was a feeling of sane, established life. An old man with a white beard was greeted by two urchins, who ran up and kissed him heartily as he beamed upon them. Grandpa, one supposes! Plenty of signs indicating small apartments to rent, four and five rooms. And down that upper slant of Broadway, as the bus bumbles past rows of neat prosperous-seeming shops, one feels the great tug and pulling current of life that flows down the channel, the strange energy of the huge city lying below. The tide was momentarily stilled, but soon to resume action. There was a magic touch apparent, like the stillness of a palace in a fairy tale, bewitched into waiting silence.

SOMETIMES on our way to the office in the morning we stop in front of a jeweller's window near Maiden Lane and watch a neat little elderly gentleman daintily setting out his employer's gauds and trinkets for the day. We like to see him brood cheerfully over the disposition of his small amber-coloured velvet mats, and the arrangement of the rings, vanity cases, necklaces, and precious stones. They twinkle in the morning light, and he leans downward in the window, innocently displaying the widening parting on his pink scalp. He purses his lips in a silent whistle as he cons his shining trifles and varies his plan of display every day.

Now a modern realist (we have a painful suspicion) if he were describing this pleasant man would deal rather roughly with him. You know exactly how it would be done. He would be a weary, saddened, shabby figure: his conscientious attention to the jewels in his care would be construed as the painful and creaking routine of a victim of commercial greed; a bitter irony would be distilled from the contrast of his own modest station in life and the huge value of the lucid crystals and carbons under his hands. His hands—ah, the realist would angrily see some brutal pathos or unconscious naughtiness in the crook of the old mottled fingers. How that widening parting in the gray head would be gloated upon. It would be very easy to do, and it would be (if we are any judge) wholly false.

For we have watched the little old gentleman many times, and we have quite an affection for him. We see him as one perfectly happy in the tidy and careful round of his tasks; and when his tenderly brushed gray poll leans above his treasures, and he gently devises new patterns by which the emeralds or the gold cigarette cases will catch the slant of 9 o'clock sunlight, we seem to see one who is enjoying his own placid conception of beauty, and who is not a figure of pity or reproach, but one of decent honour and excellent fidelity.

One of our colleagues, a lusty genial in respect of tobacco, has told us of a magnificent way to remove an evil and noisome taste from an old pipe that hath been smoked overlong. He says, clean the bowl carefully (not removing the cake) and wash tenderly in fair, warm water. Then, he says, take a teaspoonful of the finest vatted Scotch whiskey (or, if the pipe be of exceeding size, a tablespoonful of the same) and pour it delicately into the bowl. Apply a lighted match, and let the liquor burn itself out. It will do so, he avouches, with a gentle blue flame of great beauty and serenity. The action of this burning elixir, he maintains, operates to sizzle and purge away all impurity from the antique incrustation in the bowl. After letting the pipe cool, and then filling it with a favourite blend of mingled Virginia, Perique, and Latakia, our friend asserts that he is blessed with a cool, saporous, and enchanting fumigation which is so fragrant that even his wife has remarked upon it in terms complimentary. Our friend says (but we fear he draws the longbow nigh unto fracture) that the success of this method may be tested so: if one lives, as he does, in the upward stories of a tall apartment house, one should take the pipe so cleansed to the window-sill, and, smoking it heartily, lean outward over the sill. On a clear, still, blue evening, the air being not too gusty, the vapours will disperse and eddy over the street; and he maintains with great zeal that passersby ten tiers below will very soon look upward from the pavement, sniffingly, to discern the source of such admirable fumes. He has even known them, he announces, to hail him from the street, in tones of eager inquiry, to learn what kind of tobacco he is smoking.

All this we have duly meditated and find ourselves considerably stirred. Now there is only one thing that stands between ourself and such an experiment.

THERE are some who hold by the theory that on visiting a restaurant it is well to pick out a table that is already cleared rather than one still bearing the débris of a previous patron's meal. We offer convincing proof to the contrary.

Rambling, vacant of mind and guileless of intent, in a certain quiet portion of the city—and it is no use for you, O client, to ask where, for our secrecy is firm as granite—we came upon an eating house and turned inward. There were tables spread with snowy cloths, immaculate; there were also tables littered with dishes. We chose one of the latter, for a waiter was removing the plates, and we thought that by sitting there we would get prompter service. We sat down and our eye fell upon a large china cup that had been used by the preceding luncher. In the bottom of that cup was a little pool of dark dregs, a rich purple colour, most agreeable to gaze upon. Happy possibilities were opened to our mind. Like the fabled Captain X, we had a Big Idea. We made no outcry, nor did we show our emotion, but when the waiter asked for our order we said, calmly: "Sausages and some of the red wine." He was equally calm and uttered no comment.

Soon he came back (having conferred, as we could see out of the wing of our eye) with his boss. "What was it you ordered?" he said.

"Sausages," we replied, urbanely, "and some of the red wine."

"I don't remember having served you before," he said. "I can't give you anything like that."

We saw that we must win his confidence and we thought rapidly. "It's perfectly all right," we said. "Mr. Bennett" (we said, seizing the first name that came into our head), "who comes here every day, told me about it. You know Mr. Bennett; he works over on Forty-second Street and comes here right along."

Again he departed, but returned anon with smiling visage. "If you're a friend of Mr. Bennett's," he said, "it's all right. You know, we have to be careful."

"Quite right," we said; "be wary." And we laid hand firmly on the fine hemorrhage of the grape.

A little later in the adventure, when we were asked what dessert we would have, we found stewed rhubarb on the menu, and very fine stewed rhubarb it was; wherefore we say that our time was not ill-spent and we shall keep the secret to ourself.

But we can't help feeling grateful to Mr. Bennett, whoever he is.

OCCASIONALLY (but not often) in the exciting plexus of our affairs (conducted, as we try to persuade ourself, with so judicious a jointure of caution and hilarity) we find it necessary to remain in town for dinner. Then, and particularly in spring evenings, we are moved and exhilarated by that spectacle that never loses its enchantment, the golden beauty and glamour of downtown New York after the homeward ebb has left the streets quiet and lonely. By six o'clock in a May sunset the office is a cloister of delicious peace and solitude. Let us suppose (oh, a case merely hypothetic) that you have got to attend a dinner somewhere in the Forties, say at half-past seven; and it is requisite that evening clothes should be worn. You have brought them to the office, modestly hidden, in a bag; and in that almost unbelievable privacy, toward half-past six, you have an enjoyable half hour of luxurious amusement and contemplation. The office, one repeats, is completely stripped of tenants—save perhaps an occasional grumbling sortie by the veteran janitor. So all its resources are open for you to use as boudoir. Now, in an office situated like this there is, at sunset time, a variety of scenic richness to be contemplated. From the President's office (putting on one's hard-boiled shirt) one can look down upon St. Paul's churchyard, lying a pool of pale blue shadow in the rising dusk. From the City Room (inserting studs) one sees the river sheeted with light. From the office of the Literary Editor (lacing up one's shoes) one may study the wild pinnacle of Woolworth, faintly superfused with a brightness of gold and pink. From the office of one of our dramatic critics the view is negligible (being but a hardy brick wall), but the critic, debonair creature, has a small mirror of his own, so there one manages the ticklish business of the cravat. And from our own kennel, where are transacted the last touches (transfer of pipe, tobacco, matches, Long Island railroad timetable, commutation ticket, etc., to the other pockets) there is a heavenly purview of those tall cliffs of lower Broadway, nobly terraced into the soft, translucent sky. In that exquisite clarity and sharpness of New York's evening light are a loveliness and a gallantry hardly to be endured. At seven o'clock of a May evening it is poetry unspeakable. O magnificent city (one says), there will come a day when others will worship and celebrate your mystery; and when not one of them will know or care how much I loved you. But these words, obscure and perishable, I leave you as a testimony that I also understood.

She cannot be merely the cruel Babel they like to describe her: the sunset light would not gild her so tenderly.

It was a great relief to us yesterday evening to see a man reading a book in the subway. We have undergone so many embarrassments trying to make out the titles of the books the ladies read, without running afoul of the Traveller's Aid Society, that we heaved a sigh of relief and proceeded to stalk our quarry with a light heart. Let us explain that on a crowded train it is not such an easy task. You see your victim at the other end of the car. First you have to buffet your way until you get next to him. Then, just as you think you are in a position to do a little careful snooping, he innocently shifts the book to the other hand. This means you have got to navigate, somehow, toward the hang-handle on the other side of him. Very well. By the time the train gets to Bowling Green we have seen that it is a fattish book, bound in green cloth, and the author's name begins with FRAN. That doesn't help much. As the train roars under the river you manage, by leanings and twistings, to see the publisher's name—in this case, Longmans. At Borough Hall a number of passengers get out, and the hunted reader sits down. Ten to one he will hold the book in such a way that you cannot see the title. At Nevins Street you get a seat beside him. At Atlantic Avenue, as he is getting off, you propose your head over his shoulder in the jam on the stairs and see what you are after. *Lychgate Hall*, by M. E. Francis. And in this case, success left us none the wiser.

Atlantic Avenue, by the way, always seems to us an ideal place for the beginning of a detective story. (Speaking of that, a very jolly article in this month's *Bookman*, called "How Old Is Sherlock Holmes?" has revived our old ambition to own a complete set of all the Sherlock Holmes tales, and we are going to set about scouring the town for them.) Every time we pass through the Atlantic Avenue maelstrom, which is twelve times a week, we see, as plain as print, the beginning of two magazine tales.

One begins as the passengers are streaming through the gate toward the 5:27 train. There is a very beautiful damsel who always sits on the left-hand side of the next to last car, by an open window. On her plump and comely white hand, which holds the latest issue of a motion picture magazine, is a sparkling diamond ring. Suddenly all the lights in the train go out. Through the open window comes a brutal grasp which wrenches the bauble from her finger. There are screams, etc., etc. When the lights go on again, of course there is no sign of the criminal. Five minutes later, Mr. Geoffrey Dartmouth, enjoying a chocolate ice cream soda in the little soft-drink alcove at the corner of the station, is astonished to find a gold ring, the stone missing, at the bottom of his paper soda container.

The second story begins on the Atlantic Avenue platform of the Lexington Avenue subway. It is 9 A.M., and a crowded train is pulling out. Just before the train leaves a young man steps off one of the cars, leaving behind him (though not at once noticed) a rattan suitcase. This young man disappears in the usual fashion, viz., by mingling with the crowd. When the train gets to the end of the run the unclaimed suitcase is opened, and found to contain—*continued on page* 186.

EVERY now and then we take a stroll up Irving Place. It is changing slowly, but it still has much of the flavour that Arthur Maurice had in mind when he christened it "the heart of O. Henry land." Number 55, the solid, bleached brownstone house where O. Henry once lived, is still there: it seems to be some sort of ecclesiastical rendezvous, if one may judge by the letters C. H. A. on the screen and the pointed carving of the doorway. Number 53, next door, always interests us greatly: the windows give a glimpse of the most extraordinary number of cages of canaries.

The old German theatre seems to have changed its language: the boards speak now in Yiddish. The chiropractor and psycho-analyst has invaded the Place, as may be seen by a sign on the eastern side. O. Henry would surely have told a yarn about him if he had been there fifteen years ago. There are still quite a number of the old brown houses, with their iron railings and little patches of grass. The chocolate factory still diffuses its pleasant candied whiff. At noontime the street is full of the high-spirited pupils of the Washington Irving High School. As for the Irving house itself, it is getting a new coat of paint. The big corset works, we dare say, has come since O. Henry's time. We had quite an adventure there once. We can't remember how it came about, but for some reason or other we went to that building to see the chief engineer. All we can remember about it was that he had been at sea at one time, and we went to see him on some maritime errand. We found that he and his family lived in a comfortable apartment on the roof of the factory, and we remember making our way, with a good many blushes, through several hundred or thousand young ladies who were industriously working away at their employer's business and who seemed to us to be giggling more than necessary. After a good deal of hunting we found our way to a secret stair and reached our seafaring engineer of the corset factory in his eyrie, where (we remember) there were oil paintings of ships on the walls and his children played about on the roof as though on the deck of a vessel.

Irving Place is also very rich in interesting little shops—laundries, tailors, carpenters, stationers, and a pleasant bookshop. It is a haunt of hand-organ men. The cool tavern at the corner of Eighteenth, where Con Delaney tended the bar in the days when O. Henry visited it, is there still. All along the little byway is a calm, genteel, domestic mood, in spite of the encroachments of factories and apartment houses. There are window boxes with flowers, and a sort of dim suffusion of conscious literary feeling. One has a suspicion that in all those upper rooms are people writing short stories. "Want to see a freak?" asks the young man in the bookshop as we are looking over his counters. We do, of course, and follow his animated gesture. Across the street comes a plump young woman, in a very short skirt of a violet blue, with a thick mane of bobbed hair, carrying her hat in her hand. She looks rather comfortable and seemly to us, but something about her infuriates the bookseller. He is quite Freudian in his indignation that any young woman should habit herself so. We wonder what the psycho-analyst a few blocks below would say about it. And walking a few paces further, one comes upon the green twitter, the tended walks and pink geranium beds of Gramercy Park.

THERE is no time when we need spiritual support so much as when we are having our hair cut, for indeed it is the only time when we are ever thoroughly and entirely Bored. But having found a good-natured barber who said he would not mind our reading a book while he was shearing, we went through with it. The ideal book to read at such a time (we offer you this advice, brave friends) is the *Tao* of Lao-Tse, that ancient and admirable Chinese sage. (Dwight Goddard's translation is very agreeable.) "The Tao," as of course you know, is generally translated The Way, i.e., the Way of Life of the Reasonable Man.

Lao-Tse, we assert, is the ideal author to read while the barber is at his business. He answers every inquiry that will be made, and all you have to do is hold the book up and point to your favourite marked passages.

When the barber says, genially, "Well, have you done your Christmas shopping yet?" we raise the book and point to this maxim:

Taciturnity is natural to man.

When he says, "How about a nice little shampoo this morning?" we are prompt to indicate:

The wise man attends to the inner significance of things and does not concern himself with outward appearances.

When, as we sit in the chair, we see (in the mirror before us) the lovely reflection of the beautiful manicure lady, and she arches her eyebrows at us to convey the intimation that we ought to have our hands attended to, old Lao-Tse is ready with the answer. We reassure ourself with his remark:

Though he be surrounded with sights that are magnificent, the wise man will remain calm and unconcerned.

When the shine boy offers to burnish our shoes, we call his attention to:

He who closes his mouth and shuts his sense gates will be free from trouble to the end of life.

When the barber suggests that if we were now to have a liberal douche of bay rum sprayed over our poll it would be a glittering consummation of his task, we show him the words:

If one tries to improve a thing, he mars it.

And when (finally) the irritated tonsor suggests that if we don't wait so long next time before getting our hair cut we will not be humiliated by our condition, we exhibit Lao-Tse's aphorism:

The wise man is inaccessible to favour or hate; he cannot be reached by profit or injury; he cannot be honoured or humiliated.

"It's very easy," says the barber as we pay our check; "just drop in here once a month and we'll fix you up." And we point to:

The wise man lives in the world, but he lives cautiously, dealing with the world cautiously. Many things that appear easy are full of difficulties.

To a lot of people who are in a mortal scurry and excitement what is so maddening as the calm and unruffled serenity of a dignified philosopher who gazes unperturbed upon their pangs? So did we meditate when facing the deliberate and mild tranquillity of the priestly person presiding over the bulletin board announcing the arrival of trains at the Pennsylvania Station. It was in that desperate and curious limbo known as the "exit concourse," where baffled creatures wait to meet others arriving on trains and maledict the architect who so planned matters that the passengers arrive on two sides at once, so that one stands grievously in the middle slewing his eyes to one side and another in a kind of vertigo, attempting to con both exits. We cannot go into this matter in full (when, indeed, will we find enough white paper and enough energy to discuss *anything* in full, in the way, perhaps, Henry James would have blanketed it?), but we will explain that we were waiting to meet someone, someone we had never seen, someone of the opposite sex and colour, in short, that rare and desirable creature a cook, imported from another city, and she had missed her train, and all we knew was her first name and that she would wear a "brown turban." After prowling distraitly round the station (and a large station it is) and asking every likely person if her name was Amanda, and being frowned upon and suspected as a black slaver, and thinking we felt on our neck the heated breath and handcuffs of the Travellers' Aid Society, we decided that Amanda must have missed her train and concluded to wait for the next. Then it was, to return to our thesis, that we had occasion to observe and feel in our own person the wretched pangs of one in despair facing the gentle—shall we say hesychastic?—peace and benevolent quietness of the man at the bulletin board. Bombarded with questions by the impatient and anxious crowd, with what pacific good nature he answered our doubts and querulities. And yet how irritating was his calmness, his deliberation, the very placidity of his mien as he surveyed his clacking telautograph and leisurely took out his schoolroom eraser, rubbed off an inscription, then polished the board with a cloth, then looked for a piece of chalk and wrote in a fine curly hand some notation about a train from Cincinnati in which we were not at all interested. Ah, here we are at last! Train from Philadelphia! Arriving on track Number—; no, wrong again! He only changes *5 minutes late* to *10 minutes late*. The crowd mutters and fumes. The telautograph begins to stutter and we gaze at it feverishly. It stops again and our dominie looks at it calmly. He taps it gently with his finger. We wonder, is it out of order? Perhaps that train is already coming in and he doesn't know it, and Amanda may be wandering lost somewhere in the vast vistas of the station looking for us. Shall we dash up to the waiting room and have another look? But Amanda does not know the station, and there are so many places where benches are put, and she might think one of those was the waiting room that had been mentioned. And then there is this Daylight Saving time mix-up. In a sudden panic we cannot figure out whether Philadelphia time is an hour ahead of New York time or an hour behind. We told Amanda to take the one o'clock from Philadelphia. Well, should she arrive here at two o'clock or at four? It being now 5:10 by our time, what are we to do? The telautograph clicks. The priestly person slowly and gravely writes down that the Philadelphia train is arriving on Track 6. There is a mad rush: everyone dashes to the gate. And here, coming up the stairs, is a coloured lady whose anxiously speculating eye must be the one we seek. In the mutuality of our worry we recognize each other at once. We seize her in triumph; in fact, we could have embraced her. All our anguish is past. Amanda is ours!

[PP]

THOUGHTMARKS

IT IS DANGEROUS to fix undue affection on any antique landmark in New York; when you have learned to love and understand it, suddenly it disappears. Henceforward I shall have to specialize more in thoughtmarks. The other day I went to show a man that old courtyard that opened off an alley in Ann Street. There was a dark smithy there, and a round brick building which (I've been told) was the original Astor fur-warehouse. The fur cap that old Johnjake was wearing when Walt Whitman saw him probably came from there. This little *cul de sac* was much esteemed by the Three Hours for Lunch Club; occasionally, in its rambles, the Visionary Committee of the club would prowl in there and concoct schemes for founding the Ann Street Country Club. The old raftered cellar, with its open hearths, and dark corners, would make the pleasantest chop house in New York, and very unlike our many Olde English chopping houses where visiting Englishmen feel themselves so hilariously ill at ease. Upstairs would be bedrooms, the quietest in the city, for Ann Street is all darkness and dream by dinner time; the cobbled yard would be sodded for a small bowling green; it would have been the last and loveliest shred of ancient Manhattan. But going there for another look, nothing remains but a quarry of rubbled brick and stacked timbers. It is an ill thing to postpone one's dreams.

Well, I was making a little mental memorandum of the places in New York that I specially wanted to show a British visitor. There wasn't time to reconnoitre more than a few of them, because the legendary American hustle is sheer torpor compared with the agile haste of the Briton when he gets over here. Even if you do catch him for a few hours' leisurely sightseeing, he will be dodging into telephone booths every half hour to explain to someone why he will be late for the next appointment. But, for the benefit of other prowlers, I will tell you what I wanted him to see. First of all I intended him to lunch in the little unpublicitied chop house on Golden Hill (John Street) which (whatever Boston may demur) is I believe just about the place where the first rumpus occurred in the Revolution. We weren't going to eat a very heavy lunch, though, because afterward I was planning to rush him up to Morningside to have a stack of buckwheat cakes in some restaurant as near as possible to Barnard College. This because I have always been told that Barnard is built on the site of a buckwheat field where the Battle of Harlem Heights was conducted. It was a successful "attack on the flank," the history books say; and so are buckwheat cakes. After this we would go along Riverside Drive and I would point out the curious adjacent contrast of the two most notable tombs in New York—those of General Grant and of the Amiable Child. Then, from the depth of Morningside Park, beside the delightful statue of the bear and the faun, we would look up at Gutzon Borglum's angel on the roof of the cathedral.

This suggests another upward gaze I'm fond of; we would hasten downtown again to Vesey Street, and ascending to the balcony on the tenth floor of the former *Evening Post* building we'd admire Mrs. Batchelder's golden triumph on the roof of the Telephone Company. There has always been some argument as to the exactly correct name of this statue: I have heard it stated as "The Spirit of Electricity"; but I believe it symbolizes the gallant exultation of the human mind on having put in its nickel and got the right number. In St. Paul's Church, below, I would call my Briton's attention to George Washington's prayer for the American people: that they should "cultivate a spirit of subordination." He would reply, in fact did, that if they had done so there wouldn't have been any United States.

I should have taken him, but forgot while we were uptown, to the Schuyler Arms apartment house on 98th Street; I love it because I lived there for a while and also because (according to Mr. Fremont Rider's *New York City*) it is just about there that the Woodman spared That Tree and touched not a single bough. Instead, we would go to Schulte's: the bookstore, not the tobacconist, in that stretch of Fourth Avenue among so many other delightful bookshops. We would go to Schulte's because (I will make a confession) although Roger Mifflin's Haunted Bookshop was supposed to be in Brooklyn, its author actually was thinking of the darkling and savoury piled-up alcoves of Schulte's. Mr. Mifflin's place was really a sort of morganatic offspring of an uncanonized union of Schulte's on Fourth Avenue and Niel Morrow Ladd's in Brooklyn.

People who are coming to New York sometimes write to ask (and by the way, Anatole France wasn't the first writer to keep his unanswered letters in the bathtub; De Quincey used to do the same thing) where is the real bohemia. They are growing suspicious of the somewhat determined bohemianism of Greenwich Village or of Longacre. Of course every generation, every profession, has its own bohemia; bohemia is wherever you happen to be having a good time; but the place that comes nearest to my notion of what that mythical coast should look like is the old saloon on Seventh Street near the Cooper Union. It was John Sloan's drawing of it, in *Harper's Weekly* (in October, 1913), and an article by Hutchins Hapgood, that first sent me there; it is a fine old Tammany-flavoured sanctum, with Niblo's Garden playbills and that genteel air of literature and politics and sentiment that belongs to an honest saloon. I suppose the youngest generation doesn't know it at all; it is the house's pride that no woman has ever been admitted, probably it is the last place in New York where the bartender would be thoroughly scandalized if a female appeared. Bill McSorley, succeeding his father, has been behind that bar for fifty years and the house still obeys the law as it always has. A mug of one-half of one per cent at McSorley's tastes better than chemical Scotch in the surreptitious dens of the Forties.

I suppose that nowadays no enterprise can be successful without admitting the ladies. There must be some profound reason, for example, for the carvings of Aphrodite over the Cunard, White Star, and French Line piers on the North River. And when McSorley's familiar signboard—"*The Old House at Home*"—fell down a few months ago, perhaps that was an omen of future change. But even if Bill someday turns it into an eating-place, and admits ladies, let us have, complete down to the yellowest playbill, the authentic sliced onion, and the painting of Moonlight on the Wabash, our loved McSorley's, last toll-gate on the Bohemian frontier.

The last item on my brief memo was to show the visitor Barry Faulkner's murals in the lobby of the Washington Irving High School. Among them is a lovely map of Long Island, the pleasantest conspectus of that region (I wish it might be reproduced on a coloured postcard for the use of Paumanokers), and this suggested a final foray for the touring Briton. He is a Whitman enthusiast, and had been rather depressed by Walt's house in Camden which is surrounded by a dingy soot-blown slum. So it seemed agreeable, in the long sunset of a transparent June evening, after a skirmish out to Lloyd's Neck where that fine old colonial mansion stands in a blue tissue of shadows above the salty lagoon, to run Dean Swift through the forests of West Hills to Walt's birthplace. The little ochre cottage—"pumpkin-coloured," the visitor insisted—was surrounded by a wide freshness and a soft supper-time pause. Alongside a main road, and with a realtor's development (called "Dreamland") near by, and a ganglion of hot doggeries on the pike a few rods distant, it won't preserve much longer its magical feeling of solitary blessing. But it does still put one's sentiments about Walt into a gracious perspective. "And see," we exclaimed, for we wanted our friend to know that America respects its authors, "there's another American writer celebrated just across the road." We pointed to a large brilliant billboard that faces the Whitman cottage. "Surely that isn't how he spelled it," protested our guest.

The sign says "*Oh Henry!*"

[ODE]

THOUGHTS IN THE SUBWAY

I

WE HEAR people complain about the subway: its brutal competitive struggle, its roaring fury and madness. We think they have not sufficiently considered it.

Any experience shared daily and for a long time by a great many people comes to have a communal and social importance; it is desirable to fill it with meaning and see whether there may not be some beauty in it. The task of civilization is not to be always looking wistfully back at a Good Time long ago, or always panting for a doubtful millennium to come; but to see the significance and secret of that which is around us. And so we say, in full seriousness, that for one observer at any rate the subway is a great school of human study. We will not say that it is an easy school: it is no kindergarten;

the curriculum is strenuous and wearying, and not always conducive to blithe cheer.

But what a tide of humanity, poured to and fro in great tides over which the units have little control. What a sharp and troubled awareness of our fellow-beings, drawn from study of those thousands of faces—the fresh living beauty of the girls, the faces of men empty of all but suffering and disillusion, a shabby errand boy asleep, goggling with weariness and adenoids—so they go crashing through the dark in a patient fellowship of hope and mysterious endurance. How can one pass through this quotidian immersion in humanity without being, in some small degree, enriched by that admiring pity which is the only emotion that can permanently endure under the eye of a questioning star?

Why, one wonders, should we cry out at the pangs and scuffles of the subway? Do we expect great things to come to pass without corresponding suffering? Some day a great poet will be born in the subway—spiritually speaking; one great enough to show us the terrific and savage beauty of this multitudinous miracle. As one watches each of those passengers, riding with some inscrutable purpose of his own (or an even more inscrutable lack of purpose) toward duty or liberation, he may be touched with anger and contempt toward individuals; but he must admit the majesty of the spectacle in the mass. One who loves his country for a certain candour and quick vigour of spirit will view the scene again and again in the hope of spying out some secrets of the national mind and destiny. Daily he bathes in America. He has that curious sense of mystical meaning in common things that a traveller feels coming home from abroad, when he finds even the most casual glimpses strangely pregnant with national identity. In the advertisements, despite all their absurdities; in voices humorous or sullen; even in the books that the girls are reading (for most girls read books in the subway) he will try to divine some authentic law of life.

He is but a poor and mean-spirited lover—whether of his city, his country, or anything else—who loves her only because he has known no other. We are shy of vociferating patriotism because it is callow and empty, sprung generally from mere ignorance. The true enthusiast, we would like to think, is he who can travel daily some dozen or score of miles in the subway, plunged in the warm wedlock of the rush hours; and can still gather some queer loyalty to that rough, drastic experience. Other than a sense of pity and affection toward those strangely sculptured faces, all busy upon the fatal tasks of men, it is hard to be precise as to just what he has learned. But as the crowd pours from the cars, and shrugs off the burden of the journey, you may see them looking upward to console themselves with perpendicular loveliness leaping into the clear sky. Ah, they are well trained. All are oppressed and shackled by things greater than themselves; yet within their own orbits of free movement they are masters of the event. They are patient and friendly, and endlessly brave.

II

The train roared through the subway, that warm typhoon whipping light summer dresses in a multitudinous flutter. All down the bright crowded aisle of patient humanity I could see their blowing colours.

My eyes were touched with Truth: I saw them as they are, beautiful and brave.

Is Time never sated with loveliness? How many million such he has devoured, and must he take these, too? They are so young, so slender, so untutored, such unconscious vessels of amazing life; so courageous in their simple finery, so unaware of the Enemy that waits for us all. With what strange cruelties will he trouble them, their very gayety a temptation to his hand? See them on Broadway at the lunch hour, pouring in their vivacious thousands onto the pavement. Is there no one who wonders about these merry little hostages? Can you look on them without marvelling at their gallant mien?

They are aware of their charms, but unconscious of their loveliness. Surely they are a new generation of their sex, cool, assured, even capable. They are happy, because they do not think too much; they are lovely, because they are so perishable, because (despite their naïve assumption of certainty) one knows them so delightfully only an innocent ornament of this business world of which they are so ignorant. They are the cheerful children of Down Town, and Down Town looks upon them with the affectionate compassion children merit. Their joys, their tragedies, are the emotions of children—all the more terrible for that reason.

And so you see them, day after day, blithely and gallantly faring onward in this Children's Crusade. Can you see that caravan of life without a pang? For many it is tragic to be young and beautiful and a woman. Luckily, they do not know it, and they never will. But in courage, and curiosity, and loveliness, how they put us all to shame. I see them, flashing by in a subway train, golden sphinxes, whose riddles (as Mr. Cabell said of Woman) are not worth solving. Yet they are all the more appealing for that fact. For surely to be a riddle which is not worth solving, and still is cherished as a riddle, is the greatest mystery of all. What strange journeys lie before them, and how triumphantly they walk the precipices as though they were mere meadow paths.

My eyes were touched with Truth, and I saw them as they are, beautiful and brave. And sometimes I think that even Time must be sated with loveliness; that he will not crumble them or mar their gallant childishness; that he will leave them, their bright dresses fluttering, as I have seen them in the subway many a summer day.

[PP]

GRAND AVENUE, BROOKLYN

WE HAVE always been a strong partisan of Brooklyn, and when we found ourself, in company with Titania, set down in the middle of a golden afternoon with the vista of Grand Avenue before us, we felt highly elated. Just how these two wayfarers chanced to be deposited in that quiet serenity, so far from their customary concerns, is not part of the narrative.

There are regions of Brooklyn, we have always felt, that are too good to be real. Placid stretches of streets, with baby carriages simmering in the sun, solid and comfortable brownstone houses exhaling a prosperous condition of life, tranquil old-fashioned apothecaries' shops without soda fountains, where one peers in and sees only a solitary customer turning over the pages of a telephone book. It is all rather like a chapter from a story, and reminds us of a passage in "The Dynamiter" where some untroubled faubourgs of London are winningly described.

Titania was wearing a little black hat with green feathers. She looked her best, and was not unaware of it. Our general plan, when destiny suddenly plumps us into the heart of Brooklyn, is to make our way toward Fulton Street, which is a kind of lifeline. Once on Fulton Street we know our way. Moreover, Fulton Street has admirable second-hand bookshops. Nor do we ever forget that it was at the corner of Fulton and Cranberry streets that *Leaves of Grass* was set up, in the spring of 1855, Walt doing a good deal of the work himself. The only difficulty about getting to Fulton Street is that people will give you such contradictory instruction. One will tell you to go this way; the next will point in the opposite direction. It is as though Brooklynites suspect the presence of a stranger, and do not wish their sacred secrets to be discovered. There is a deep, mysterious freemasonry among the residents of this genial borough.

At the corner of Grand and Greene avenues we thought it well to ask our way. A lady was standing on the corner, lost in pleasant drowse. April sunshine shimmered all about: trees were bustling into leaf, a wagonload of bananas stood by the curb and the huckster sang a gay, persuasive madrigal. We approached the lady, and Titania spoke gently: "Can you tell me—" The lady screamed, and leaped round in horror, her face stricken with fearful panic. She gasped and tottered. We felt guilty and cruel. "We were not meditating an attack," we said, "but just wanted to ask you the way to Fulton Street." Perhaps the poor soul's nerves were unstrung, for she gave us instruction that we felt instinctively to be wrong. Had we gone as she said (we now see by studying the map) we would have debouched into Wallabout Bay. But undoubtedly it was the protective instinct of the Brooklynite, on guard before strangers. Is there some terrific secret in Brooklyn that all residents know about but which must never be revealed to outsiders?

Making a mental note not to speak too suddenly at the next encounter, the two cheerful derelicts drifted along the sunny coast of Grand Avenue. A shining and passionless peace presided over the streets. A gentle clop-clop of hooves came trotting down the way: here was a man driving a white horse in a neat rubber-tired buggy without a top. He leaned back and smiled to himself as he drove along. Life did not seem to be the same desperate venture it appears round about Broadway and Wall Street. Who can describe the settled amiability of those rows of considerable brown houses, with their heavy oak doors, their pots of daisies on the stoop, their clear window panes, and now and then the face of a benignant grandmother peeping from behind lace curtains? The secret of Brooklyn, perhaps, is contentment, and its cautious residents do not want the rest of us to know too much about it, lest we all flock over there in swarms.

We then came to the bustle of Fulton Street, which deserves a book in itself. Some day we want to revisit a certain section of Fulton Street where (if we remember rightly) a rotisserie and a certain bookstore conspire to make one of the pleasantest haunts in our experience. We don't know exactly what the secret of Brooklyn may be, but we are going to spend some time over there this spring and lie in wait for it.

[P]

ALICE AND THE *AQUITANIA*

SHIPPING BUSINESS is bad; it is grievous to see so many good vessels laid up in the Erie Basin and in the alcoves of the Gowanus Canal. But *Alice M. Moran*, "of 29 net tons measurement," says her certificate, still puts in a lively twelve-hour day.

We were talking to Buck McNeil at the Battery Pier. If you have ever fallen—or jumped—overboard from the Battery sea-wall, you know Buck. He is the fellow who pulled you out. In his 26 years as boatman at that pier he has rescued 290 people. At least he has been credited with 290; the number is really more than that, for Buck has a habit of walking away when he has got the pessimist ashore. He keeps in his pocket the certificate of the U. S. Life Saving Medal of Honor, "for acts of Unusual Heroism," and on his watch-chain is the gold medal of the Dock Department, given him by Mayor Hylan. But in spite of hard times, people don't seem to go off the deep end so much nowadays. Buck hasn't had to go into the harbor for anyone in the last two years. He's just as pleased, for he says there are occasional twinges of rheumatism. We wanted to ask Buck whether the Carnegie Medal committee knew about all this, but just then *Alice M. Moran* came steaming across from Jersey City with a bone in her teeth. This was the Club's first chance in many years to go tugboating, and we hastened aboard.

We are not the first to raise a small chantey of praise in honor of *Alice*, for her skipper, Anton Huseby, proudly showed us an admirable article written about her by Roy Crandall in *Gas Logic.* No one could improve on Mr. Crandall's excellent story, which Captain Huseby keeps in the pilot house, and which includes also a lifelike photograph of *Alice*'s snug galley with the skipper, and Mr. Banks, the mate, and Mr. Anderson, the chief, and I think also Selverson, the rope-artist on deck, sitting down to chow, with Bill Paton, the Scotch cook, in the background. The deck-hand is the lad who can toss a four-inch hawser so that it loops itself right round the big iron cleat when *Alice* comes alongside a pier. And Bill Paton is still a leal Scot though he admits it's a long time since he tasted haggis. We apologize to Bill for having thought he said he came from Canarsie. It wasn't Canarsie but Carnoustie, which is near Dundee. This record of the Three Hours for Lunch Club's visit doesn't attempt to compete with Mr. Crandall's narrative. But all days on a tugboat are different, and this one happened to be our own.

We were remembering that it was just 45 years ago this month that the Lords of Committee of Privy Council for Trade granted to a certain Conrad Korzeniowski his "Certificate of Competency as Master." For that reason I was the more interested in Captain Huseby's own license. It reads that he "can safely be entrusted with the duties and responsibilities of master of freight and towing steam vessels of any gross tons upon the waters of bays, sounds and rivers and to Dumping Grounds off Scotland Light, and Pilot of any Steamer of any tonnage upon New York Bay and Harbor to Yonkers, Staten Island Sound, South Amboy, Newark Bay and tributaries of the East River to Stepping Stones." The commander of a tug is a more important navigator than a lubber perhaps realizes. He is a seaman to his finger-tips, and performs dexterities of manœuvre that astound any lover of craft. And when he takes a steamship in or out of dock he climbs to the big fellow's bridge and takes charge up there. Even if she's as big as the *Aquitania*, it's the tugboat captain who is up aloft giving the word to his leash of soft-nosed whelps, nuzzling like beagles under her tall side.

Alice had already done a good five hours' work when we boarded her. She left her berth in Brooklyn at 6 A.M. First she went to pier 57 North River and brought the *Jacques Cartier* to Pier 3, Army Base. Then she docked the steamer *Tergestea*, and the transport *St. Mihiel* just in from Honolulu. Then she took the barge *Dwyer 17* across to Pier 7, Central Railroad of New Jersey. It was there, I suppose, that she got the surprising news from her home office that four members of the Club had received permission to come aboard. In older days the owners of tugboat fleets sometimes signalled their captains by intricate codes of waving from the office windows in Battery Place. Perhaps there still is an emergency signal that means Visitors for Lunch.

We were hardly in the roomy pilot house before sturdy *Alice* was again about her affairs. The first thing one noticed was that tugboats, by old tradition, steer backward: unlike social craft the wheel preserves the old theory of the tiller. When the wheel is turned to starboard, the tugboat turns to port. So the ordinary merchant seaman or yachtsman is a dangerous fellow at a tugboat helm until he has learned this difference by instinct.

We went down past Governor's Island, which seemed empty and peaceful. A solitary officer was riding on a horse beside the big polo field. Captain Huseby recalled with some amusement a thing that happened (but not to his own clients) a few years ago. A big cattle-barge for the Union Stock Yards was rounding the Battery when someone hit her amidships, "right in the belly." She began to founder and the nearest safety was the army pier at Governor's Island. She was got alongside just in time and drove off several hundred terrified steers and sheep who fled in panic among barracks and parade grounds, putting major generals and polo players to flight. That day Governor's Island's dignity was badly shaken. It must have looked like a Wild West show. We had always wondered at the origin of the name Buttermilk Channel for the strait between Governor's Island and Brooklyn. Did it imply that mariners of softer temper kept in that sheltered reach while men of strong gizzard plowed up the main slot? No; Captain Huseby thinks it was named when the Brooklyn shore was all farmland and there was a rustic refreshment stand for thirsty boatmen near where the Hamilton Avenue ferry is now.

At Erie Basin and along the Gowanus Inlet one observes the curious transition in the naming of ships. There we saw old-timers like the *Buccaneer*, romantic names like *Silver Scandal*, *Western Ocean*, *Munamar*, alongside the *Commercial Guide*, the *Bird City*, the *Commercial Trader*, the *Cities Service Empire*. The *Eastern Temple* is a sulphur trader from Louisiana. The *Gibraltar* of Glasgow, a sturdy British tramp with salmon and black funnel, showed an active riffle of steam from her escape. The *West Isleta* was canted far over to starboard so we supposed she was loading. Among many idle bottoms it was encouraging to see these signs of activity. The *Cities Service Empire* was evidently very much on the job, but some of her neighbors lay rusting and forlorn. What a setting for a mystery story, one of these grim idle freighters. We lay off Owl's Head, an old mansion on the hill at Bay Ridge, waiting for the *Alaskan*. Two old wooden hulks are on the beach there, surely a disgrace to the pride of New York Harbor. They have been there many years, and boatmen are sensitive about these things. Why doesn't the Port Authority destroy them?

In the sunny noon, which seemed more like April than November, we tarried for our client. The great heights of Manhattan showed faintly through soft haze. Along that Brooklyn shore one is aware of the enormous auxiliaries of power and service that lie behind the tall frontages of the office world. The Bush piers, the Edison plant, the Long Island Railroad freight terminal, give one plenty to think about. The incredibly vast warehouses of the Army Base add a vibration of anxiety. Then the *Alaskan* of the American–Hawaiian Line came striding up the Narrows, in light from Boston. We had thought she might be the original *Alaskan*, whom F. R. had met years ago in the Straits of Magellan. But she must be a younger vessel, and her bow showed traces of a previous name, *Wheaton*. It was fine to see *Alice* slide alongside of her, running parallel and at exactly the same speed, and gently edge in with hardly a creak from the log fenders. Bill Banks took the wheel, Captain Huseby ran up the tall green ladder *Alice* carries at her side. With unbelievable address she was swung and pushed to her berth. Her neighbor there was a well-known Bermudian friend, the *Fort St. George*. Not far away were the handsome

Eastern Prince and *Japanese Prince* with their emblems of the Prince of Wales' three feathers. Just above was the pier of the Brazilian Lloyd, and a very handsome ship the *Niel Maersk* of Svendorg. A few hours round the waterfront make geography very real.

Now it was time for lunch. Tugboat meals are a noble tradition, and Bill Paton, even though four guests had been put upon him unexpectedly, was ready for the test. No one ever tasted better corned beef and cabbage, boiled potatoes, spinach, coffee with condensed milk. The bowl of apples had been polished until they glittered. Bill's doughnuts, little balls of crisp fluff, compare to the average doughnut of commerce as Bacon's essays to a newspaper editorial. When we asked him if he ever gave his crew a Scotch haggis he replied that there was hardly enough room to compound one in that galley, where the stove warms the backs of the eaters as they sit. But I think he could do it if it were laid upon him. His eyes shone as we recalled how Captain Bone has the haggis played in with pipers aboard the *Transylvania*, and the cook is honored for his art with a tumbler of neat Highland elixir. The next time *Transylvania* comes up the harbor I think if Bill Paton happens to see her he will look out from his galley, see her commander high aloft in gold stripes and yellow gloves, and say to himself "Yon's the skipper wha kens aboot a haggis."

What's our next job? we asked, already feeling that for one day *Alice*'s affairs were our concern. We were to take out the *Ashburton* of London, said Captain Huseby. We had noticed her at Pier 2, flying her Blue Peter, and her house-flag, with the emblem of a swan. "The Hungry Goose they call it in the Old Country," said Bill Paton.

But the *Ashburton* wasn't quite ready for us yet, so we tied up and lay comfortably in a warm drowse. Grey gulls were squealing, New York shone faintly through a yellow veil of sun. The radio in the pilot house was turned on, and through peaceful siesta some humorist from Newark was singing hunting songs about view halloos and gentry in scarlet "galloping, galloping, galloping." We ourselves felt more like snoring, snoring, snoring. Another member of the Moran family, *Eugene F.*, sidled in and lay alongside us with calm brotherly affection. One member sat on the stringpiece of the pier, sketching the pair. Others walked along beneath *Ashburton*'s comely stern, watched the last of her cargo going aboard, learned from her mate that she was bound for Newport News and then Australia. A Diesel barge called *Corning* went buzzing fussily in and out of various piers, carrying only one huge case which looked like a crated automobile. It was like a small dog with a bone he hasn't decided where to bury. *Corning* barked every now and then with a loud and very unship-like-sounding horn. From *Alice*'s pilot house we heard the radio cry "This quaint minuet is re*dol*ent with the atmosphere of bygone days."

Then suddenly there was a hail from *Ashburton*'s stern. We woke from our drowse on the pierhead. *Alice* and *Eugene F.* sprang to life. One of the Club's own members, master mariner himself, cast off *Ashburton*'s stern lines from the big iron cleat. Water boiled under her counter. We took her out and swung her toward open sea, feeling we had done well. But our greatest adventure was still to come.

We came up harbor again in the pink light of late afternoon, too wise even to try to match words against that cluster of stalagmites that will never be described by deliberate intention; only, if ever, by accident. Perhaps James Bone came as near it as anyone: "The City of Dreadful Height." It is a much steeper view from the deck of a tug than from the high terraces of a liner. We steered for the deep notch of Broadway, as the big ships do, and rounded the bend of the island. F. R. remembered that the last time we had come up the bay in a tug was the night President Harding died, when some great building in Battery Place had left its lights burning toward sea in the pattern of a huge cross. "I'm afraid they wouldn't do it again for poor old Harding," was someone's comment. Yet no man need be grudged whatever light he can get as he heads down those dark Narrows.

We passed the *American Farmer* at her pier: a

merchantman of letters in spite of her bucolic name. The other day she brought over from London the new edition of Sir Thomas Browne; and is it not her commander, good Captain Myddleton, who told us long ago that he always keeps the General Catalogue of the Oxford University Press in the chart-room, for momentary relief during hours of fog or soundings? But our minds were on other matters. The *Aquitania* was now at Quarantine and would be up shortly—a full day late, after a bad voyage. *Alice* was to help dock her.

At Pier 42 is a little rendezvous where the *Moran* family and their friends the *Barretts* wait for the prima donnas to come in. We tarried there in a plain, undemonstrative family group. From the various errands of the day these stout workwomen of the harbor came puffing in. They seemed to wipe their hands on their aprons and sit rocking gently on beamy bottoms to talk things over before the big job. They filled water coolers, the men took a sluice at the fresh-water hose. There was *Joseph H. Moran*, bigger than ourself; and *Helen B. Moran* with a small white dog on board, very alert and eager of eye, much aware of his responsibility as the only dog among so many informal human beings. He stood up with front paws rigid against *Helen B.*'s bulwarks and watched the other kinsmen arrive with critical attention. Oliver (who notices everything) says the small white dog was furiously annoyed when in the middle of his supervisions one of the men sprayed him humorously with a mouthful of drinking water. Certainly it was a liberty, and the more so if it was done by someone on the *Howard C. Moore* or the *Downer X*, who were not *Moran*s or *Barrett*s. But I did not see this myself, for at that moment F. R. was telling me of his excitement in reading Defoe's *Journal of the Plague Year* and asking me (so it seemed to my morbid mind) why none of us could write as well as Defoe.

We lay in a knot, haunch to haunch, at the end of Pier 42. *Eugene F. Moran* had followed us faithfully from Brooklyn. *Grace Barrett* was there, and *Richard F. Barrett*, and *R. J. Barrett.* It must be fun to have a big family and a tugboat to name after each of them. *John Nichols*, however, kept a little in the offing. He was too proud to join our little gab, for it is *John Nichols*'s captain who goes aboard the big liner and commands the whole fleet of tugs. The rest of us sociabled our soft noses together, our upward poking bows muzzled with the big fenders tht look like a brown bear climbing aboard. Above the soft aroma of the North River was a good smell of cooking. We lay in an eddy of it, for all galleys were busy.

Aquitania loomed up in the haze. Only someone very important could arrive so quietly, so steadily, so sure of herself. We had the oblique profile of her, best for both women and ships. Every slant of her seemed to accept homage. She took it as her due, yet not wholly unconscious of it, for she was still a little sore from discourtesies outside. At sea, alone with grey trigonometry, she is only a little thing. Here she was queen. In that soft light she did not come, she grew. But these were the thoughts of lubbers. The urchin tugs (I am sorry to switch metaphors so often) have no time for awe. They swarm about her skirts and hustle her with sooty grasp.

Our little fleet throbbed into action. It was like letting a pack of well-trained beagles out of a kennel. No one needed to be told anything. The routine has been perfected in every detail. *John Nichols* turned downstream to meet her. *Joseph H.* and *Helen B.* shot up ahead of us with a scurry of froth. *Grace Barrett*, pirouetting on her solid heel, twirled across our bow and took the inside track along the pierheads. Behind this interference *Eugene* and ourself and *Howard Moore* followed upstream. There was a very strong ebb, Captain Huseby had told us. But there was no difficulty of wind, a gentle breeze from S.W. It was pink November dusk at its mildest.

Alice and *Eugene* went outward to join her. She came huge above us, steadily increasing. Now we had no eyes to note the movements of the other tugs, only to study this monstrous nobility of a ship. It must have been a bad voyage, for she looked dingy, rusted, and salted from water-line to funnels. High on her sloping stacks were crusts of salt. Her white-work was stained, her boot-topping green with scum. The safety nettings were still stretched along her steerage decks, even high on the promenade we could see them brailed up. Passengers at her rails looked down incuriously as we dropped astern. Just one more landing, they supposed.

We passed the notice board—*Propeller 8 feet beneath surface. Keep Clear*—and with *Eugene* slid in under her magnificent stern. Her bronze fans, turning unseen, slipped her cleanly along; we nosed busily into the very broth of her wake. Almost beneath the overhang we followed, dipping in the great swelling bubbles of her shove. It was like carrying the train of an empress. AQUITANIA, LIVERPOOL! Only the sharks have followed her closer than that. She was drawing 33½ feet at the rudder-post. The smooth taper of her hull, swimming forward ahead of us, made her seem suddenly fishlike. Beneath that skin of metal you could divine the intricate veinings and glands of her life: silvery shafts turning in a perspiration of oil, hot bulbs of light, white honeycombs of corridor, cell-like staterooms suddenly vacated. All the cunning structure of vivid life, and yet like everything living so pitifully frail. Then Bill Banks the mate went forward with a boathook. He stood under her colossal tail with his rod poised like a lance. "My God," said Oliver, "he's going to harpoon her." We looked at *Eugene F.* and there, too, stood one with boathook pointed. Like two whaleboats we followed *Moby Dick*.

She swam steadily. A uniformed officer and two sailors looked down at us from the taffrail far above. There was superiority in that look, but *Alice M.* takes condescension from none. "Give us your rope," she cried. They said nothing. We continued to follow. A breath of anxiety seemed to pass over Captain Huseby and Bill Banks, for now we were almost abreast of the pier. Perhaps that ebb tide was on their minds. To deal with that ebb was our affair. They repeated the invitation. "Wait till we get word from the bridge," replied the officer calmly. The devil with the bridge, we could see *Alice* thinking. Her job is to get hold of a line and the sooner the better. At last it came, snaking downward. Bill Banks caught it, partly on the boathook and partly on his neck. The big hawser drooped after it, five inches thick of new rope. There was fierce haste to get it looped on the towing bitts astern. It was *Alice* who took *Aquitania*'s first line, from the port quarter. "You've got to be careful taking a rope under way like this," said Captain Huseby spinning his wheel. "These big ships have a powerful suction."

Eugene F. took the second line. The next thing we realized a quick hitch-up had taken place, and we were towing in tandem. *R. J. Barrett* was coupled ahead of *Alice*, *Richard Barrett* was in line with *Eugene*. The quartet headed diagonally upstream.

The big hawsers came taut and creaked. *Alice* trembled. Up at *Aquitania*'s port bow were three other tugs pushing forward, side by side. Seven of us altogether on the port side. There must have been half a dozen to starboard, but what was happening there we couldn't see.

Alice shook with life. The churn from *R. J. Barrett* boiled past us. The mass of *Aquitania*'s stern plus the flow of the whole Hudson watershed hung on a few inches of splice hooked over the bitts. The big ship stood unmoved as a cliff, while our quartet strained and quivered. *Moran*s and *Barrett*s dug their twirly heels into the slippery river and grunted with work. Steam panted with hot enjoyment. *Aquitania* didn't seem to care. She wasn't even looking at us. Her port side was almost deserted. Passengers were all to starboard looking for someone to say hullo to. Lights began to shine from the ports. One was blocked with a wooden deadlight, proof of smashing weather. A single steward looked out calmly from the glory hole. It was all old business to him. For several minutes nothing seemed to happen. In midstream a big Socony tanker, almost loaded under with weight of oil, stood by to bring in fuel as soon as she was docked. John D. ready for business, we thought. There was no time to lose: she must sail again only 31 hours later. And in this, the very stress of the battle, they asked us, "How about some supper?" *Alice* had hold now.

Apparently she could do practically all the rest of it herself. Captain Huseby was surprised when we said we were too excited to eat.

Gradually the big hull swung. The downward sweep of the tide crisped in a smacking surf against her side as she straightened out across the river. Her great profile brightened with lights in the thickening dusk. Now she was straight onto the opening of the pier. She blew once, very short, a deep, mellow rumble. Thanks! We all answered in chorus, with equal brevity. Sure! Our quartet slackened the pull, wheeled off at wider angles to safeguard her stern as she warped in. She had pivoted round the corner and was slowly easing against the camels, those floating rafts that keep her from rubbing. Captain Huseby now did his steering from the wheel at *Alice*'s stern. The rest were at supper.

It was blue dark, 5:10 P.M. New Jersey had vanished except for the bright words LIPTON'S TEA. *Aquitania*'s stern was flush with the outer end of the pier. Her ensign came down. We could hardly believe it was all over.

Bill Paton was a little disappointed we could not stay for supper. But we had seen too much—and eaten too much lunch—to be hungry yet. "Next time let us know a day ahead," he remarked, "and we can really give you a meal." We tried to compliment the deck-hand on his sure skill with a hawser. He was embarrassed. "I'm glad you were pleased," was his modest reply. They put us ashore at the end of the pier.

Why do people build or buy big steam yachts, we wondered. Surely a tugboat is the perfect craft. They build them on the Great Lakes—Green Bay, I think they said, was where *Alice* came from. You can get one like her for something like $100,000. A maiden voyage in a tugboat from Green Bay to New York would be a good trip to take.

Aquitania lay there, a blaze of lights, stewards busy carrying off baggage. *Alice* backed off with a curtseying motion, and vanished into the dark. She sleeps in Brooklyn.

[IR]

DOWAGER OF THE SEA

"England's dear-bought Queen . . . the state of Normandy
Stands on a tickle point."

Shakespeare, 2nd Henry VI, I, 1.

OF HER QUALITY AS A SHIP, or as a commercial venture, we can suspend judgment. Ships are not proved in the newspapers. But as international gesture *Queen Mary*'s arrival was magnificent. By miracles of good luck none of the flocking airplanes collided, none of the hideously overloaded excursion steamers foundered. As the whole armada (or pacificada) came smoking up the Bay it was a gorgeous spectacle. The Moran flotilla of towboats, whose privilege none ever disputes, led the parade. Behind us the harbormaster's launch and the coastguard greyhounds controlled and chivied the wallowing array, yelping horns of warning. The terrific *Mary*, fiscally as fantastic as the *Flying Dutchman*, came tall and solid; dignified as her godmother. I counted twenty-three planes gnatting about. (Her natural welcomers, the seagulls, were nowhere to be seen; they were frightened off the river.) At the Battery a fireboat jetted bridal veils of white water. Then the blue afternoon rocked under a lid of sound. And beneath all, barely audible in the yell of the world's most enthusiastic city, the deep deep growl of the dowager herself. Like the voice of Neptune, muttering in his beard. That note, said to be A two octaves below middle C, is almost off soundings for the human ear. It's the same note, Jim Bone said, as that of the *Normandie*, so deep can call to deep. There was something more than New York's usual tribute to Size. Everyone remembered, I think, that huge vessel was once a naked hull which lay rusting and abandoned for three years on the ways at Clydebank. Without even a name, just Number 534, a monument of dismay, hopeless as the Tower of Babel. So our wholehearted yell of welcome must have thrilled in all her ten million faithful rivets; Glasgow workmen who tightened their belts while she lay idle must have heard it on the pub's wireless and tilted a pledge of beer. That was the true miracle of this great scene: tribute to those workmen and builders who didn't know when they were licked; the greatest gesture of come-back that our weird economy has seen. Now she came gravely by, her water-line forward scoured to naked steel by the sluice of the bow-wave at more than 30 knots. Under the great roar of New York I think she still heard the homely accent of Clydeside voices.

The excursion boats, filing on both sides, leaned toward her with their watching crowds; rolling in the harbor swell they seemed to curtsey; and every craft in the wide array wore a stiff aïgrette of saluting steam, as if for court presentation. Like a fan of ostrich feather came the great waft of silver from the Queen. Far above a sky-writing plane struggled with his Q and U, but the breeze was too keen. Nobody but God could read what he was trying to spell.

It was *Alice M. Moran* who took the first line. She put her padded nose square against the spine of the bulging cruiser stern. The line dropped across Bill Bank's boathook and the big hawser followed. *Alice* had the position she likes best—on the port quarter; least spectacular but most arduous. *E. F. Moran, Jr.* and *Dalzellido* and *Eugene F. Moran* tandem'd up ahead of us. The *Mary*, riding high, was drawing 36. Tide was at low slack, but the flood had just made. That, and a breeze up-river, made her swing astonishingly fast. Too fast, for an instant. We had to check it and take her ahead a bit. Hudson mud, black and creamy, churned up thick along her steep side. She was actually parallel the pier in 35 minutes, but we had to hang on quite a while longer. Captain Tony Huseby, master of the *Alice*, explained that it takes time to fit a lot of untried gangplanks to their openings.

The whole Moran fleet was out for the *Mary*. We went round and round her as she lay at Quarantine. Passengers arriving for the first time may well have supposed that the word *Moran*, like the Japanese *Maru*, was some nautical suffix in the name of every American towboat. Aft of the enormous *Mary* lay little *M. Moran*. The Queen, disregarding so small a creature, might have been surprised to learn that *M. Moran* had crossed the Atlantic twice as often as herself. Most of the tugs were dressed with pennants, but not *Alice*. This was a working day for her, and as flagship of the squadron she was too serious to pretend that docking the *Mary* was a picnic. But we had two brilliant flashes of color. One was the red axe with which Bill Banks stood by the great hawser when we took hold. The other was the necktie of Mr. Bill Hall, the Three Hours for Lunch Club's official photographer. Mr. Hall, combing his lively wardrobe, had chosen a scarf appropriate to the day—the tartan of the clan MacQueen.

That was a braw notion, for the *Mary* is unmistakably Scottish. As James Bone said, she's Sandy's idea of a ship; and Sandy has been building them a long time. She's magnificent, conservative, stately, but not stylish. She makes—outwardly—no concession of streamline design. Seen from forward angles, a royal shape, but viewed broad-on she is too enormously vast, slapsided, and high-built in her stern topsides. The contrast between her and the *Normandie* (merely in exterior profile, which is all I know) is interestingly characteristic of the two national temperaments.

I am, as you may have noticed, no enthusiast for big and crowded ships. Of what use is it to save a few hours in actual passage when you lose as much again in longer embarcation, lying at Quarantine, and getting baggage through the Customs? As much again in meals too, I daresay, when the steward has to travel 85 yards from kitchen to table.

It was queer—it almost seemed intentional—that there were no other big ships anywhere in port. Had they made themselves scarce, not to intrude on royal ceremony? The *Washington*, one of our own few first-ratings, dipped salute from her pier, and the *Mary* roared reply. I rather wished the Queen had said a word of homage for the handsomest hull in the river, the perished *Leviathan.* But it might have been thought condescension. Near *Leviathan* the trimly crossed yards of the *Tusitala* were watching. Did the *Mary* know that *Tusitala* was built on the Clyde, 55 years ago? Also on the Hoboken side was the adorably smart little *Batory*, our new Polish visitor (built on barter, not on tick). She catches the eye of any lover of shipshape. But of all steamers seen afloat that day, the one I'd like to travel in was a freighter, *Port Darwin*, outward bound. The name sounds Australian, and I read that she had cleared for Brisbane.

Just above the *Mary*'s pier, another Clyde-built ship, Captain Bone's *Transylvania*, had loyally dressed herself in flags. And there was one of the Swedish liners also, her pale yellow funnels darkening at the top like the bowl of a meerschaum pipe. All these were gossiping together, and what they said privately to each other only shipping men would understand. Most of all I'd like to have heard the exchange of comment between *Leviathan* and *Tusitala.* "She'll never go where I'm getting ready to," said *Tusitala.* "Where's that?" "Round the Horn," said *Tusitala.*—"And I hope it'll be a long time before she knows how they treat you when you're no longer fashionable," said *Leviathan.* "Well, here's luck to her anyhow, and plenty of subsidy," they both agreed. Meanwhile all the New York newspapers were writing editorials on the Shame of the U. S. Merchant Marine and asking why *we* don't build Queen Maries of our own. But we've got the Empire State Building, haven't we?

Anyhow, the Three Hours for Lunch Club feels that the *Mary* is half its own ship anyhow. Mr. Pigott, the managing director of John Brown's at Clydebank, is the uncle of the Club's seagoing bookseller, Miss Niehoff of the Wakefield Book Shop. And Mr. Ben Morris, the Club's official architect, supervised her interior decorations. And George Blake, the Club's consul in Glasgow (author of that fine Clydeside novel *The Shipbuilders*), was aboard her to do broadcasting. And James Bone, the Club's fulcrum in London, was aboard to report her behavior for his two papers, the Manchester *Guardian* and the Baltimore *Sun.* Mr. Bone was disturbed that the biggest Scotch ship should have a Welshman as Chief Engineer. "And what do you suppose he has in his cabin?" he cried. "A leek," we suggested, but he misunderstood us.—What he meant was that Mr. Roberts, the Chief, has a framed poem by Masefield in his quarters.

There was no British reticence about her maiden voyage. That period of mist which slowed her down (to 25 knots) was not I think pukka fog but an induced fog of syllables, a cloud of radio witnesses. (Her only heavy rolling was the R's of George Blake's broadcasting.) I read in the papers that 90,000 words of press dispatch were emitted; 62,591 words of private radio messages were sent out (and 18,826 received); 312 minutes of wireless telephone talk outgoing, 241 minutes incoming. The British Broadcasting Company had put on board 15,000 feet of cable and 22 mikes; 33 separate programs were volleyed from the ship. The only serious damage of the voyage was a radio clerk who stood on duty for 36 hours until his legs had to be bandaged for varicose veins. This interests me, for it is in line with the general tendency of human beings nowadays to make things as difficult as possible for themselves and for each other. Man, in the grip of economic law and machinery which he cannot control, is evidently compelled to do things which reason rejects in horror. The band of ladies in white uniforms playing God Save the King on the overcrowded excursion steamer, might occasionally have played God Save Ourselves; it was terrifying to the onlooker to see the peril of those dangerously topheavy nautical grimcracks. But *Alice*, with her customary quiet attention to business, did one good act. Some broadcasting people had set up elaborate apparatus on board the tug, and prepared a snappy description of the arrival. But, for some technical reason, they could only broadcast above 42nd Street. It happened that *Alice* found it desirable to go down the Bay instead of loitering upstream; so the broadcast stayed in the batteries.

I repeat, as an international salute it was great stuff. To my private thinking, ships like that are not Cunard–White Star but Cunard–White Elephant. But many valuable phases of national pride entirely transcend reason. That she has plenty of horsepower still up her sleeve, or in her thrust-blocks, no one doubts. At 185 r.p.m. she was developing 165,000 h.p., said to be better than expected. It's a sure thing that she'll break the record, even if (as vulgar shipping men said of the *Normandie*) the tourist passengers have to wear double brassières.

Here and there round the streets you'll see gentlemen wearing handsome black neckties with narrow diagonal stripes of gold and red. These, Jim Bone explained to me, are the most expensive neckties in the world. They're only sold on board the *Mary*, so they cost at least £35, the minimum price of passage.

She docked at 4:30, and privileged passengers

(franked through the customs) looked at their watches when they left the pier. Just time for a cocktail, they thought; but it was more of a coincidence than that. It was a memory of Clydeside courage and patience. It was 5:34.

[CMB]

COLDEST AND HOTTEST

(Recollections of the Two Days when New York Thermometers Broke the Record Both Ways)

FEBRUARY 1934

IT ALWAYS ABASHES ME to think how many experts one would have to call on in order to tell anything in full. I would need Sir Josiah Stamp to explain why 25 million dollars' worth of English gold was hustled into the strong-room of the *Berengaria* and why every hour's delay cost someone money. (You and me, probably, eventually.) I would need the Weather Man to explain why 14° below zero that morning, though crystalline clear on Manhattan, caused a fog in the Ambrose Channel. It was February 9, the coldest day New York City has ever recorded, and the vapor steaming up from the much warmer sea-water wrapped *Berengaria* in fog up to B deck. So there she lay waiting; and the *Mauretania* and the *Rotterdam* too, and stubby little *Pan-America*.

The Federal Reserve and the Old Lady of Threadneedle Street may have been tapping their toes impatiently but all this was fine for F. R. and me. We had planned to go to the Cunard pier to meet a kinsman known irreverently as the Loch Ness Monster. When we learned that the ship was going to be hours late we had a great idea. Perhaps we could go down to Quarantine in the customs cutter. We asked permission in the proper quarters, and they said yes—if we could get there in time. We hastened to the subway. When we reached the office of the Collector, that magnificent room in the Custom House which has so often been for us a prelude to adventure, Mr. Stuart and Mr. Lessing had a pass ready for us but feared the cutter might have left. There was a moment of acute anxiety while waiting for a telephone connection. Accustomed these several years to successions of bad luck, Felix and I almost assumed ourselves frustrated. But no: we got to the Barge Office just on the tick. Commander Dempwolf saw us safely aboard the cutter *Raritan*. We looked at each other. From now on, we said to ourselves, things are really going to be better. So nice a conjunction of times and chances puts one in a better vibration. Every living creature, I read in the newspaper, has its own special wave-length; which, if tuned in upon, may produce extraordinary results. Perhaps 1934 was going to be somewhere closer to our own frequency.

It was 12:30; the cabin was packed tight with ship-news men and customs officers who had been waiting patiently for several hours. We slipped into the galley where a good-natured mess boy allowed us huge mugs of the best and hottest coffee. It was good to hug the stove, looking over the open half-door at the ice-choked slip. But when we got under way we went outdoors. The harbor was clotted with floating cakes. Shaped in jigsaw patterns (mostly great trapezoids) they outlined the mechanics of surface tension more clearly than I had ever seen before. When a tug went creaming through the broken floe inshore you could see the wave building up ahead of her, and the hollow sucking behind her stern. Except a couple of news-reel men, always the hardiest, we had the deck mostly to ourselves, and kept to leeward. It was cold; it really was. Felix, a veteran of the Arctic (he once spent a winter in Spitzbergen), said this seemed more bitter than that. We grinned to recall that the last time we had been on shipboard together was in the *Malolo*, a balmy day at San Pedro in Southern California, nearly a year ago; and that we were both wearing the same clothes as then; for good and sufficient reason. "How would you like to be abandoning ship in weather like this?" asked Felix, who has made a professional study of the details of sea courage. For the first time in a long while I thought affectionately of some long woollen underwear I bought in Halifax.

Berengaria lay massive at Quarantine. We came alongside the *Rotterdam* first, to put her inspectors aboard. As we did so a tall well-known figure came riding up the Narrows. At first we thought she was plated in ice, she shone so white; then realized she was painted so for tropical cruising. It was *Mauretania*, in from the West Indies. Famous old lady of the seas, she went smoothly by, lowering her blue ensign in courtesy. The particular pleasure of her four high funnels, closely set and with a sort of onward suggestion, is too subtle ever to have been justly described. She seems delightfully old-fashioned already, so much tall hamper to catch resistance; but what a history she has. Much of those upper works is streamlined away in the new ships. Later in the afternoon we saw the *Bremen* at her berth uptown; it was odd to note how much smaller she looks than older ships of considerably less burthen. On *Mauretania*'s white hull we first observed something we saw closer when we came alongside the other ships. Paint was flaking off in great strips. On *Berengaria*'s deckhouses the thick ivory coating was crackled in loose slabs. The steel underneath, contracting with cold, had buckled it loose by the yard. The next day I saw the same thing on many big motor trucks round the city. That must have been a profitable weather for the paint makers. Ourselves, hard-working proletarians, could not resist a small grin at the feelings of the West Indies trippers, coming back from the dulcet Caribbean in their lightest gear. Some of the loveliest knees in New York may well have been chapped that afternoon on the pier at 14th Street.

I did not like the look of the ladder they put down from *Berengaria*'s side. Just a skinny wooden trellis, freshly varnished, and there was a drip from somewhere above that froze shinily on the rungs. I think it was then that Felix made his remark about abandoning ship. There was a gap of unpleasantly cold-looking water between the hulls. A ruddy and competent mariner was on the lookout at the top of the climb—but I noticed that the prudent customs men mostly wore rubbers for better footing. Anyhow, up we went without a miss. I saw no more of the news men, who hastened to the First Class. It is an old newspaper tradition, and a wrong one I think, that the First Class always has the important tidings. It has at any rate the more luxurious grub, which is reasonably in the mind of a reporter who has hung about the harbor for six hours. Felix and I, knowing the ways of members of the Club, made for the more congenial Tourist. Numb as we were, the big idea was something hot and Scotch. We found our quarry finishing his lunch and took him cleanly by surprise. But it was an ironic moment, though. He was digging into a plate of strawberry ice cream.

As a matter of statistics, let one more detail be recorded. Even hot double Scotches in the smoke-room didn't seem as calorific as we had expected. After sitting a while we noticed a thermometer.

This was indoors, mind you, and full steam circulating. The mercury said 48.

JULY 1936

I have no idea how hot it is in the city, but today's amusement here has been watching the thermometer. It went to 116° when placed on the sun-dial at full meridian, has been 96° all afternoon under the trees in the garden. Even the dogs realize it's warm and have been mercifully mute.

The ideal reading for hot weather is Max Beerbohm. If I were the French Line I'd get out a little reprint of his "On Speaking French" and sell it to the passengers in the *Normandie*. You'll find it in the volume *And Even Now*. In the same book is his essay on Laughter.—The three Bon Voyage readings we have always hankered to put in steamer baskets are Beerbohm's *And Even Now*, Santayana's *Soliloquies in England*, and Nevinson's *Farewell to America*.

But, for reasons of my own, I found myself on this hot day re-reading here and there in Shakespeare. As usual, I came upon all sorts of appropriate excitement. I wondered again, as I have before, why no radio company has ever used as a motto the lines of Glendower:—

> "Those musicians that shall play to you
> Hang in the air a thousand leagues from hence."
> (1st Henry IV, III, 1, 226)

That reminded me of Walt Whitman's line in the 1855 Preface, which I always hanker to see at the head of a newspaper radio timetable:—

"The broadcast doings of the day and night."

Of course we can go much further back and find (in the *Aeneid*, Book VI, 847) the great passage I hoped might be used as a motto for Radio City:—

Orabunt causas melius, caelique meatus
Describent radio, et surgentia sidera dicent.

If you allow yourself to ramble at large in Shakespeare there's no knowing what you'll come upon. Thinking about the sun-dial made me think of marigolds, because there used to be some clumps of that flower near it. And hunting up Shakespeare on the subject of marigolds, I note that he says they are the flowers to give to middle-aged men (because they blossom in middle summer). This, unexpectedly, in the *Winter's Tale*. Of course sun-dials send one to Hazlitt, who wrote so pleasant an essay; he says the thing to plant near them is sun-flowers; which I never thought of. (My own sun-dial, because I pointed the gnomon to magnetic North instead of True North, is just an hour wrong: but it marks perfect Daylight Saving Time.)

Shakespeare comes into that again. This sun-dial is my only remaining relic of the Hoboken production of *After Dark*; it stood in the garden of what was supposed to be "The Lilacs, Montclair," and the hero rested his tall hat on it in a romantic scene. Well, *After Dark* had a subtitle, "Neither Maid, Wife, Nor Widow," which I tagged onto it and thought I had invented it myself. Years afterward, rummaging in *Measure for Measure* (V, 1, 173) I found that Shakespeare had used the phrase "Neither maid, widow, nor wife." Skelton also, in the enormously amusing *Philip Sparrow*.

Thinking about warm weather, there is that remark of Falstaff's hoping it won't be a hot day when the armies come together; because, he says, he's only taking two shirts with him.—And the immortal line in the greatest of all tavern scenes: Doll Tearsheet, when she wipes his face and says: "Poor ape, how thou sweatest."

[CMB]

EPISTLE TO THE COLOSSIANS

LETTERS DROPPED in the mail chutes at the top of the Empire State Building fall so far and so fast that they must be slowed down to prevent scorching. At the 65th and 38th floors (so I once read in a newspaper article) there are devices to retard the drop. When I think about New York, and the grotesquely accelerated behavior some of us show, that seems symbolic. Surely we need occasional slow-down devices or zones of pause, to avoid burning up. The Three Hours for Lunch Club was founded for that purpose, but I fear its influence is not very wide.

An expert English observer of political doings, who was in charge of urgent relief works during the War, remarked the other day that in Washington lately she had seen the affairs of peace proceeding at a war-time pace, and men exhausting themselves in fatigue and pressure.

My own recourse when I find excitements too intense is riding in the subway. It is the most interesting cloister in New York, for it is there that one is most alone. Only two or three times, in twenty years of subway travel, have I ever met anyone I knew. One is completely and blissfully anonymous; and what a gallery of portraiture.

What a school, also, of good manners. Physically the conditions are not ideal, but mentally the subway passengers are well bred. No one dreams of forcing his ideas upon you, of interrupting your meditation or trying to get you to sign books or read manuscripts. The subway is perfect spiritual privacy.

I am reminded, irrelevantly, of the grand saying attributed to Mrs. Patrick Campbell by Alexander Woollcott in his mischievously witty book *While Rome Burns*. Mrs. Campbell, congratulated on her marriage, said how pleasant it is to sink back "into the deep, deep peace of the double-bed after the hurly-burly of the chaise longue." —And now I see in the paper that the young Emperor of Manchukuo began his reign with three days of purification and thought. (He'd better take it while he can, for the destiny of a buffer state is not always easy.) It suggested to me also to stay away from the office today and meditate these things. But so subtly infectious is the damned tohu-bohu it becomes as alluring as tipple. One wants to begin telephoning around and find out what's going on. Nothing is so admirable as to see our own G., sweet-natured mistress of the switchboard, when calls begin to rise to the forenoon peak and perhaps she has also a lap full of correspondence to deal with at the same time and some Visiting Fireman is looking through the little hatchway (like Shere Khan at the mouth of the cave in the grand old *Jungle Book* picture) and the whole excitement and *brio* of the publishing season seems to be coruscating around her small corner. I myself am very likely a bit haywire at that moment, maybe it's the day when the Book of the Month Committee meets, but I catch G.'s eye and we both burst out laughing. "Well, Gittel, life gets a bit complicated," I remark, and she replies, "Yes, but we have fun." The world of books and magazines may be small potatoes in turnover but it is enormous in comedy.

It seems to be much the same in most offices; and not only in offices but in domestic and social life too. Perhaps *thought*, in any strong intuitive sense, is gradually being eliminated. Often a whole day will go by without anything that can properly be described as cerebration. And certainly there are many writers who have mistaken for thought what was only bad temper. Perhaps purposeful and intentional thinking is overestimated. I wonder if economic processes can be reduced to simple diagrams of physics as a recent book pictorially suggests. I wonder about "planned economy." (I'm just wondering, not concluding.) I find that many believe Franklin D. Roosevelt to be a great leader not for any far-reaching schemes of rehabilitation but because he seems to be flexibly opportunist. Perhaps the Great Man is not so much he who imposes his will on the Time, but the one who divines the destiny of the Time and lets it impose on him. The danger of such a course is in too sudden and impulsive decisions where the event is subject to hazard.

Perhaps bookstores are not sufficiently appreciated as slow-down devices or zones of pause. They are rarely crowded; even the humblest of them always has something one hasn't read and which may well startle the mind. Publishers and editors and reviewers have mostly too little time to think; booksellers perhaps too much. It seems odd to me that the bookseller doesn't try to do more of the publisher's thinking for him.

Last night a group of men were discussing the general hysteria of the present age; the great rapidity with which all means of communication have outrun the value of whatever we have to communicate. (I must re-read Kipling's Bandar-log, one of the greatest of satires.) It is even significant that News was once called Intelligence; but not so often nowadays. In our anxiety to talk constantly with all parts of the world, by cable, radio, telephone, and newsprint, we almost forget the best kind of talk there is, with one's self. The bookseller has that chance; I wish we heard more of his musings.

By chance I discovered another place of pause. On Sixth Avenue near 47th Street, unspoiled and uninfluenced by the eccentricities of that neighborhood (the Bowery of uptown), is a demure little bazaar of notions and dressmaking materials. A bookseller friend was leaving, in snowy weather, for vacation in Mexico, and I thought to buy her a handkerchief in case of rheum. I went into this delightful elderly place where you recognize the muslin and linen smells of shops you visited in childhood with your mother. There are dress patterns, scissors, ribbons, spools of thread, Victorian underwear, all sorts of feminine falbalas and fixtures. Gentlewomen of established mien serve you with an air of soft surprise; and best of all, there are the antique cash-carriers that sing on overhead wires back to the cashier's cage. I begged permission to pull the handle and ejaculate the money myself. I hadn't worked one of those air-line carriers since I was a young clerk in the original Old Corner Book Store in Boston. The haberdash ladies said they would let me do it again, so I shall solicit my family for small millinery commissions.

A thought in my mind lately has been, if I were going away from New York and might not return, what would I most wish to remember? The motto for such a memorandum would be appropriately, in the Epistle to the Colossians: "Yet am I with you in the spirit, joying and beholding your order . . . the head of all principality and power." I think of a photograph printed in the *Herald-Tribune* in October 1932 showing a line of workmen, in a warm autumn lunchtime, sitting at ease on an awful girder over 800 feet of space at the top of the RCA building. I think of those superb photographs of the city taken by Samuel Gottscho, which specially show the strange light-effects of our Babylon and make one see our heights and distances with new eyes. The camera with its art to hold the moment in spell, to drench it in crystalline streams of stillness, suggests the sadness that is inherent in every glimpse of beauty. The lens of the eye can also summon up those visions of millennium when we have seen (gazing aside hastily at the wheel of a hurrying car) the East River from the Queensborough Bridge, in a pinkish dusk; or pigeons near the City Hall and people strolling in the noonday pause; or lights reflected in Central Park reservoir on a night of fog. Or would it be the strange silence of Riverside Drive in a summer dawn, broken only by the chirp of crickets and the ambling hoof-clops of milk and roll deliveries? Sometimes in middle darkness, below Riverside, one is startled to hear the shrill heroism of cockcrow. Even in the fatal coops of the poultry-train, waiting on the New York Central freight-track, bruised and weary chanticleer has heart to salute the turning planet. Nor would I forget the glimpse of Manhattan's peaks seen from far out on the Northern Boulevard of Long Island. From twenty miles away, as the car comes over the rise between Roslyn and Manhasset, you see them glitter toward the morning, and wonder what the Colossians are doing today. Strange Etruscan and Babylonian touches in her design are part of her oddity; humorous ingenuities too: once on the Manhattan Bridge I applauded an advertiser who had rigged a huge electric coffee-cup sign so that the exhaust rising from someone else's chimney behind it made the imaginary coffee steam with savor. *Verweile doch, du bist so schön*, I have said to her a thousand times in pauses of amazement; but I would not idealize her in memory.

(*March, 1934*)
[Sl]

*BARABBAS**

AMONG THE OBSCURE New York hotels to which, for reasons of my own, I have sometimes made sentimental pilgrimage, is the Aberdeen on 32nd Street. It was an occasional overnight refuge for Grub Street Runners when I first had a publishing job. In those days there were a number of publishing offices on 32nd Street. I wonder if anyone else remembers a little chop-house on that street called the Blossom Heath Inn? It was almost next door to Doubleday's office at 11 West, and often—with a Pink Slip cashed by Angie Murphy (now as then Doubleday's admired exchequeress in the New York office)—promising authors were well gruntled there at lunch time. Surely the great success of Ken Roberts's fine historical novels on Doubleday's list really dates from an all-afternoon lunch at the Blossom Heath twenty years back. Dear old Guy Holt, who died a year ago, would remember those lunches. There was a brand of cigar obtainable there, called *Nabocklish*; the name sounds Gaelic, I have no notion what it means, but it became a kind of password among us; it had a sort of carefree sound and became an ejaculation suggesting "We should worry." Among the

**Chronicles of Barabbas, 1884–1934*, by George H. Doran. New York: Harcourt, Brace & Co., 1935. $3.50.

young writers who were entertained there were two who happened later to write two very different books with the same title. One, a novel now known to all the world; the other, earlier by several years, a little book of agreeable verses. Both were called *Main Street.* It was disturbing to learn, after cajoling Miss Murphy to O.K. the pink slip for Editorial Expense, that these two authors belonged to a rival house. Joyce Kilmer was faithful to George Doran; and Sinclair Lewis was at that moment Doran's literary scout.

But what I am leading toward are not my own small recollections but those of a much livelier fellow. I mentioned the old Aberdeen Hotel because George Doran once lived there to be handy to his office at number 15. It was from the Aberdeen that he looked down and saw his office building on fire—just after he had providentially paid a premium for $10,000 extra insurance. It was there too, I think, that the most important accident of his whole publishing career took place. It was in 1908, soon after Mr. Doran had started his own business. Mrs. Doran, ordered by the doctor to take a few days' complete rest, needed some books to read. Among those sent up for her by G. H. D. was Arnold Bennett's *Old Wives' Tale*, newly out in England. After a day's reading she telephoned her husband and begged him to cable for the American rights. He did so, and 1000 sheets were ordered.

It is pleasant to hear that it was the enthusiastic selling of young Fred Melcher, then a clerk at Lauriat's in Boston, which exhausted the first importation and started the book moving. Not only for Bennett's own books, and the intimate friendship that ensued, but also for the succession of brilliant young writers who came to Doran at Bennett's suggestion, this was a turning point in the publisher's career.

George's book is one which will have very great interest for all who are concerned or curious about our little world of publishing. Memoirs of publishers are always exciting because there is no other career that brings a man so intimately and frequently in touch with egregious people; and on terms of immediate social freedom. George tells a delightful anecdote of sprightly little Buffy (Elizabeth) Cobb, Irvin's daughter, when the Dorans arrived as strangers to live next door to the Cobbs in a well-mortgaged Suburban-on-Hudson. "They must be nice people," said Buffy, who had been watching the new neighbors' kitchen premises; "they have such nice garbage." Even the garbage of the publishing business, if you'll condone the phrase, is attractive. Combining the charm of the arts with all the hilarity and headache of commerce, in a trade of great social influence, it is a business of compelling allure. It is overcrowded, and it breaks hearts, but those who know it would exchange for no other.

And George's book is George himself. To tell you the truth I had no idea he would be so good a writer. Except for an occasional overuse of the word "precious" or for the description of Mary Roberts Rinehart's smile I would not edit away any of his vivacious zeal. The homage to Mrs. Rinehart is well-deserved—not only for their affectionate personal relation as grandparents of the same child, but because she was at that moment autographing innumerable books for customers at Marshall Field's. And George is not only a sentimentalist but also an intensely alert business man. This book, which describes 50 years of adventure in the book trade, has the same quality of infectious impulsive charm, high spirits, mixed Irish emotionalism and mischief, together with something hard and canny at bottom, which we have always relished in G. H. D. I find a parable of sadness in the book reaching us just at the time that the *Mauretania*, which George loved and travelled in so often, sails to be broken up.

And George himself was not unlike the *Mauretania*—a handsome craft on a smart schedule, making a quick turn-around and carrying important passengers.

The pleasantest phase of this excellent book is its spirit of youthfulness, its sympathy with the younger generation in publishing. There was always a touch of gallantry, swank, panache, in G. H. D. When he carried a cane he swung it and went along the street as if he were going somewhere. Young authors were fascinated by him at sight. When beautiful and powerful booksellers came to town, his handsome car was at their disposal. In his own office I rather guess he might be a pretty exacting taskmaster. I remember that poor Ivan Somerville, his manufacturing man, used to look pretty haggard sometimes. He made a very bad mistake (he admits it handsomely) in not understanding Gene Saxton who is one of the real editorial geniuses of our time. I hope all this doesn't sound like epitaph; but George speaks with such honest candor in his book that he invites his friend to talk blunt shop. On the final and fantastic error of the Doubleday merger he touches only lightly. It was an error of the first magnitude on both sides. George thought he was safeguarding the future of his young men. Doubledays' thought they were securing the remarkable literary prescience which had marked the Doran imprint. But the publishing business is (on its creative side) an intensely individualized affair. Like the theatre it revolves on hunch and temperament. It's all very well to draw up stock agreements, but personalities, diverse ambitions and methods, don't merge so easily. The long illness of Frank Doubleday, and then the era of declining business, helped to complicate matters. The union was entered into in good faith on both sides. It didn't work. In the detached perspective of the outsider its most important result was the founding of one of the ablest and most successful of younger houses, Farrar & Rinehart. I keep, as a rather pathetic souvenir, one of the special copies of Tarkington's *Claire Ambler*, bound in white bridal vellum, issued in 1928 as a consummation of the marriage. "This first volume over the new imprint," it says, "has been autographed by the author and the publishers." In 1930 George fled to the embrace of the Iron Maiden, Mr. Hearst—where he became a "notable prisoner." That, by the way, is St. Matthew's description of Barabbas. The line "Now Barabbas was a robber," which Lord Byron jocularly altered to "was a publisher," occurs in St. John XVIII, 40. George, as an old Bible salesman, should have checked this.

It's odd that a man who was himself a brilliant salesman says nothing in this book of his own sales boys who helped him build up so remarkable a business. It grew from $200,000 in 1908 to 2½ millions in 1927. I wish there were space to suggest the whole story, which he tells with most infectious good humor, and with many vivid little character sketches of his authors and associates. It begins in the familiar way: the ambitious boy of 14 who sees the sign SMART BOY WANTED. That was in Toronto, where G. H. D. was born of North of Ireland Presbyterians in 1869. He just escaped being christened, for his mother, George Oliver Doran, which would have given him embarrassing initials. After early experience in a Tract Depositary he joined an evangelistic publisher in Chicago, "the predatory Fleming H. Revell." Nothing in this book is more agreeable than George's deliciously ironic and yet fair-minded description of the humors (and occasional hypocrisies) of evangelical publishing. As a boy of 15 in Toronto he had met old Matthew Hodder of the famous English firm Hodder & Stoughton. Twenty years later he became the official representative of H. & S. in America, and their publications were the nucleus of his list. His description of old Hodder, and his brilliant grandson the lamented Ernest Hodder–Williams, is rich in mirth and affection. Dulac's edition of the *Rubáiyát* horrified old Mr. Hodder until he learned it was earning £800 a year profit. The early connection with pietistic publishing helped to tinge the Doran list for many years, and sometimes was a source of humorous incongruity—as when G. H. D. was reproached for bringing out, almost simultaneously, Moffatt's New Testament and *The Green Hat*.

The chronicles of this very lovable Barabbas are full of good stories. His first capture outside the devotional field was Roswell Field's *Bondage of Ballinger*. He became an American citizen; heard Bryan give the Cross of Gold speech. Like all publishers he has errors of judgment to look back on. Ralph Connor was Revell's big fiction seller, but G. H. D. agreed with his employer to turn down

Harold Bell Wright and also Sheldon's *In His Steps*—showing that even then our young editor had germs of admirable literary taste. His valiant attempt to find a public for Mary Webb was an example. There is refreshing candor in some of his confessions: that he never understood why all the excitement about *Revolt in the Desert*; that Marie Corelli's pique (because he did not mention her name in an interview) caused her to cancel her contract and saved him $20,000 in promised advances; that he was always incapable of appreciating really great poetry. (He is evidently at a loss to know how to comment on Elinor Wylie, the greatest poet on his list.)

I have given you no notion of the richness of anecdote and comment in this valuable book. George's lively blend of British and American temperaments makes him a unique officer of liaison between the two countries.

Similarly his paradoxical mixture of sacred and profane makes him the most enchanting of companions. Vivid and frank as his chronicle is, he has been more discreet than you might suppose. I think of many things he might have told; some of them were generous kindnesses done by him to people in trouble. He says that the book he would best like to have written is *Of Human Bondage*, which tells much of himself. Ambitious, highstrung, sensitive, sometimes a bit of a snob, a multiple soul. It is impossible to believe that he will not again have his suite at the Savoy and throw the most intelligent frolics in the publishing business. Blessings, George, from a friend and beneficiary of long standing! If some of the copies of *Barabbas* look a little worn in the shops it will be because the booksellers themselves have been reading them.

[Sl]

ON BELONGING TO CLUBS

I WOKE UP just now laughing and talking to myself. It must have been amusing, because I heard acoustic (and caustic) whispers from upstairs. "Quiet! You'll wake the baby." (A grandson, here on visit.)

I am a collector of risibilia, and I have two recurring dreams that always take me comic. They come mostly in what Oscar Firkins called "the warm little hollow between Christmas and New Year."* Then, by overeating and overreading, the triple expansion impulse-reaction turbines of the mind† slip a few steamy vanes and the mind has fun on Queer Street. My annual rereading in the Christmas Octave is always instinctively the same: Conrad, Conan Doyle, W. W. Jacobs, Leonard Merrick, George Gissing, and C. J. Cutcliffe Hyne. These dreams are rubricated with flushes of innocent bibliography. I see myself in a bookstore, say about 1903, and scream with mirth at the embarrassment of the Trade (and the authors) when they find that without warning two books have been almost simultaneously published so ridiculously con-

**Memoirs and Letters* (University of Minnesota Press, 1934), p. 91.

†*The New R.M.S. Caronia*, Cunard White Star booklet, 1949.

fusable as Conrad: *Youth*, and *Conrad in Quest of His Youth.* That alone is enough to keep me happy until I wake, when I reflect how grim Mr. Conrad must have been if he noticed that Mr. Merrick was never quite sure what is a taffrail.‡

But this time I was dreaming the dream called Belonging to Clubs. What put it into my turbines must have been talking to a distinguished man of affairs who was offering the hospitality of his own club for a literary dining-group that needed a room for decorous assembly. Actually it was the Baker Street Irregulars, who carry bibliography to the verge of anesthesia. My friend found the steward of his club (the Marrow & Squash) rather cagey. The steward wished to know, were the proposed visitors really mature? The club had catered a dinner for some young Wall Street men, where furniture and epithets were thrown and $400 damage done to fine old English linenfold panelling.

My friend was appalled. He explained that the coterie he sponsored were (was) a sodality of middle-aged Victorian literateurs. Most of them practically *are* old English panelling. But I remember (from my days about town) that the Marrow & Squash has (have) to be careful. I knew one of their members whom they didn't like to wash out because he came of ten lineal offsprings of Harvard (some of them badly sprung), but he was only allowed inside the club as far as the cloak room

‡See *When Love Flies Out o' the Window*, and *One Man's View.*

(left of the lobby) and the steward's desk where he could buy (for cash) the club tie. Even that he gave up, because people thought it meant (red and blue) the University of Pennsylvania. He also gave up oldfashioneds, and now he is in *Who's Who in America* and *Bartlett's Quotations*.

I used to think (this is what I was laughing about) how wonderful it must be to belong to a Club. When I was 26—you can guess when that was—my dear old friend A. Edward (Amenity) Newton, as kind as wealthy, decided I should join a famous club of great collectors. You bibliophiles know the De Vinne Club. It has about 500 members, the most princely paramours of print and champagne in the western hemisphere. According to A. Edward they had decided they wanted a Baby Member, but among the engraved protocol they forgot it might be embarrassing to the nominee. Walter Gilliss, bless his old heart, was also a mover in the matter. Walter was so pleased by my having not only praised but memorized his inscription for the Printers' Sundial at Country Life Press,* it never occurred to the saintly old celibate that a young man complete with family might not only wear purple patches in his prose but also in his pants. As Bob Holliday and I used to say to each

*"May thy unerring finger ever point
To those who printed first the written word."
See footnote, p. 1053, *Bartlett*, 12th edition.

other, Where breek meets breek, there comes the tug of war.

The very day our first child was born, and I was digging like a dachshund in a badger-den, came the accolade, and a bill for initiation.

The honor (honour) of Letters, of Oxford, and even of Eddie Newton, was at stake. I borrowed money on the Morris (it should have been William Morris) Plan, and stalled doctor and hospital and nurse as long as I could. Soon, full of pride and terror, I went to one of those Sunday Night Suppers that were famous and cathartic at the De Vinne Club. Those meetings were Big Rubric and entirely democratic: all you had to do was bring one of your own most precious *ex libris carissimis* and give it a terse collation to the assembled Lorenzoes. It might be a quarto Hamlet, or a Songs of Innocence in unique color, even a Breeches Bible or some unbreeched Ben Franklin. I sat, *scelerisque purus*, between J. P. Morgan and Owen D. Young. The only rarissima I had on me was the final punch of a tentrip ticket to Queens Village, L. I.

As a matter of fact I made very good friends with Mr. Morgan; he had forgotten his tobacco pouch, and borrowed some of my *Serene Mixture.* His pipe had a large bowl, I remember. I used to see him sometimes afterward, on the L.I. train, and he remembered me as the man who had mild tobacco. He was pleased that my only other convert to that blend was dear old Hilaire Belloc. I used to say to him, it's like my books, it has never been advertised; and he replied Morgan's don't advertise either.

But I don't think the De Vinne Club has had a Baby Member since. As soon as my initiation fee expired I did also. I went there once, 30 years later, to see an exhibition of Max Beerbohm. I am sure that though the members know Max is a satirist they don't quite know what he is satirizing.

I moved, slightly foxed and shaken, to Philadelphia; and again dear Eddie Newton got busy. I found myself a member of that delightfully clannish little tavern on South Camac Street, and I don't mean the Poor Richard. There were only 100 members, but almost every one had written a book on Our Colonial Heritage. Therefore they didn't speak to each other, but only to me; and at length. Still (1949; it is my only social triumph) you will find over the hearth at the Philmagundi a church-warden clay that, reluctantly, I was forced to smoke at a fire of prerevolutionary billets. It is a sweet old club; nothing should be allowed to disturb it; nothing will. I wrote a book about Philadelphia (long before poor *Kitty Foyle*) which I had no heritage to do, and fled.

I got back to New York, two hours later, and Don Marquis said I must join The Mummers. That was a club of actors and writers and collectors and boblishers. They played pool, in the basement; once a week they had curried mutton and some delicious new wisecrack by Oliver Herford. It was difficult, though, for a young member, because the shibboleth was you mustn't say anything about plays or actors or writers because almost any other member might be implicated. I had always dreamed that a Club was where you could drop in about dusk (which comes early in winter) and after a Hard Day at the Office (if you could find an office) knock back a few at the bar, tell the agreeable Nubian at the phone to call the Little Woman (who seemed to get bigger as hours went by) and sit down to a sidetable under nineteenth-century playbills, and alongside nineteenth-century actors. You could sign the check for someone else's drinks, and lounge in professional gossip. But the inscription over the hearth expressly forbade gossip (which is the germ of creation) and even dear old Edwin Booth had been thrombosed by one of the very mild but agreeable verses of Tom Aldrich. The book was still open at the fatal page, in his bedroom upstairs.†

I never had the nerve to ask the Nubian to phone Long Island. If I didn't get home, say by 7 P.M., to put the furnace to bed, and help wash the dishes and the baby, who would?

†*Poems of T. B. Aldrich.* Hougton Mifflin & Co., 1882.

Came the horrors of 1929–30. I would have liked to go to The Mummers, but I was managing a theatre, and the Club was full of actors out of work, and managers out of angels. One could always buy an apple on a street-corner, and eat it in the Club, which was warm; even sometimes carve a drink out of a publisher, but according to the laws as by Edwin Booth and Mark Twain laid down you mustn't talk critical shop in the clubhouse. I resigned, just one two-cent stamp ahead of the Treasurer. But dear old Don Marquis, who had been my sponsor in 1920, was then chairman of the committee. "We can't possibly accept your resignation," he said. "Just carry on and forget about it." I did; I had plenty to carry, including what was then known as the Decline and Fall of the Hoboken Empire. I still remember (and would like to have the clipping buried with me) an editorial in the New York *Sun* which said the only bankruptcy it ever sentimentally regretted was that of the Hoboken theatres. The *Sun*'s politics never moved me much, but its instinct toward the arts was always "Soyez gentil avec."

(What a genial topic, by the way, for a COLOPHON essay: the Attitudes of Various Papers toward Literature. I have seen, for instance, in 35 years, so many zigs and zags in the New York *Times* in book criticism that I don't know what not to believe. As Simeon Strunsky once said to me, the only subjects he felt were absolutely safe to praise in his then Topics of the Times were Sherlock Holmes, or Walking to Work (which John Finley had consecrated).

But à propos that Club in Gramercy Park. Fifteen years after resigning I had a notion to give it a MS, in honor of affectionate memories. It is now framed (they contributed the frame) near the bar; a letter written by F.D.R. about Don Marquis. I sent it, by a trusty hand, as a gift to the Club. They wrote: "We are delighted to have your gift; but we remind you, your name is still on the books and you owe the Club $250" (or something like that).

I must be brief, and very likely you also. There was the dignified Centipedes Club. One day of 1920, in the doublahvay of the *Evening Post* (there may be still in N.Y. a couple of hundred people who remember when New York had an evening paper that was liberal, literate, and lepid), dear old Sandy Noyes (the financial editor) told me they wanted a Baby Member. They had scanned their lists and found they had no one under Fifty. (I was then 30.) Even Henry Canby, Van Wyck Brooks, Elmer Davis, Leonard Bacon, and John Marquand weren't babyish enough for what they wanted. They wanted someone who would amuse Major Putnam, Henry Holt, and Nick Butler, without always contradicting them. My sponsor was that enchanting octogene Will H. Low, who had been a member for 50 years.‡ With a taxi driver I carried Will in to the meeting, on a tripos of canes. I saw I was about to be elected, and resigned at once. I was beginning to learn. Nothing gives me more malice and delight than when Henry Canby, or other much later members of that Club, ask me if I wouldn't be thrilled if they would Put Me Up.

I knew by then (say 1921) that clubs weren't for me, unless I invented them myself. I was quite happy, for a while, at dear old Frank Crowninshield's Café Noir on 45th Street, but if you didn't write for, or talk like, his *Vanity Fair*, you were gently eased out. Even Thackeray would have been greyballed.

I had to invent the Three Hours for Lunch Club, which existed only one meal at a time. We found ourselves owners of a full-rigged sailing ship, *Tusitala*. Something had to be done about that. Then we invented The Foundry, in the ruins of an old ironworks in Hoboken. We had a gorgeous suite of Chinese Chippendale furniture in the skeleton of an abandoned machineshop, with several residual blondes in the attic. In a few months, and after many impromptu lyrics in the old engine-room crankpit, we found ourselves putative owners of some lithographed stock-paper, a contract for a

‡ **Have you read his delightful *Chronicles of Friendship*? Scribner, 1908.**

Night Club, and a traffic in canned Mulligan. Something had to be done, and I had to do it. You'd be surprised to learn how intricate are the laws of New Jersey for Amicable Receivership. The canned soup of Eire was for a while transferred to the East 50's of Manhattan, where our business manager alternated singing "Mother Machree" and soliciting stock subscriptions; but even that, in the desiccations of 1931, blew away. Yet there are still occasional bohemians who remind me of the mixture of Irish sentiment and Irish bacon.

And still, poor soul, I had this morbid hanker for inventing clubs. Surely the most innocent impulse of my life was my boyish passion for the corn of Conan Doyle. I invented something called the Baker Street Irregulars; a simple group of a dozen devotees who met, Dutch, to discuss what amused them. It was taken up by that resonant sounding-board Woollcott, and then by *Life* magazine. The quiet speakeasy where we met was trampled into covercharge by runners and readers and their dames. Our scrapbook of minutes was stolen by some biblioklept; our simple punchinello (Christ Cella) died of ambitious hypertension. Truly, men in Clubs have an urge toward Deficit, Damnation, and Death. Now the scholarly group of Baker Street find themselves swaddled, or saddled, with a publishing business, an annual meeting, and a province of pulp. They have about 30 scionist branches whose letters have to be answered. But not by me.

So you mustn't wonder that I found myself shocked, some dozen years ago, at being elected to the National Institute of Arts and Letters. I have never attended a meeting. I have a horror it might turn out to be a Club.

One has one's weaknesses. When I was last in London I was thrilled to see the fine old Athenaeum being repainted, a dazzling oyster-white, Elgin frieze and all. I did have a curiosity to know who now has hat-peg number 33 (which was Kipling's) or whether Henry Canby's order for iced-tea (which horrified the steward) has ever been repeated. I bet in there you could say what you think about acting, or editing, if you could get anybody to talk to you. The Savile and the Garrick must also be pleasant memberships. My friend James Whitall still yammers about the crumpets at the Savile; I think of it as the place where conscientious old Sidney Colvin was so excited to meet R.L.S. unexpectedly that he forgot a portfolio of valuable Italian drawings (belonging to the British Museum) and left them in the cab and they disappeared.* At the Garrick, as Baby Guest, I had the excitement of sitting at dinner between J. M. Barrie and Anthony Hope; our host was E. V. Lucas. But that was as foreigner and guest, which is the thing to be. I am proud to be an honorary member of the Omar Khayyam Club, partly because its annual din-

*See that most delightful of *meminisse juvabits*, Sir Edward Marsh's *A Number of People*. 1939.

ner was poor George Gissing's only social jamboree. Gissing's usual instincts were far from festive. I love to remember that when he first went to Paris one of his earliest pilgrimages was to the Morgue.†

There are two clubs in London that not even their own members know apart. One is the Oxford and Cambridge, and the other the United Varsities. I have visited both, as a guest. I was agitated when in the coffee room of one or other my host (a cousin of mine, well over six feet six and well over sixty) said, "You're a varsity man, you should let me Put You Up, we need fresh blood." Next to us, at a lovely Queen Anne breakfront desk (they have lovely replicas of it at Abraham & Straus for $124.89), was an elderly parson making notes from a hidebound quarto and smoking a pipe and sipping a quarto of pale socialized India Ale.

The immortal story on this theme is of course James Bone's, done with his perfect concinnity in two lines:—

> "Drive me to the Caledonian Club."
> The taxi-man's face fell.

It was a shock to me when I realized I am not by temperament a clubman. It looks well in obits. But generally speaking (as I am) I prefer them vast and impersonal (like the Book-of-the-Month Club) or unsociable and imaginary, like the Diogenes Club

†*Letters of George Gissing* (Constable, 1927), p. 177.

where Mycroft spent every afternoon from 4:45 to 7:40.‡

There was a club once (about 33 years ago) that had only two members. To them I dedicate this feeble echo of a laughing dream. It was the Porrier's Corner Club, near Doubleday's press on Long Island. It was a saloon where Robert Cortes Holliday* and I used to have a shell of beer (we could afford only one apiece) on our way home from work. We used to talk about Literature, which we loved and in our humble ways ensued. We talked about George Gissing and Richard Jefferies, about Don Marquis and Simeon Strunsky, and all the gorgeous things young men in publishing houses talk about. We would hammer the bar as we intoned our favorite war-cry, *I was a great solitary in my youth* (we always misquoted it).† One day an old man, I bet he was over fifty, who had been watching our antics, doddered up to us and said, "What do you boys talk about all the time? The Death of the Essay?"

"Mister," we cried, "them's fighting words."

[IB]

‡*Memoirs of Sherlock Holmes*: "The Greek Interpreter."

*He was then putting together his delightful collection of *Walking-Stick Papers*.

†Stevenson: *The Pavilion on the Links*.

THREE NEWS-REELS

I. August 6, 1928

IN THE SMOKING CAR, whose etiquette is that you keep quiet and let men read the morning paper, it occurs to the student that future historians might value a casual abstract of one day's marginalia on the book of life. I take a New York morning newspaper, on a Monday in August, 1928, and quote some of its minor items. It is not for me to offer comment; I leave that to the historian of 2028.

The Mayor of New York, who, "despite the weather, wore a vest," returned from a six weeks' absence, mostly on the Pacific coast. "After travelling 10,000 miles," he said, "I wasn't in one place where there was any difficulty to see and get liquor. I didn't take advantage of this, however." It is still news, by the way, when a Mayor of New York carries a cane.—The United States Air Transport, Inc., advertised daily air service to Washington: leave Teterboro Field 4 P.M., arrive Washington 6:15 P.M. Fare one way, $30. Equipment, Ryan Brougham, Monoplanes, sister ships to "Spirit of St. Louis," carrying four passengers and express.—In the *Public Notices* column, which lists mostly Inquiries for Missing Persons, and "not responsible for debts contracted by my wife," the voice of Hazard can always be heard: "Party going to jungles of South America on sporting and film-taking expedition wants man to join them. K. R., 104 East 14." "Two outdoor-loving girls desire join family on boat trips, week-ends, paying own expenses." "Gentleman driving to Denver, closed Packard, can accommodate three gentlemen." "$15,000 Hispano-Suiza and man who knows how to use it, awaits instructions in England for European or world tour; hirer pays $250 weekly. Cable Methven Gear-box, Hackwick, London."

A piano company, having a clearance sale, remark that "The sour tones of an old piano disastrously affect family dispositions. A tin-panny, untuned old piano makes you 'mad' every time you hear it. Imagine what friends and neighbors think of you."—The Consolidated Automatic Merchandising Corporation will send you a booklet on "The Automatic Age in Merchandising." The Company's program for the next 5 years "calls for the installation of 80,000 additional Sanitary Postage Machines. Supplying the public with loosely handled finger-printed postage stamps, a danger to public health, will practically cease to exist."—The same corporation controls the Schermack Talking Automatic Merchandising Machines—"The Machines not only make change and deliver the merchandise, but also say *Thank you* together with the Manufacturer's slogan. The machine does everything but slap the customer on the back and ask him how his family is."—The Eastman Kodak Company made a full-page announcement of its "Kodacolor" process: "Home movies in full color, as easy to make as ordinary pictures in black and white."—Paul Block, the publisher, announced that he had bought the Brooklyn *Standard Union*, and printed a whole page of messages from all sorts of people, including Douglas Fairbanks, Charlie Chaplin, Babe Ruth, Calvin Coolidge, and Otto Kahn, all apparently steady readers of the *Standard Union*.

The weather was hot. People slept on the beach at Atlantic City. It was 96 in Baltimore. It was 102 in Phoenix. It was 94 in Boston and Philadelphia. It was 96 in Washington. It was 66 in Montreal, 64 in San Francisco. The Fall River Line said, "When torrid summer days turn offices into ovens, take a cool invigorating trip. The water is the great fan whose never ceasing breezes will keep you refreshed and stimulated. Hot and cold running water in all staterooms. $4.50 to Fall River." Much geography could be learned by studying the sailing schedules of steamships. The *President Harding* was listed to sail for Bremen on the Wednesday: "Mail for Canaries, Senegal, Gambia, Sierra Leone, Liberia, Ivory Coast and Gold Coast must be specially addressed." The transcontinental air mail left New York at 11 A.M., arrived Chicago 7 P.M., arrived Omaha 20 minutes after midnight, arrived Cheyenne 4:30 A.M., arrived Salt Lake City 10

A.M., arrived San Francisco 4:30 P.M. The Pennsylvania Railroad urged you to travel through "that most beautiful valley of the Juniata, theme of Indian song and story. On the east slope of the main ridge of the Allegheny Mountains is the Horseshoe Curve, indescribably beautiful in the approaching twilight. Enjoy all this on the Pennsylvania Limited, the 20 hour 50 minute train, with a midday departure from New York and an early morning arrival in Chicago. Club car, valet service, ladies' maid, writing desk, current papers and periodicals, ball scores, stock quotations."—Incidentally I wish Mr. Pedrick, the cheerful passenger agent of the Pennsy, would put a copy of the *Saturday Review* on his limited trains, for a train is one of the few places left in the world where one can read in peace.

Peaches Browning (it will give the historian of 2028 some research to account for her news value) was playing at a theatre in Brooklyn. 34 motorists in Brooklyn, during a two-weeks' period, had their driving licenses suspended—21 of these for driving while drunk. At Rockaway Beach 20 summonses were served on people for undressing in motor cars. The matter of public undressing, the future historian will observe, is one of the quaintest of American phobias. It is only safe if done on the stage. The police of Rockaway were asking property owners at street intersections to keep their hedges trimmed low to prevent traffic accidents. Emergency dressing stations, with doctors and nurses, were urged for the White Horse Pike between Camden and Atlantic City, because the hospitals of New Jersey cannot accommodate all the people who bash themselves up in week-end motoring to the shore.—*The Ladder*, that much revised play (said to have been written in red ink), presented gratis for many months, was still in existence at the Cort Theatre with audiences supposed to average about a dozen people. The job of running the Cort box office must be very tranquil; I wonder if the ticket-wallah would like some books to review in his spare time? The ad says "Money Refunded if Not Satisfied with Play."

The parsons had been busy in their Sunday sermons. Dr. Roach Straton said that Governor Smith had a lovable disposition but "whether wittingly or unwittingly was a friend of vice." Rev. Everett Wagner said that the stream of automobiles on the highways on Sunday was evidence that people "find expression for the finer sense of freedom and quiet meditation." Rev. William C. Judd said it would be all right for men in the congregation to take off their coats and be comfortable, but only one usher at the back of the church did so. Rev. John McNeill "deplored the prevalence of profanity. What particularly pained him was the fact that the practice of using unseemly language had spread to the feminine world." Professor Luccock of Yale, preaching at a theological seminary, said that the much-touted American efficiency was dubious. "We build an $8,000,000 moving picture temple in which to show 30-cent pictures." The International News Company urged you to buy English religious journals (sample copies 12¢ each) to keep abreast of "the prayerbook controversy raging within the Church of England."

An "overnight bag" containing a black coolie coat, a navy blue dress, and a typewritten manuscript was lost in a taxicab outside a restaurant on 58th Street. Telephone Spring 1910. I wonder what the MS. was? (Incidentally I wish we might use the abbreviation TS. for a typescript to distinguish from actual penmanship.) The Parisian modistes had concluded their showing of fall and winter modes. The colors for this autumn were said to be scarlet, brick-dust red, and tangerine. Picturesque robes will be the style. Short-waisted bodies with extremely circular skirts flaring to the floor behind. The favorite trimming consists of strings of graduated buttons set thickly with rhinestones or tiny mirrors.—The Marathon race in the Olympic Games was won by an Arab from Algeria. "It is the strange irony of destiny," says the A. P. dispatch, "that the only athlete who won for France shuns her wines, drinks nothing but milk and water." Marathon dancers, the biological oddities of the year 1928, were still going strong. A pair of them had just reached the outskirts of New York after having danced down the Post Road all the way from Bridgeport. An alumnus of the Bunion Derby (perhaps that will puzzle 2028?) ran backward from Bridgeport to Stamford, 35 miles, in 7½ hours, "breaking all previous records for backward running."—Electric refrigeration was highly spoken of in the ads. There seemed to be plenty of apartments to let, and plenty of Household Situations Wanted. A couple, Japanese man and Scotch wife (unusual combination, surely?), would go anywhere as cook–valet and waitress–chambermaid. Russian gentleman, highly educated, wished a position as private secretary or major domo with a gentleman desiring to shed all responsibilities of home duties. The Childs Restaurant Company desired a limited number of intelligent English speaking young ladies, ages 18 to 25. The Mayfair Mannequin Academy assured you that Attractive Girls can become professional models in a few inexpensive lessons. "If you earn less than $50 weekly you should become a Wilfred Beauty Expert at once; learn the famous Wilfred System of Beauty Culture during the DAY or EVENING. Prepare you for the best positions in smart beauty shoppes."—Christmas card salesmen were wanted, a new kind of beautiful Christmas card; cards sell on sight.

"Salesmen to assist on membership drive, strictly private golf club."—"*Free*, A short course in salesmanship to every one attending the 10 o'clock sharp Monday morning Barton System lecture on Master Salesmanship; learn how to analyze yourself and prospect—108 different difficult situations charted out" . . . "and if you are weary tired of stubborn resistance you can join the Harry Levey Graphic Homesite Organization: learn how the California Lecture and Excursion system solves the hot weather problem, breaks down the resistance."

The world of finance and investment is one of which this anthologist has no knowledge, he refrains from excerpt—mentioning merely that Brooklyn–Manhattan Transit 6s, the only investment he ever made, and a very satisfactory one, were quoted at 98½. He watches them just now with attentive eye, as he is about to part with some of them to pay for a piece of waterfront.—Real estate ads are always interesting. Out in Huntington, L. I., for instance, we notice William E. Gormley calling attention to "An old farmhouse, 10 rooms, 3 open fireplaces; 2¼ acre plot; Lloyd Neck, overlooking Lloyd Harbor; magnificent old trees; a good purchase at $15,000." In that case, as I know by personal observation, the word "magnificent" is not misused; just in front of that farmhouse is the finest tree I have seen in America.—At 246 5th Avenue a gentleman advertises "Mail received, telephone messages taken, confidential, $5 monthly." Most services of this sort hail from Fifth Avenue: there seems to be a certain flavor about an Avenue address that is highly relished.—There was a "Forest-Farm in Pomerania, Germany" for sale: 3400 acres of which 1977 acres are timber-forest, 1234 acres best farmland. Modern castle with all comforts. Fixed price $290,000.

There were 14,007 students in the Columbia Summer School. And the American Booksellers' Association calculated that in the United States twice as much money is spent for candy as for books. 6.9 pounds of candy are sold for each volume of reading matter, but as the newspaper adds "more than one person may read each book, a situation which is not paralleled in the field of candy."

These, then, were some of the items that caught the eye of a reader of the New York *Times* on August 6, 1928. Undoubtedly a Keyserling in 2028 will be able to deduce all sorts of theories from them; mostly fallacious. But whatever 2028 may say about our present skirmishes he mustn't think we don't enjoy 'em.

II. Rain on the Roof
(*May 29, 1931*)

An uncle of my acquaintance has a small nephew who confided to him, with the candor of childhood, that there were three sounds he liked to hear when in bed at night. They were the sound of rain on the roof, the radio playing downstairs, and the toilet flushing. These sounds, the child said, suggested a sense of being at home, of life going on, and of someone being near-by to take care of him.

Perhaps grown-ups get somewhat that same feeling of reality—though not always of safe care and protection—by reading the newspaper. Once every two or three years I take a copy of the New York *Times* and sit down with it to study it intensively. The last time I did so was in 1928 when things were riding high. And now, cleaning up in my study in hope of a small vacation, I find the issue of May 29, 1931. I had set it aside because it seemed to contain a specially high proportion of interesting news. Let's report briefly on it, for students of living. It contains all those three symbolic elements of human life which the wise child mentioned. There is no harm in civilization sometimes lying awake in bed to listen to the rain on the roof.

Professor Piccard, Swiss physicist, now a teacher in Brussels, and his assistant Kipfer, descended safely on the Gurgl Glacier in Austrian Tyrol after a balloon ascension of approximately ten miles. Professor Piccard was very pale after their eighteen hours' flight and asked for some hot tea when they reached the village of Obergurgl. The newspaper men reached Obergurgl at 2 A.M. and waked him up to ask questions, which he said was more agitating than the flight itself. Augustine Courtauld, a young British meteorologist who spent five months in solitude in a snow house on the Greenland icecap, reported his experiences. Except for the pain of frost-bites he said he had been very comfortable; he had "plenty to eat and drink, an excellent supply of classical and other literature, good tobacco, and a fine lamp." The last six weeks of his stay however he had no light; he ate a mixture of cocoa, oats and snow and spent most of his time "day-dreaming" in his sleeping bag. I wish he would let us know what books he read. A man's body was found floating in the Seine near Paris with a bullet wound in the head. The only clue to identity was the label of John David, a New York clothier, and the lot mark 5659–37, in a brown suit. Eight such suits had been sold in the John David stores in May and June, 1929; five of these had already been accounted for and a conjectural identification suggested. Sir James Jeans, English physicist, speaking at a dinner of scientific societies at the Hotel Astor, said that "Today if anyone asks a question about the universe it cannot be answered except by a mathematician, and when the answer is given no one except a mathematician can understand it." In the immediate adjoining column was an advertisement of a book called *Our Gods on Trial*, announced as the "Freethought Book Club Selection for June," with this deliciously naïve blurb quoted from Clarence Darrow: "A bully good book, convincing to anyone who wants to know the truth about the Bible and the Gods."

The first "heat wave" of the season had arrived and everyone was thinking of the Decoration Day week-end. The thermometer in New York City went to 85 the preceding afternoon and there were one death and one prostration. The deficit of the Federal Treasury now exceeded one billion dollars, but treasury officials believed that "an upward turn in economic conditions was near at hand." But one of Mr. Babson's statistical staff was reported as saying that business was not likely to reach the 1918 status until 1945. Two aviators (Lees and Brossy) flying in Florida established a new world's record for non-refuelled flight, 84 hours 33 minutes. Their motor was a Packard-Diesel. Lees, aged 43, was the driver of a horse-car twenty years ago. The 143rd general assembly of the Presbyterian Church, meeting in Pittsburgh, was arguing whether or not to include an endorsement of birth control in its transactions. Mr. Adolph Lewisohn, the distinguished financier, sang three songs at a dinner given him in honor of his 82nd birthday. The sky armada of 672 U. S. army airplanes, which had been exhibiting spectacular airoeuvres over large cities, was preparing to hop off for Washington for a Decoration Day flying bee. Two Italians were shot in front of the Parody Dance Hall on 116th Street by gunmen in a dark-colored sedan, who escaped. It was said to be a by-play of the beer racket. The Putnam bookstore advertised "You 'Trade in' Your Automobiles, Why Not Your Books?" Only 56 members of the G.A.R. were left to join the Memorial Day parade in New York; in 1930 there had been 81. Seven airplane expeditions were said to be waiting for favorable weather to attempt transatlantic flights. A group of mayors of American cities, visiting France as guests of the French government, were arousing some merriment by their naïve antics. The mayor of Los Angeles had walked out from an official luncheon because champagne was served. The mayor of Portland, Oregon, had broken a tradition of silence by delivering a speech (described as "vibrant") at the tomb of the Unknown Soldier. The New York *Times* in an editorial (probably by Simeon Strunsky) advised him to "go and chin no more."

Prices were said to be at the lowest level in many years. John Wanamaker advertised "Cowhide Overnight Cases at the lowest point since 1910! $5." Hand-Sewn Silk Panties $2.95. Gotham Gold Stripe Silk Stockings were eloquent about their seven inches of adjustment space to fit every length of leg. The new Spanish republic voted $230,000 to build schools. The Vickers Company in London opened a new show-room for the public display of war equipment, including machine guns, tanks and torpedo-airplanes, round the corner from the headquarters of the Peace Society. Joseph Stalin, general secretary of the Russian Communist party, congratulated the tractor stations on the successful completion of the spring sowing program. A book about the Russian Five-Year plan was selling well in the bookstores. In Brooklyn marriage licenses were granted to sixteen young women; their ages ranged from 18 to 29 and their names were Brennan, Cohn, Feinstein, Gross, Herkowitz, Kofsky, McCarthy, Montrose, Oakley, Paul, Pogarelsky, Rabinowitz, Rose, Schoenfeld, Solotaroff, Williams. The Hollywood Gardens, Pelham Parkway, advertised that it was America's largest open-air restaurant, seating 5,000. "Make up a party of 4 or more persons, hail a Keystone taxi anywhere in Manhattan or Bronx, and drive to the Hollywood Gardens. We pay your fare upon arrival." Twelve men were dropped from the Yale rowing squad for breaking training rules; they were said to have smoked. The *Empress of Britain*, 42,500 tons, the largest passenger liner built in Britain since the War, was making her maiden voyage from Southampton to Quebec. A lunch was held at the Walt Whitman Hotel in Camden, N.J., to celebrate the launching of the *Excambion*, a 7,000 ton passenger and cargo steamer, the fourth of four sister ships built there in ten months for the Export Steamship Company. By purchasing a rag-paper copy of the New York *Times*, of which a limited edition is printed each day, "records of births, deaths, engagements may be preserved indefinitely." This special perdurable edition costs 75 cents on weekdays, $1.25 on Sundays.

The Vice-President of the United States, whose name was Curtis, was to give the Decoration Day address at Gettysburg and then have his summer vacation. George Arliss was sailing in the *Majestic*,

Otis Skinner in the *Bremen*; Gutzon Borglum in the *Berlin* to attend the unveiling of his statue of Woodrow Wilson at Poznań in Poland. Apartments at 2 Beekman Place, 2 to 8 rooms, were offered at rentals ranging from $1,150 to $8,600. For a good many children the day began as usual at 7:45 A.M. by the Cream of Wheat broadcast about "Jolly Bill and Jane." Too many radio broadcasters were attempting to ingratiate themselves with their hearers by a soupy whine of simulated tenderness. Arthur Murray the dance teacher—"rates lowest in our history"—offered ten minutes' lesson and a dancing analysis gratis. Hilaire Belloc, lecturing at Oxford, said that translations were more numerous and worse done than ever before. The Players' Club were rehearsing Congreve's *The Way of the World* for their tenth annual revival. President Nicholas Murray Butler of Columbia University unveiled a portrait of the late Henry R. Seager, professor of economics, who died last year while making researches in Russia. Dr. Butler said of Professor Seager that he had died while acquiring information on "the most important happening of our time or of any time." 235,791 stock-holders of the P.R.R. were receiving their quarterly dividend. The U. S. Marine Corps was asking for bids on furnishing 60,000 pairs of cotton socks, 70,000 pairs of woolen socks, 100,000 cotton undershirts. Among new corporations reported by the secretary of state at Albany were the Adirondack Log Cabin

Co., The Shreddy Coconut Co., the Adorable Hat and Accessory Co. The American Merchant Lines offered weekly sailings to London for $100. The Universal Tours suggested Free Booklet H, "Honeymoon Haunts, contains 80 Honeymoons 3 to 30 days." The advertisement carried a small cut of Cupid aiming his arrow. The Munson Lines suggested Tourist Cabin to Rio de Janeiro and return for $275. Henry Werner of 75 West Street advertised that he had left two books in a taxi arriving at Grand Central Station, viz., a biography of Charles Darwin and ditto of Walter Bagehot.

The Viennese film operetta *Zwei Herzen im ¾ Takt* was playing its 9th month. Of the Dressed Poultry market it was said:

> Broilers cleaning up well and tone firm. Fowls slow, but held steady. Old cocks steady. Turkeys quiet. Ducks easier. Squabs steady. Frozen broilers easier for small but large firm. Fryers and roasting chickens firmer. Fowls well sustained. Turkeys steady.

The trade depression had made the real estate advertisers more folksy than ever. For instance:

> Silvermine, Norwalk
>
> Cute little bargain, 5 rooms, all improvements, big fireplace; large plot; $9,700. More real bargains now.

> *SOUTHAMPTON*—I own a location where I desire a good neighbor still time for that Summer vacation home; ideal surroundings for the wife and kiddies; safe bathing, boating and restricted social as-

sociations; for the man, golf, yachting, best fishing and gunning in season; why not run down and investigate? $2,000, your terms. Write for particulars. Room 820. George Washington Hotel, 23 Lexington Av., New York City.

68TH ST., 60 WEST (The Cambridge Hotel)—It's hard to say how big our apartments are; we have a 1-room apartment, but the closets are so large and the room so spacious it looks like two rooms. Then there's one of those special 2-room suites with brand-new, homelike furniture and a smart colored tile bath; and we're accused of underestimating its size—so there you are. If you want to live a few steps from Central Park in either a one or a two room apartment, completely furnished, with full hotel service, electric refrigeration, at truly payable prices come in and see Mr. Spear.

NEAR BEAUTIFUL STAMFORD, N. Y.

Adaptable for man who contemplates retiring or for a semi-retiring business man; 70 acres; fully equipped furnished modern house, 8 rooms, bath, gas and electricity; A1 condition; 6-car garage; barns, trout stream, pine forest, apple orchard, lawn, shrubbery, fruit, berries, etc.; 2 saddle horses; excellent riding country and wonderful mountain scenery; 1,800 feet elevation, on State road.

Will sacrifice for $12,500; terms.

But one realtor in the Sayville neighborhood was trying to keep up the tone of Long Island. "ULTRA REFINED ESTATE, for refined people." I looked for, but did not find, advertisements of the admired Long Island realtors, Upjohn and DeKay. How often, in recent months, have I said to myself secretly that in business there was too much DeKay and not enough Upjohn. I apologize!

III. July 20, 1933

THE paper before me is the New York *Times* of Thursday, July 20. Giving ourselves the privilege of detachment, what can we deduce of the state of the world?

It happens that there is one big news story which of course gets preferred position. Italian Air Minister Balbo, with his "air armada" of 24 big seaplanes and 96 men, has just arrived at Floyd Bennett Field beside Jamaica Bay, Long Island. His magnificent mass flight, after one tragic accident at Amsterdam, came smoothly via Londonderry, Reykjavik, Labrador, New Brunswick, Montreal, to Chicago—where the "Century of Progress" exposition is being celebrated. That was about 6100 miles; actual flying time, 47 hours 52 minutes. Yesterday his fleet came down the Hudson—we could see them plainly from the *Saturday Review* office, two squadrons of twelve planes each, in little triangles of three. Everyone, admiring that superb triumph, must have had a pang to recall that one plane didn't get beyond Amsterdam.

Bearded General Balbo, aged 37, "took a bath,

donned a suit of white pyjamas and sat comfortably in his suite at the Hotel Ambassador" to be interviewed. His gallantry has almost restored the beard to favor in America. The *Times* calls it brownish red, the *Evening Post* calls it black. He dined at the Columbia Yacht Club where he was hailed as a second Columbus. He said gracefully that Columbus hadn't had Weather Prophet Dr. Kimball to warn him against storms. He liked to hear the sirens of his police escort. The reporters asked him what he thought of the New York skyline, and of American women.

Coming closer to the ground, various industries were busy in formulating their Codes of Fair Competition as required by NIRA—the National Industrial Recovery Act. General Hugh Johnson, the toiling administrator of said Act, must smile grimly at the idea of a 40-hour week. The Ladies' Garment Workers, the Rayon Industry and the National Millinery Council had submitted their codes. The milliners said "No employee shall work more than 40 hours per week except during the peak periods which occur in the spring and fall occasioned by seasonal changes in the styles of women's hats." Shipbuilders, electrical manufacturers, coal operators and theatre people were trying to formulate codes. One theatrical producer was quoted: he didn't believe they could codify a business which was essentially a gamble. But the American people were taking up Codes with their usual enthusiasm.

We even hear of a "blanket code," which I believe is to cover and sum up all others—a supercode, a code to end codes.

Meanwhile the Recovery Cabinet was anxious lest prices should rise faster than purchasing power could catch up. There was a sudden wabble in the stock market which had been climbing steadily since April. The only stock I had been watching was Union Pacific, because crossing the plains in the Overland Limited in mid-April I got a definite feeling that things had turned a corner. When I began writing about the U. P. in April its shares were in the 70's. Three months later they reached 132. The Bowling Green was pleased to see its sentiment so promptly reflected on 'change. But anyhow it appears that on July 19 there was a jitter down town. Senator Thomas of Oklahoma naïvely telegraphed to the president of the Stock Exchange that it mustn't happen again. There's a good deal of talk of guaranteeing increased buying power. But how? Saks–Fifth Avenue took a full page to announce a 10% rise in salaries. The Crowell Publishing Co. (Springfield, Ohio) said they'd increased their payroll $500,000 annually. Wage increases were reported also in Detroit, Cleveland, and Youngstown. London taxi-fares were raised. At the University Club in Washington, D.C., an assistant secretary of state (not Prof. Moley, but Mr. Harry Payer) outlined the Ten Commandments of the so-called New Deal. 1st, "Thou shalt not live, my dear country, beyond thy means" . . . 8th, "Thou shalt not suffer the paradox of poverty amid plenty . . . since the age of scarcity hath passed to return no more." (The angel of record pauses a moment to meditate that.) At Reading, Pa., 11,000 "full-fashioned hosiery workers" were on strike. Governor Pinchot of Pennsylvania was protesting the use of tear-gas on hosiery strikers at Lansdale. In international exchange the dollar had "an indicated gold value of 69.4 cents."

An Essex car climbed Mount Washington with its gear-shift lever locked in high. Remembering my glimpse of Mount Washington a few days ago I shuddered. The Cunard Line begged us not to think First Class so terribly expensive: first cabin room and bath in *Aquitania* for $230. Hamburg–American Line said First Class in the motor-ship *Milwaukee* (a profitable name for a German ship) from $166 up. The North German Lloyd was saying steadily "Fastest Way to Europe, *Europa* and *Bremen*." Capt. Nillsson of the tanker *Gulf Gem* died of exhaustion after rescuing 34 men from another tanker, the *Cities Service Petrol*, afire and sinking off the coast of Florida.

Evidently, the detached observer would note, something had been happening to Prohibition. Arkansas and Alabama had voted for Repeal, making 18 states to vote so. The Board of Higher Education authorized beer to be sold at the symphony concerts in the Lewisohn Stadium. And here's an ad:—"Gentleman of social standing wanted to sell beer to fashionable clubs and hotels." If the visitor from a distance depended on our quinquennial summaries he would notice other queer changes. Five years ago we were all familiar with those delightful little advertising essays on thrift, virtue, sobriety, careful management, the irresistible cumulation of interest, etc., under the name of the Harriman Bank. But what do we see now? "Harriman Bank depositors to get 50¢ on the dollar." "Joseph W. Harriman being studied for sanity in psychopathic ward at Bellevue." Well, they've got all the latest equipment in that fine new ward. In our summary of five years ago I remember that Mayor Jimmy Walker was riding high. On July 20, 1933, Jimmy Walker seems absent; but friends of another Mayor, John Purroy Mitchel, now 15 years dead, made their annual pilgrimage to put flowers on his grave at Woodlawn.

As one moves deeper into this fascinating maze of printed paradox we realize that only the merciful opium of habit makes it possible for the pensive citizen to skim all this every morning and not go haywire. Everywhere he turns is the perfection of astonishment. The Blind Women's Club, 100 members, went in the steamer *Belle Island* on their annual outing to Roton Point. 250 picked bridge players played a tournament in the Abraham & Straus store in Brooklyn. The same store says of its new Envelope Beret (a hat) "It's reckless! It's vital!" The 72-story RCA building in Rockefeller Center opened an observation promenade 850 feet up. People in the Chrysler Building elevators were stalled for 41 minutes, suspended between floors. The management said only about 20 people were caught. One of the elevator boys said about 300. Mrs. Franklin D. Roosevelt in the *Woman's Home Companion* invited people to write and tell her their problems. President Roosevelt had had a cold, but would be able to receive General Balbo. A Prince from Ethiopia was to lunch at the White House on Friday, but the White House kitchen was warned that for reasons of piety he can't eat meat, milk or butter on Fridays. Six circus lions housed in a barn on East 221st Street kept the neighbors awake. An unemployed chauffeur has two beehives on his roof in Brooklyn. One stung a neighbor's child and he is brought to court. The bees produced 435 lbs. of honey last year, worth 25¢ a pound. Trotzky was on his way from Turkey to live in France. "The official eye would be kept discreetly closed so long as he lives in such a manner as not to awaken it." In the Yangtse Valley it was very hot—115° reported. In New York the day before showed 86 high, 69 low. London maximum same day 80; Paris 74. Phoenix, high 108, low 82. Bismarck, 100 and 60. Los Angeles, 76 and 60. San Francisco, 76 and 52. Washington, 90 and 64. Portland, Maine, 72 and 66. Chicago, 90 and 68.

"Dignified Funerals as low as $150." European

publicists, considering that American changes of plan had blown up the Economic Conference in London, lamented that it is very difficult to complete any negotiations with the U. S. government. George Ennis, distinguished painter, writes from Eastport, Maine, that three talented young American artists, all pupils of his, who have been jailed in Majorca, can hardly have been guilty of anything more than a boyish prank. Macy's welcomed General Balbo in an advertisement and assured him that if he should be homesick for *formaggio reggiano* or any other cheese, they can supply it—and have 1200 persons of Italian descent on their staff. Gimbel's continued their series of humorous advertisements which have ventured—with gratifying success—to toy with the public's sense of merriment. The British Air Force decided—wisely—not to attempt to regain the record for air speed, now held by Italy at 423 m.p.h. A deer, strayed somehow into the streets of Rochester, N. Y., was chased into a garage and there died of fright. Arthur Henderson, president of the world disarmament conference, was going to Munich to meet Chancellor Hitler. The British Labor Unions suggested a boycott of German goods until Germany should repudiate Hitlerism. Saks–Fifth Avenue "extended its hands" to its employees in appreciation of their talents and loyalty. Kidnapping was evidently the current racket. John J. O'Connell Jr. of Albany still unfound after 13 days. Even in peaceful old Haverford township, Pa., there was an attempted kidnapping of a real estate broker. Abercrombie and Fitch bathing suits have "that delightful next-to-nothing feeling when you swim." Princess Mary was suffering from acute fatigue brought on by too many public engagements. A Scottish pastor said that the "new morality" of Bertrand Russell was a return to animalism. A committee of critics published a rather hasty list of the 100 best books written in the past century by American women. Only 2 titles in Science were listed—one of these was *An Atlas of the Medulla and Mid-Brain.* Why, I wonder, didn't they list Louise Imogen Guiney among the poets? Obviously because they never heard of her—as, 20 years ago, they would never have heard of Emily Dickinson.

Babe Ruth muffed a fly and the Yankees lost, ending their winning streak of 9 games. Jack Lovelock, Oxford student from New Zealand, had lately made the world's record mile at Princeton in 4:07⁶⁄₁₀ but on a wet track in Canada was ten seconds slower.

More than 13,000 parcels of real estate were advertised for sale in Jersey City for delinquent taxes. The list filled 12 pages of agate type in Jersey City newspapers. The New Jersey Bell Telephone Co. reported that in June, 1933, their net loss in number of telephones in service was only 159; in June, 1932, it was 5766. The Neustadt Brewing Corporation of Stroudsburg, Pa., brewers of beer under the trade name *Gesundheit!* recorded the offering of 29,000 shares of common stock at $12.50 a share. "This advertisement appears as a matter of record and is not to be construed as a solicitation to buy." 13 major railroads reported 262,614 freight cars loaded the preceding week, as against 204,023 same week last year. The Bank of France withdrew 5 millions of gold from "ear-mark" here and shipped it to Paris. Fishermen at Montauk were going to try for swordfish with bow and arrow. The consul general of Jugoslavia announced that the State Mortgage Bank of Jugoslavia, "as a result of the world-wide economic crises," would temporarily interrupt service payments on the 7% Sinking Fund Gold Bonds. The Basement Managers of the Retail Dry Goods Association were addressed by Mr. Propper of Mandel Bros., who said that higher retail prices had evoked no customer complaint. Other speakers advised caution, lest there be a buyers' strike this fall. In Fur Trimmings, these were wanted by buyers: Gray Foxes, Fitches, Chinese Weasels, Squirrel Belly Plates, Kit Foxes, Marminks, and Silver Fox Paws. Other buyers wanted Rayon Sand Crepe, plain and waffle piqués, Silks Damaged and Tender. *Arrival of Buyers*: Miss A. Chaloux was here from Jordan Marsh (Boston) to buy corsets. Miss L. Bailey from Stewart & Co. (Baltimore), women's, misses', stouts', coats, suits. Mr. G. S. Samsel of Idaho Falls, to buy ready-to-wear. C. Schneider of Chicago for handkerchiefs, notions, hats, towels, boudoir caps. The City of New York, Department of Purchase, wanted Propeller Shafts, Spruce Lumber, Liquid Chlorine, and Muslin Sheeting (this last for the Dept. of Correction).

The delights of the various classified advertising are always the best part of the paper. Why did I leave them until space is short? *Business Opportunities*: "Partner with capital to invest in beer and wine business in New Jersey territory; surface only scratched." I wonder; New Jersey has been scratched pretty deep in that trade. "Legitimate Broadway Play, small amount capital wanted to complete financing immediate production. Chelsea 2-7715." *Public Notices*: after the usual crop of My Wife having left my bed and board, will not be responsible, etc., we find "Wanted—Air Passengers for Maine, leaving every Friday P.M. returning Monday A.M.—Clarence Chamberlain, Times Bldg." A duplex penthouse apartment of 15 rooms and 7 baths at 1115 Fifth Avenue was sold to "a well known New Yorker whose name is not revealed." The Pennsylvania Drug Co. leased space on the ground floor of the RKO building in Rockefeller Center. The Mavis Bottling Co. needed more space in Sunswick Street, L. I. City—I'm glad, I love the stuff. Bronislaw Zglobicki bought 3 vacant lots on Carlton Ave., Jersey City. 123 West 57 St. is "a midtown residential hotel with the distinctive Rue de la Paix atmosphere." 140 East 28 is an unusual 3-room apartment with 31-foot living room, wood-burning fireplace, bright gayly decorated bath, four huge closets. The Hotel Taft, Single Rooms $8 a week. "A room you'll enjoy; writing desk, full length mirror, easy chair, bedhead reading lamp, circulating ice water—nightly organ recitals." Gimbel's has a few openings for elevator girls of good appearance; must be at least 5 feet 5 inches tall and under 25 years. IDLE NEWSMAN, depression victim, university graduate, experienced legman, humorous columnist; service record includes *Time*-advertised Des Moines Register. X 2026, *Times Annex.* (Good luck, old son.)

Wills for Probate: "John Markle, to six nieces and nephews, $200,000 each."—And quite at the other end of the scale, "Thos. F. Kelley, estate $760. To Matilda Kelly, widow. Other heirs, seven children." There might be a little mutual adjustment here. "Frank Huebl, to granddaughter Helen Huebl, $800 in trust until 16 years of age when $200 a year is to be spent for her education." In New Rochelle a Mathematics Tutor is wanted; college student preferred; exchange for room and board.—The Banford Beauty Culture Academy is "Endorsed by Cosmetologists' Association and Guild of Master Beauticians of America. Summer Rates Now in Effect."

Estates Appraised: John A. Wade must have been a loyal alumnus. His net estate was $1938, and $1000 of it goes to Yale University. *Fire*

Record: In Brooklyn, at 8:15 P.M. Atlantic and Williams Avs., fence; Long Island Railroad; Loss Slight. *Movements of Naval Vessels*: "The commander of Submarine Squadron 3 has shifted his broad command pennant to the S-11." *Sailing Tomorrow*: *American Banker*, *Clan Macbeth*, *Europa*, *Lafayette, Minnetonka, Statendam*—and the *Cristobal Colon* to Vigo, Coruna, Gijon, Santander, Bilbao, Cadiz and Barcelona. . . .

With an atlas, an encyclopaedia, and a shelf of histories one might adequately absorb one issue of a newspaper. Like the New Jersey vintner, I have hardly scratched the surface. If one really did, perhaps—like the deer in Rochester—he might die of fright. Anyhow these notes are now filed away; hopefully—though a little doubtfully—referred to the end of July, 1938.

[IR]

BLUE CHINA

IT'S ONLY the thinking about it beforehand that is tedious; the actual writing is great fun. All morning I had been commiserating myself because I would have to write this on the train; and now, sitting in one of those delightful and almost-empty B. & O. smokers, I am enjoying it. Years ago I began my modest (and unsubsidized) campaign to convince New Yorkers that the way to go to Philadelphia, Baltimore or Washington was by the Jersey City routes, but thank goodness they didn't pay any attention, and the smokers and dining cars are still uncrowded. The Max Beerbohm Special we used to call one of the New Jersey Central trains to Philly, because there were usually only Seven Men in the smoker. (I find a surprisingly large number of people who have never read that book of Max's.) To a Long Island commuter, finding a smoker with hardly anyone in it seems like a fairy-tale.

When I say smoker, of course I mean the day-coach, with smooth leather seats. I have no use for Pullmans, unless you can afford a "drawing room." How grievous are the plush chairs that feel like the back of your head just after a hair-cut. I am always for extremes. Just as in religion I would be either a Quaker or a full-blooded Papist (surely religion isn't anything to be rational about?) so on a train I prefer either the humble day-coach smoker or a luxurious private compartment.

I saw a newspaper item the other day saying that Primo de Rivera, former dictator of Spain, was traveling incognito in France under the name of the Duke of Montgomery. . . . I pause here for an instant, realizing that we are just passing Neshaminy Falls. I don't suppose you ever heard of it, but it is to me a place of happy memory. Titania and I had a picnic there all by ourselves one time, and I wrote a piece about it which even got printed in a book . . . why Primo chose that name I can't imagine; I feel that I have more right to it than he, for I was born in Montgomery County, Pennsylvania, among all those nice Welsh place-names. And as I came down Liberty Street about lunch time, on my way to the ferry, I felt that I also had that happiness that lies in an incognito voyage. I thought of myself as the Duke of Montgomery, deposed from a castle in Spain (what is the opposite of a grandee? A minimee?) and out to see what things look like. It was a bright noonday, last night's sleet was thawing, and the sun-and-shadow chequer under the L was all a flicker of falling drops, a veil of wavering sparkle. I walked on the south side of Liberty Street because I remembered once having known an excellent speakeasy there, with a green door. I felt that after a busy morning and to celebrate a journey, the Duke of Montgomery might well have relished a small glass of dry sherry before lunch. That speakeasy had apparently vanished, but I discovered instead a building called INNS OF COURT which had an unexpectedly English sound; as I am always startled to see, at Brooklyn Bridge, elevated trains marked KING'S HIGHWAY.

I got aboard the ferryboat *Wilkes-Barre*. It was Thursday, always (I don't know why) a peaceful sort of day. I had my shoes shined by a kneeling minion (again that ducal feeling). The ferry nested quietly in her slip for some minutes, like a squatting hen. A few passengers strolled leisurely aboard. No one hurried. The streets were calm—in fact at that time most of the office population are in the telephone booths. The first thing young women do when they get out for the lunch hour is flit into a booth and begin making dates for the evening. Life is very full of excitement, and you would be wrong to forget it. It is to deal with the enormous down-town fever of lunch-time phoning that the booths have now all been equipped with dials.

The *Wilkes-Barre* seethed her way out into the river. In the distance I could see the modest spire of the Piazza San Lackawanna in Hoboken, and the *Leviathan*'s three huge funnels looming over the ancient Foundry. The only important traffic we passed was a barge of freight-cars, one of which bore the legend CANADA DRY. This made me think what a blessing the revived ginger ale industry must have been to the makers of gold foil. No bottle of ginger ale would dare look a jobber in the face nowadays unless it had a gold collar on its neck, like a Lord Mayor.

Primo de Rivera, by the way, has had his connections with literature. It was he, I believe, who banished Unamuno from Spain—the Unamuno who wrote "The Tragic Sense of Life" and many fine essays. Unamuno has long been one of my trump cards; you can lead him in almost any literary gathering and not find anyone who has read him. And now Primo is "out on the hoof with nothing but scarcity," as the line in *The Blue and the Gray* said, and Professor Unamuno has returned to Salamanca. By the way, I thought that was a gorgeous pun in Mr. Adams' column in *The World* this morning: someone wrote from Spain that "Spanish wine and women are a snare Andalusian."

Alongside the Liberty Street ferry slip are the piers of the Great White Fleet, where the United Fruit steamers are berthed; and I remembered how in the old days Endymion and I used to go down to lunch aboard those ships with McFee and the well-loved Dr. Walker. Dr. Walker has been dead these several years, but I had a surprising reminder of him the other day in Bogota, New Jersey. My host brought out a little chaser-glass with a pleasant grape-pattern frosted on it. He said that Dr. Walker had given it to him as a souvenir of one of those ship-lunches. It was a glass that the Doctor had been drinking from in a pub in some Caribbean port when a fight broke out. The Doctor, not looking for trouble, walked out quietly, carrying the glass with him as he had not finished his drink. It was good to meet that unexpected memory of our old wily Ulysses in a quiet suburban household. My host filled the little crystal with some extraordinary nectar he had jugged up years ago from a still in Virginia; we drank John Walker's memory.

The air of the river was brisk, and the lunch counter in the Jersey City station was a temptation; but I had vowed to wait for the dining car on the 1:30 train—the National Limited, it calls itself. I was glad I did, for not only is the 85-cent plate lunch of the B. & O., served in one of those amusingly subdivided platters, adequate for any midday appetite, but also I made my first acquaintance with the famous Blue China with which the B. & O. celebrated its recent centennial. Among the various literatures with which the dining-car *Catherine Greene* was supplied was a charmingly printed booklet about the Blue China, which is decorated with B. & O. scenery and pictures of the locomotives of various eras. To eat roast pork on blue china would have pleased Charles Lamb. When I learned that the ingenious B. & O. not only feeds you on these attractive dishes but actually lets you buy them afterward, I was enchanted. It happened to be a Birthday in my family, so I immediately bought a "medium platter" for one of my young women. She is only seven, so it will be plenty big enough. It is wrapped up now in a likeness of Harper's Ferry.

There is nothing so pleasant as giving an advertisement where it is gratuitous and unexpected; so I take pleasure in rendering this small homage to the B. & O., romantic road of my youth. It has imagination and a real sense of the poetry of travel. Its engineers rarely shake the fillings out of your teeth as do some other lines; it is, in my experience, always courteous and never crowded. It had the good sense to pick out some of the loveliest scenery in America to travel through; and best of all for the meditative rambler it begins with a ferry ride.

I noticed that the two Pullmans I passed through on the way to the diner were called *Helianthus* and *Portulaca*. There are a lot more up ahead, and I have a real curiosity to know what they are called; but I am very comfortable here in the last car. J'y suis, j'y reste. There is a color and foreboding of spring upon these soft country slopes. We have left Wilmington already, and I shall renew my acquaintance with the names of stations I had forgotten to remember. And presently comes Mount Royal Station, Baltimore—one of the most romantic railroad stations in the world.

[IR]

TO A NEW YORKER A HUNDRED YEARS HENCE

I WONDER, old dear, why my mind has lately been going out towards you? I wonder if you will ever read this? They say that wood-pulp paper doesn't last long nowadays. But perhaps some of my grandchildren (with any luck, there should be some born, say twenty-five years hence) may, in their years of tottering caducity, come across this scrap of greeting, yellowed with age. With tenderly cynical waggings of their faded polls, perhaps they will think back to the tradition of the quaint vanished creatures who lived and strove in this city in the year of disgrace, 1921. Poor old granfer (I can hear them say it, with that pleasing note of pity), I can just remember how he used to prate about the heyday of his youth. He wrote pieces for some paper, didn't he? Comically old-fashioned stuff my governor said; some day I must go to the library and see if they have any record of it.

You seem a long way off, this soft September morning, as I sit here and sneeze (will hay fever still exist in 2021, I wonder?) and listen to the chime of St. Paul's ring eleven. Just south of St. Paul's brown spire the girders of a great building are going up. Will that building be there when you read this? What will be the Olympian skyline of your city? Will poor old Columbia University be so far downtown that you will be raising money to move it out of the congested slums of Morningside? Will you look up, as I do now, to the great pale shaft of Woolworth; to the golden boy with wings above Fulton Street? What ships with new names will come slowly and grandly up your harbour? What new green spaces will your street children enjoy? But something of the city we now love will still abide, I hope, to link our days with yours. There is little true glory in a city that is always changing. New stones, new steeples are comely things; but the human heart clings to places that hold association and reminiscence. That, I suppose, is the obscure cause of this queer feeling that impels me to send you so perishable a message. It is the precious unity of mankind in all ages, the compassion and love felt by the understanding spirit for those, its resting kinsmen, who once were glad and miserable in these same scenes. It keeps one aware of that marvelous dark river of human life that runs, down and down uncountably, to the unexplored seas of Time.

You seem a long way off, I say—and yet it is but an instant, and you will be here. Do you know that feeling, I wonder, (so characteristic of our city) that a man has in an elevator bound (let us say) for the eighteenth floor? He sees 5 and 6 and 7 flit by, and he wonders how he can ever live through the interminable time that must elapse before he will get to his stopping place and be about the task of the moment. It is only a few seconds, but his mind can evolve a whole honeycomb of mysteries in that flash of dragging time. Then the door slides open before him and that instantaneous eternity is gone; he is in a new era. So it is with the race. Even while we try to analyze our present curiosities, they whiff away and disperse. Before we have time to turn three times in our chairs, we shall be the grandparents and you will be smiling at our old-fashioned sentiments.

But we ask you to look kindly on this our city of wonder, the city of amazing beauties which is also (to any man of quick imagination) an actual hell of haste, din, and dishevelment. Perhaps you by this time will have brought back something of that serenity, that reverence for thoughtful things, which our generation lost—and hardly knew it had lost. But even Hell, you must admit, has always had its patriots. There is nothing that hasn't—

which is one of the most charming oddities of the race.

And how we loved this strange, mad city of ours, which we knew in our hearts was, to the clear eye of reason and the pure, sane vision of poetry, a bedlam of magical impertinence, a blind byway of monstrous wretchedness. And yet the blacker it seemed to the lamp of the spirit, the more we loved it with the troubled eye of flesh. For humanity, immortal only in misery and mockery, loves the very tangles in which it has enmeshed itself: with good reason, for they are the mark and sign of its being. So you will fail, as we have; and you will laugh, as we have—but not so heartily, we insist; no one has ever laughed the way your tremulous granfers did, old chap! And you will go on about your business, as we did, and be just as certain that you and your concerns are the very climax of human gravity and worth. And will it be any pleasure to you to know that on a soft September morning a hundred years ago your affectionate great-grandsire looked cheerfully out of his lofty kennel window, blew a whiff of smoke, smiled a trifle gravely upon the familiar panorama, knew (with that antique shrewdness of his) a hawk from a handsaw, and then went out to lunch?

[PS]

ROUND MANHATTAN ISLAND

WE WERE TALKING with an American who had just come back after living several years in Europe. He expressed with some dismay his resensitized impression of the furious ugliness and clamour of American life; the ghastly wastes of rubbish and kindling-wood suburbs fringing our cities; and suggested that the trouble is that we have little or no instinctive sense of beauty.

To which we replied that perhaps the truth of it is that the American temperament is more likely to see opportunities for beauty in large things than in small. But we were both talking bosh. Only an extraordinarily keen and trained philosophic perception—e.g., a Santayana—can discuss such matters without gibbering. A recent book on young American intellectualism recurs to us as an example of the futility of undigested prattle about æsthetics. Even the word *æsthetics* itself has come to have a windy savour by reason of much sophomore talk.

But, though we have laid by our own copy of that particular book as a permanent curio in the realm of well-meant gravity, its author was obeying a sound and praisable instinct in trying to think about these things—beauty, imagination, the mind's freedom to create, the meaning of our civilization. We are all compelled to such an attempt: shallow, unversed, clumsily intuitive, we grope into them because we are sincerely hungry to understand. The same wise, brave, gracious spirit that moved Mr. Montague to write his exquisite book *Disenchantment* is tremulously and tentatively alert in thousands of less competent minds. And we, for our own part, grow just a little impatient with those who are quick to damn this wildly energetic and thronging civilization because it shows a poverty of settled, tranquil loveliness. We look out of our window into this morning where Mrs. Meynell's "wind of clear weather" tosses the Post Office flags and the rooftop plumes of steam; we see the Woolworth pinnacle hanging over our head—and ask, is it possible that this great spectacle breathes from her towers only the last enchantments of a muddled age?

Aristotle remarked that "the flute is not an instrument which has a good moral effect; it is too exciting." And very likely New York civilization falls under the same reproach. But even if it is all madness, what a gallant raving! You cannot see the beauty in anything until you love it for its own sake. Take the sightseeing boat round Manhattan if you want to get a mental synthesis of this strangest of islands. From a point in the East River off Coenties Slip you will see those cubed terraces of building rising up and upward, shelves and ledges of rectangular perspective like the heaven of a modernist painter. Nor do we deny the madness and horror. Farther up the river you will see the ragged edges of the city, scows loading their tons of jetsam and street scourings, wizened piers, grassless parks, all the pitiful makeshift aquatics of the Harlem region. And yet, all along that gruesome foreshore, boys—and girls, too—bathing gayly in the scum-water, flying ragged kites from pier-bollards, merry and naked on slides of rock or piles of barrels. Only on the three grim islands of Blackwell, Ward, and Randall will you see any touch of beauty. There, grass and trees and beds of canna and salvia (the two great institutional flowers) to soothe the criminal and the mad. When your mind or your morals or your muscles give way, the city will allow you a pleasant haven of greenery and air. It is odd to see the broad grounds of the Children's Hospital—on Randalls Island, is it?—with no child in sight; but across the river the vile and scabby shore is thick with them. And the bases of the Harlem swing-bridges, never trod by any one, are carefully grassed and flowered.

So the history of every modern city consists of a painful, slow retracing of its errors, an attempt to undo painfully and at vast expense the slattern stupidities it has allowed to accumulate. But to see only these paradoxes and uglinesses is to see less than the whole. He cannot have lived very long or thoughtfully with humanity for neighbour who does not ruefully accept greeds and blindnesses as part of its ineradicable habit. It takes a strong stretch of the imagination to grasp this island entire; to see, even in its very squalors and heedlessnesses, an integral portion of its brave teeming life. You must love it for what it is before you have a right to love it for what it may be. We have never been able to think this thing out, but there seems to us to be some vital essence, some miraculous tremor of human energy and folly in the whole scene that condones and justifies the ugliness. It is queer, but the hideous back-lots of the city do not trouble us so greatly: we have a feeling that they are on their way towards being something else. We do not praise them, but we feel in an obscure way they are part of the picture. Zealous passion and movement always present, to the eye of dispassion, aspects either grotesque or terrible, according to that eye's focus. In this ugly hurly-burly we feel daily (though we cannot define it) that there is a beauty so overriding that it does not depend on beautiful particulars. And, to feel that beauty fully, one must discard all hankerings to improve humanity, or to preach to it, or even understand it—simply (as Uncle Remus said) "make a great 'miration"—accept it as it thrillingly is, and admire.

[PS]

THE CONSTANT NYMPH

BEFORE ME is a newspaper photograph of her; great ropes taut round her waist and under her armpits; lashed to the wrecking company's derrick like the skipper's daughter on the *Hesperus*, or Andromeda on her roocky jut. She is coming down to-day; and New York University is the only Perseus who has volunteered to rescue this Constant Nymph.

The day Diana came down from the tower of Madison Square Garden something went away from New York. It is foolish to grumble about saying good-bye to anything we love. The Technique of Saying Good-bye is one of the great unwritten poems. But for me she will always leave, like Mr. Markham's cedar tree, a lonesome place against the sky.

The day Diana came down all continued in its

usual course. In the slack morning hours people were riding in the subway, picking up jettisoned newspapers to pass away the time. The *Berengaria* turned her great nose toward sea. Editors were busy sending back MSS., with courteous letters explaining why the poems were unavailable. One of these editors happened to tell me that he was stiff all over from a day spent in his garden, planting laurel. (Planting laurel! Exactly what an editor should be doing, I thought.) Six-cylinder cars were making that magnificent rich droning hum as they shifted into second speed. (Only a man who is just driving six-cylinders for the first time knows how splendid that sound is. Yes: Dame Quickly has a younger sister: her name is Dean Swift. The new Everyman edition of the *Journal to Stella* is carried in one of her door pockets as a talisman. We hitch our wagon to Stella.) Between the acts of great plays—such as *Rosmersholm*—people talked busily to avert the painful impact of thought. In the Thirty-fourth Street region gross terraces of building stood magnificently in soft blue air. A new anthology of poems was published—Burton Stevenson's *Home Book of Modern Verse*. A book so fascinating that in spite of its eleven hundred pages I could not resist toting it around with me all day, to read on the train and in the subway. For, absurdly enough, I felt that the publication of that book was the consolation, the counterpoise, to Diana's come-down. Eros is gone from Piccadilly Circus, Diana is gone from Madison Square, but at least in poetry books the gods still live. No one shall tip them the black spot.

The day Diana came down something went away from New York. I don't know just what; no one can say. Whatever it was, it could only be suggested in verse. A friend of mine told me that he is taking singing lessons, because, he said, You can say so many things in singing that you couldn't possibly utter in ordinary speech. There never was a truer word. In an anthology like Mr. Stevenson's (a codicil to his fat and famous *Home Book of Verse*) you can find out what people are really thinking about. The world has long since agreed that in poetry you may say what you mean; no one is offended at poetry. It is only in prose that you must be wary. It is like the old saying (Joseph Conrad makes a splendidly urban reference to it somewhere) about one man being able to steal a horse without scandal, whereas another may not even look wistfully at a halter. But it is true (Conrad adds) that some people have a particularly irritating way of gazing at halters. This is true also in the stable of the horse called Pegasus.

The day Diana came down something went away. I suppose that some day I may see her again at New York University, but I would almost rather not. For me she must always live in that particular eddy of sky that hangs above Madison Square. When it has to be done, I can say good-bye with the rest of them. But there's no law against my thinking of the old house on Madison Avenue (gone also) where three young men once lived with causeless merriment and regarded Diana as their patron deity. They would be as chaste and lofty as herself; offensive to their decent minds were the rumours of stag parties associated with the goddess. What did she mean to them? Who could say? Perhaps they felt, dumbly, that scheme life as you will, intersperse it with jocular palaver and consoling hurry, there remains above all the fierce principle of beauty, the untamed goddess of the hunt, pursuing the wild animals of desire with her sharp arrow of reason. And yet she never shoots her arrow. Ah, how that bothered those meditative young men! And a later generation of bipeds, the balloon-trousered squires of N. Y. U., will probably brood the same awkward analogue. What, meanwhile, has become of the winged mischief of Piccadilly Circus? As I remember him he was not aiming a never-to-be-shot-off dart. He was skipping on the very tiptoe of exultant malice: he had actually sped the shaft. As Eros, of course, would have; everyone knows how much more hasty they are on the incontinent of Europe. One could imagine the prickling wand transpiercing someone in that throng; yes, even some hale and fresh-bathed Briton, in silk hat and morning coat, trembling with that naughty fixture in his breast. Or better still: some docile young American, hastening through the Circus, who suddenly found the daintily feathered shaft stuck right through him. How he implored the door-man at the Trocadero to pull it out, and the latter thought him surprisingly tight for so early in the afternoon. How he dodged zigzag through the crowd, to avoid poking his awkward skewer into other people. My advice to that young man would be to hurry to George Santayana and beg him to pluck it out.—Or suppose this had happened to Henry James? Perhaps that is exactly what *did* happen to Henry James; he had to stand off a bit from the world lest people should see his arrow.—I must look up the legend of St. Sebastian.

The day Diana came down something went away from New York. Some little shuddering pang of loveliness and loneliness, something that I hear sometimes between the strident jangles of a street-organ tune or in the voices of ships in the river. Perhaps I'm glad they've taken her away; it is good to have beautiful things near you for a while, and then lose them, for only so (I suppose) can you be properly disciplined. Only so (again, perhaps) can you remember that men write poetry for other reasons than because *dust* rhymes with *thrust* and *star* with *far*. The day she went away things went on much as usual. The traffic beacons twinkled in unison up and down Fifth Avenue, the great tide of cars (six-cylinders) carried "women of the better class" (see Oliver Herford's gorgeous poem, p. 537 of Burton Stevenson's anthology) about their delightful mundanities, Congreve and Ibsen taught contemporary playwrights that neither lust nor chastity were entirely post-war inventions. No more shall I see her distant grace against heaven, tightening her arrow toward a rising moon, threatening our thick air with her gay pagan archery. Perhaps, near at hand, she was not beautiful at all.

Since writing the above I have walked up Fourth Avenue and seen her with the workmen round her, about to lower her from the skeleton remnant of her tower. Madison Square was black with Actæons. I dare say they were making ribald jokes; but worse than that a Life Insurance Company had attached its initialed house flag to her. I was glad O. Henry, who loved her, was not there to see. Yet there are always various interpretations. Perhaps the life insurers intended the flag to drape round her and shield her as she descended. But I can't help thinking that her sister of Ephesus had the more glorious fate. I wished there had been some Zoning Law to forbid those great ropes so tight about her lovely waist.

The day Diana came down something went away from New York. There was no multitude all with one voice crying out Great is Diana of the Manhattans. But the arrow she never shot sticks in my heart.

[RS]

THE EDITOR AT THE BALL GAME

(WORLD'S SERIES OPENING, 1922)

AT THE Polo Grounds yesterday $119,000 worth of baseball was played. Of that, however, only a meagre $60,000 or so went to the players. We wonder how much the accumulated sports writers got for writing about it. They are the real plutocrats of professional athletics.

We have long intimated our inflexible determination to learn how to be a sports writer—or, as he is usually called, a Scribe. This is to announce progress. We are getting promoted steadily. In the 1920 World's Series we were high up in the stand. At the Dempsey–Carpentier liquidation we were not more than a parasang from the ring. We broke into the press box at the 1921 World's Series, but only in the rearward allotments assigned to correspondents from Harrisburg and Des Moines.

But our stuff is beginning to be appreciated. We are gaining. Yesterday we found ourself actually below the sacred barrier—in the Second Row, right behind the Big Fellows. Down there we were positively almost on social terms (if we had ventured to speak to them) with chaps like Bill McGeehan and Grant Rice and Damon Runyon and Ring Lardner. Well, there are a lot of climbers in the world of sporting literature.

One incident amused us. We heard a man say, "Which one is Damon Runyon?" "Over there," said another, pointing. The first, probably hoping to wangle some sort of prestige, made for Mr. Runyon. "Hullo, Damon!" he cried genially. "Remember me?"

It must have been Pythias.

So far we have only been allowed to shoot in a little preliminary patter—what managing editors call "human interest stuff." When the actual game starts they take the wire away from us, quite rightly, and turn it over to the experts. But, being inexorably ambitious, we sit down now, after the game is over, to tell you exactly how we saw it. Because we had a unique opportunity to study a great journalist and see exactly how it's done. It was just our good luck, sitting in the second row. The second sees better than the first—it's higher. You have to use your knee for writing desk, and you have to pull up your haunches every few minutes to let by the baseball editor of the Topeka *Clarion* on his way back to Harry Stevens's Gratis Tiffin for another platter of salad. But the second row gave us our much needed opportunity to watch the leaders of our craft.

It was just before the game began. The plump lady in white tights (a little too opulent to be Miss Kellermann, but evidently a diva of some sort) was about to begin the walking race around the bases against the athletic-looking man. She won, by the way—what a commutrix she would make. Suddenly we recognized a very Famous Editor climbing into the seat directly in front of us. He was followed by two earnest young men. One of these respectfully placed a Noiseless typewriter in front of the Editor, and spread out a thick pile of copy paper.

This young man had shell spectacles and truncated side-whiskers. Both young men were plainly experts, and were there to tell the Editor the fine points of what was happening. The Famous Editor's job was to whale it out on the Noiselesss, with that personal touch that has made him (it has been said) the most successful American newspaper man.

This, we said to ourself, is going to be better than any Course in Journalism.

We admired the Editor for the competent businesslike way he went to work. He wasted no time in talking. After one intent glance round through very brightly polished spectacles, he began to tick—to "file," as we professionals say. Already, evidently, he felt the famous "reactions" coming to him. He looked so charmingly scholarly, like some well-loved college professor, we could not help feeling it was just a little sad to see him taking all this so seriously. He never paused to enjoy the scene (it really is a great sight, you know), but pattered along on the keys like a well-trained engine.

The two young men fed him facts; with austere and faintly indignant docility he turned these into the well-known pseudo-philosophic comment. It was beautifully efficacious. The shining, well-tended typewriter, the plentiful supply of smooth yellow paper, the ribbon printing off a clear blue, these were right under our eyes; we couldn't help seeing the story rolling out though most of the time we averted our eyes in a kind of shame. It seemed like studying the nakedness of a fine mind.

"Jack Dempsey's coming in," said the young man. Or, "Babe Ruth at bat." The Editor was too busy to look up often. One flash of those observant (and always faintly embittered, we thought) eyes could take in enough to keep the mind revolving through many words. "I'll take them, and correct the typographical errors," remarked young Shellspecs, gathering up the Editor's first page. Thereafter the Editor passed over his story in "takes" and young Shellspecs copyread it with a blue pencil. Once the Editor said, a little tartly: "Don't change the punctuation." From Shellspecs the pages went smoothly to the silent telegraph operator who sat between them.

Our mind—if we must be honest—was somewhat divided between admiration and pity. Here, indeed, is slavery, we said to ourself, watching the great man bent over his work. Babe Ruth came to the plate. Judge Landis is named after a mountain, but Ruth looks like one. There was pleasant dramatic quality in the scene: the burly, gray figure swinging its bat, the agile and dangerous-looking Mr. Nehf winding up for delivery, the twirl of revolving arms against a green background, the flashing, airy swim of the ball, the turbine circling of the bat, the STRIKE sign floating silently upon the distant scoreboard . . . but did the Editor have time to savour all this? Not he! One quick wistful peer upward through those clear lenses, he was back again on his keyboard—the Noiseless keyboard carrying words to the noisiest of papers.

And yet, we had to insist, here was also genius of a sort. The swiftness with which he translated it all into a rude, bright picture! But he was going too consciously on high, we thought. Proletarianizing it, fitting the scene into his own particular scheme of thinking, instead of genuinely puzzling out its suggestions. He was honest enough to admit that the game itself was mostly rather dull—and in so far he was much above most of the Sporting Writers, those high-spirited lads who come back from a quite peaceable game and lead you to believe that there have been scenes of thunder and earthquake.

But, like most of us, he tended to exaggerate those things he had decided upon beforehand. He made much of the roaring of the crowd—which, after all, was not violent as crowds go; and he wrote cheerily of the bitterness of hatred manifested towards the umpires, the deadly glances of players questioning close decisions. He seemed to view these matters through a pupil dilated with intellectual belladonna (if that's what belladonna does).

He wrote something about the perfect happiness of the small boy who was the Giant mascot. Heaven, he said, would have to be mighty good to be better than this for that urchin. But to us the boy seemed totally calm, even sombre. What does baseball mean to him? More interesting, and more exact, we thought, would have been to note the fluctuating sounds of the spectators; a constant rhythm of sound and silence—the hush as the pitcher winds up, the mixed surge of comment as the ball flicks across, the sudden unanimous outcry at some dramatic stroke. Or the ironical cadenced clapping and stamping that break out spontaneously at certain recognized moments of suspense.

But the Editor was going strong, and we felt a kind of admiring affection for him as we saw him so true to form. He picked reactions out of the ether, hit them square on the nose, and whaled them to Shellspecs. Shellspecs recorded faultless assists, zooming them in to Western Union.

In the third inning the Editor hoisted a paragraph clean over the heads of the bleachers by quoting the Bible. Mr. Bush, the red-sleeved Yankee pitcher, was at bat and lifted a midfield fly. Bancroft made a superb tergiversating catch going at full speed. It was beautifully done.

For the second time, we thought, history has been made in America by a Bancroft. "The human body is a wonderful machine," ticked the busy Editor. We watched Mr. Bancroft more carefully after that. A small agile fellow, there was much comeliness in the angle of his trunk and hips as he leaned forward over the plate, preparing for the ball.

In the fourth inning the Editor was already at page 13 of his copy. The young man with truncated side-whiskers then drew the rebuke for inserting commas into the story. The other young man, sitting behind, kept volleying bits of Inside Stuff. Scott came to bat. "This fellow," said Inside Stuff, "is known as the Little Iron Man; he's played in one thousand consecutive games." This was faithfully relayed to the Editor by Shellspecs, and went into the story. But the Editor changed it to "almost a thousand." This pleased us, for we also felt a bit skeptical about that item.

By this time, having noted the quickness of the Editor at "reactionizing," we were very keen to get something of our own into his story. An airplane came over. Inside Stuff announced that the plane was taking pictures to be delivered in Cleveland in time for the morning papers. How he knew this, we can't guess—very likely he didn't. This also faithful Shellspecs passed on. The plane was a big silvery beauty—we remarked, loudly, to our neighbour that she looked as though made of aluminum. A moment later the Editor, having handed a page to Shellspecs, said: "Add that the plane was aluminum." Shellspecs wrote down in blue pencil: "It's an aluminum flying machine." But we mustn't be unjust. Very likely the Editor got the reaction just as we did. It was fairly obvious.

Sixth Inning—The Editor hit a hot twisting paragraph to the outposts of his syndicate, but troubled Shellspecs by saying—Mr. Whitey Witt's name having been mentioned—"Is he a Yankee or a Giant?" "He's an albino, has pink eyes," volunteered indefatigable Inside Stuff. The flying keys caught it and in it went, somewhat philosophized: "Lack of pigment in hair, skin, and retina seems not to diminish his power." Inside Stuff: "It's the beginning of the Seventh and they're all stretching. It's the usual thing." But no stretching for the Editor. He goes on and on. Twenty pages now. When his assistants put a fact just where he likes it his quick mind knocks it for five million circulation.

"Stengel, considered a very old man in baseball," says the cheery mentor. "He's thirty-one years old." To none of these suggestions does the Editor make any comment. He wastes no words—orally, at least. He knows what he wants—sifts it instanter.

We left at the end of the Eighth. The Editor was still going strong. He didn't see the game, but we think he was happy in his own way.

We hope we haven't seemed too impertinent. We want to be a Scribe—not a Pharisee. But our interest in the profession is greater than our regard for any merely individual sanctity. We've given you a faithful picture of what has been called supreme success in journalism. Take a good look at it, you students of newspapers, and see how you like it. We'll tell you a secret. It's pretty easy, if that's the sort of thing you hanker for. In a way, it's rather thrilling. But (between ourselves) it's also a Warning.

[PS]

FIRST LESSONS IN CLOWNING

A MEDLEY of crashing music, pungently odd and exhilarating smells, the roaring croon of the steam calliope, the sweet lingering savour of clown-white grease paint, elephants, sleek barking seals, trained pigs, superb white horses, frolicking dogs, exquisite ladies in tights and spangles, the pallid Venuses of the "living statuary," a whole jumble of incongruous and fantastic glimpses, moving in perfect order through its arranged cycles—this is the blurred and ecstatic recollection of an amateur clown at the circus.

It was pay day that afternoon and all the performers were in cheerful humour. Perhaps that was why the two outsiders, who played a very inconspicuous part in the vast show, were so gently treated. Certainly they had approached the Garden in some secret trepidation. They had had visions of dire jests and grievous humiliations: of finding themselves suddenly astride the bare backs of berserk mules, or hoisted by blazing petards, or douched with mysterious cascades of icy water. Pat Valdo had written: "I am glad to hear you are going to clown a bit. I hope you both will enjoy the experience." To our overwrought imaginations this sounded a little ominous. What would Pat and his lively confrères do to us?

We need not have feared. Not in the most genial club could we have been more kindly treated than in the dressing room where we found Pat Valdo opening his trunk and getting out the antic costumes he had provided. (The eye of a certain elephant, to tell the truth, was the only real embarrassment we suffered. We happened to stand by him as he was waiting to go on, and in his shrewd and critical orb we saw a complete disdain. He spotted us at once. He knew us for interlopers. He knew that we were not a real clown, and his eye showed a spark of scorn. We felt shamed, and slunk away.)

A liberal coating of clown-white, well rubbed into the palms before applying; a rich powdering of talcum; and decorations applied by Pat Valdo with his red and black paint-sticks—these give an effect that startles the amateur when he considers himself in the mirror. Topped with a skull-cap of white flannel (on which perches a supreme oddity in the way of a Hooligan hat) and enveloped in a baggy Pierrot garment—one is ready to look about and study the dressing room, where our fellows, in every kind of gorgeous grotesquerie, are preparing for the Grand Introductory Pageant—followed by the "Strange People." (They don't call them Freaks any more.) Here is Johannes Joseffson, the Icelandic Gladiator, sitting on his trunk, with his bare feet gingerly placed on his slippers to keep them off the dusty floor while he puts on his wrestling tights. As he bends over with arched back, and raises one leg to insert it into the long pink stocking, one must admire the perfect muscular grace of his thighs and shoulders. Here is the equally muscular dwarf, being massaged by a friend before he dons his pink frills and dashing plumed hat and becomes Mlle. Spangletti, "the marvel equestrienne, darling of the Parisian boulevards." Here is the inevitable Charley Chaplin, and here the dean of all the clowns, an old gentleman of seventy-four, in his frolicsome costume, as lively as ever. Here is a trunk inscribed *Australian Woodchoppers*, and sitting on it one of the woodchoppers himself, a quiet, humorous, cultivated gentleman wtih a great fund of philosophy. A rumour goes the rounds—as it does behind the scenes in every kind of show. "Do you know who we have with us to-day? I see one of the boxes is all decorated up." "It's Mrs. Vincent Astor." "Who's she?" interjects the Australian woodchopper, satirically. "It's General Wood." "Did you hear, Wood and Pershing are here to-day?" Charley Chaplin asserts that he has "a good gag" that he's going to try out to-day and see how it goes. One of the other clowns in the course of dressing comes up to Pat Valdo, and Pat introduces his two pupils. "Newspaper men, hey?" says the latter. "What did you tell me for? I usually double-cross the newspaper men when they come up to do some clowning," he explains to us. We are left wondering in what this double-crossing consists. Suddenly they all troop off down the dark narrow stairs for the triumphal entry. The splendour of this parade may not be marred by any clown costumes, so the two novices are left upstairs, peering through holes in the dressing-room wall. The big arena is all an expanse of eager faces. The band strikes up a stirring ditty. A wave of excitement sweeps through the dingy quarters of the Garden. The show is on, and how delirious it all is!

Downstairs, the space behind the arena is a fascinating jostle of odd sights. The elephants come swaying up the runway from the basement and stand in line waiting their turn. Here is a cage of trained bears. In the background stands the dogcatcher's cart, attached to the famous kicking mule. From the ladies' dressing quarters come the aerial human butterflies in their wings and gauzy draperies. On the wall is a list of names, *Mail Uncalled For.* One of the names is "Toby Hamilton." That must mean old Tody, and we fear the letter will never be called for now, for Tody Hamilton, the famous old Barnum and Bailey press agent, who cleaned up more "free space" than any man who ever lived, died in 1916. Suddenly appears a person clad in flesh tights and a barrel, carrying a label announcing himself as *The Common People.* Someone thrusts a large sign into the hands of one of the amateur clowns, and he is thrust upon the arena, to precede the barrelled Common People round the sawdust circuit. He has hardly time to see what the sign says—something about "On Strike Against $100 Suits." The amateur clown is somewhat aghast at the huge display of friendly faces. Is he to try to be funny? Here is the flag-hung box, and he tries to see who is in it. He doesn't see either Wood, Pershing, or Mrs. Astor, who are not there; but a lot of wounded soldiers, who smile at him encouragingly. He feels better and proceeds, finding himself, with a start, just beneath some flying acrobats who are soaring in air, hanging by their teeth. Common People shouts to him to keep the sign facing toward the audience. The tour is made without palpable dishonour.

Things are now moving so fast it is hard to keep up with them. Pat Valdo is dressed as a prudish old lady with an enormous bustle. Escorted by the clown policeman and the two amateurs, Pat sets out, fanning himself demurely. Hullo! the bustle has detached itself from the old lady, but she proceeds, unconscious. The audience shouts with glee. Finally the cop sees what has happened and screams. The amateur clowns scream, too, and one of them, in a burst of inspiration, takes off his absurd hat to the bustle, which is now left yards behind. But Pat is undismayed, turns and beckons with his hand. The bustle immediately runs forward of its own accord and reattaches itself to the rear of the skirt. You see, there is a dwarf inside it. The two amateur clowns are getting excited by this time and execute some impromptu tumbling. One tackles the other and they roll over and over desperately. In the scuffle one loses both his hat and skull-cap and flees shamefaced from the scene. It is asserted by our partner that "this went big." He swears it got a laugh. Pat Valdo hurries off to prepare for his boomerang throwing. Pat is a busy man, for he is not only a clown, but he and Mrs. Valdo also do wonderful stunts of their own on Ring Number One.

And there are moments of sheer poetry, too. Into the darkened arena, crossed by dazzling shafts of light, speeds a big white motor car. Bird Millman descends, tossing aside her cloak. "A fairy on a cobweb" the press agents call her, and as two humble clowns watch entranced through the peepholes in the big doors the phrase seems none too extravagant. See her, in a foam of short fluffy green skirts, twirl and tiptoe on the glittering wire, all grace and slenderness and agile enchantment. She bows in the dazzle of light and kisses her hands to the crowd. Then she hops into the big car and is borne back behind the scenes. Once behind the doors her gay vivacity ceases. She sits, wearily, several minutes, before getting out of the car. And then, later, comes Mlle. Leitzel. She, like all the other stars, is said to have "amazed all Europe." We don't know whether Europe is harder to amaze than America. Certainly no one could be more admiringly astounded than the amateur clowns gazing entranced through the crack of the doorway. To that nerve-tightening roll of drums she spins deliriously high up in giddy air, floating, a tiny human pinwheel, in a shining cone of light. One can hear the crowd catch its breath. She walks back, all smiles, while her maid trots ahead saying something unintelligible. Her tall husband is waiting for her at the doorway. He catches her up like a child and carries her off, limp and exhausted. One of the clowns (irreverent creature) makes a piteous squawk and begs us to carry him to his dressing room.

A trained pig, trotting cheerfully round in search of tidbits, is retrieved from under the hooves of Mrs. Curtis's horse, which is about to go out and dance. The dogcatcher's wagon is drawn up ready to rush forth, and the trained terrier which accompanies it is leaping with excitement. He regards it as a huge lark, and knows his cue perfectly. When the right time comes he makes a dash for a clown dressed as an elderly lady and tears off her skirt. One of the amateurs was allowed to ride behind the kicking mule, but to his great chagrin the mule did not kick as well as usual. Here are Charley Chaplin and some others throwing enormous dice from a barrel. No matter how the dice are thrown they always turn up seven. Into this animated gamble the amateur clown enters with enjoyment. All round him the wildest capers are proceeding. The double-ended flivver is prancing about. John Barleycorn's funeral procession is going its way. "Give me plenty of space," says Charley Chaplin to us, "so the people can watch me." We do so, reverently, for Charley's antics are worth watching. We make a wild dash, and plan to do a tumble in imitation of Charley's. To our disappointment we find that instead of sliding our feet dig into the soft sawdust, and the projected collapse does not arrive. Intoxicated by the rich spice of circus odours, the booming calliope, the galloping horses, we hardly know what we are doing half the time. We hear Miss May Wirth, the Wonder Rider of the World, complaining bitterly that someone got in front of her when she was doing her particularly special stunt. We wonder dubiously whether we were the guilty one. Alas, it is all over but the washing up.

Pat Valdo, gentlest of hosts, is taking off his trick hat with the water cistern concealed in it. He has a clean towel ready for his grateful pupils.

The band is playing "The Star-Spangled Banner," and all the clowns, in various stages of undress, stand at attention. Our little peep into the gay, good-hearted, courageous, and extraordinary world of the circus is over. Pat and his fellows will go on, twice a day, for the next six months. It takes patience and endurance. But it must be some consolation to know that nothing else in the world gives half as much pleasure to so many people.

[P]

THE RETURN TO TOWN

IT WAS with somewhat a heavy heart that we prepared to leave Salamis for the winter. Yet inscrutable lust of adventure spurred us on; the city, also, is the place for work. In the country one is too comfortable, and there are too many distractions. Either cider, or stars, or the blue sparkle of the furnace fire—all these require frequent attentions. But it was hard to part with Long Island's charms in November, loveliest of months. The copper-coloured woods, the chrysanthemums, the brisk walk to the morning train, the yellow crackle of logs in the chimney, the chill dry whisper of the neighbouring belt of trees heard at midnight from an airy veranda—these are some of the excitements we shall miss. Most of all, perhaps, that stony little unlit lane, traversed in pitch darkness towards supper time, until, coming clear of the trees, you open up the Dipper, sprawled low across the northern sky.

It is hard, too, to leave Salamis just when its winter season of innocent gayeties was commencing. You would hardly believe how much is going on! Did you know that that deathless old railroad station is being (as they say of ships) reconditioned? And there's going to be a drug store in Salamis Heights. The new Methodist church is nearly finished—and, most glamorous of all, we now have an actual tea-room at the entrance to the Salamis Estates. When you are motoring out that way you can see if we don't speak the truth. In another five years, most likely, we shall have street lights along our lovely wood road to Green Escape—and pavements—and gas to cook with. But there never will be quite as many fairies in the woods as there have been these past three years.

But, perhaps fortunately, the day set for moving into town was wet and drizzly. And the labour of piling into Dame Quickly various baggages, hampers, toys, a go-cart, and the component railings, girders, rods, springs and mattresses of two cribs was lively enough to oust from the mind any pangs of mere sentiment. The mind of one who has accomplished that task, in shirt-sleeves under a dripping weather, is heated enough to make him ready for any sort of adventurous foray. The Dame, also, grossly overloaded, and travelling smartly on greasy ways, was skiddish. As is ever our fortune, we found the road through Astoria torn up for repairs. This involved a circuit along a most horrible bypath, where our ill-adjusted freight leaped crazily with every lurch, go-cart and mattresses descended on our neck, and the violence of the bumping caused the crib-girders to burst through the rear of the Dame's canopy. Also we incurred, and probably deserved, a stern rebuke from a gigantic policeman on Second Avenue. To tell the truth, in a downshoot of rain and peering desperately through a streaming wind-shield, we did not know he was a policeman at first. We thought he was an L pillar.

Yet, when both voyages were safely accomplished—one for the baggage, and one for the household: it would be harder to say which lading was the tighter squeeze—what an exhilaration to move once more in the city of our adoring. It is true that we began by making an immediate enemy in the apartment house, for, as we were quite innocently taking a trunk upstairs in the elevator, assisted by the cheerful elderly attendant, a lady living in the same house entered by chance and burst into violent reproach because *her* baggage had had to go aloft in the freight elevator. She accused the attendant of favouritism; to which he, quite placidly, explained that this particular baggage had been delivered at the front door in a private car. This compliment to the Dame pleased us, but knowing nothing of the rules, and being wet and pensive, we pretended to be an expressman and said naught.

The only other shock was when we took the Dame to a neighbouring garage to recuperate for a few days. (We were glad, then, it had been raining, for the well-loved vehicle looked very sleek and shiny, and it was too dark for the garage man to notice the holes in her top. We wouldn't want him to sneer at her, and his garage, we observed, was full of very handsome cars.) When he said it would cost the Dame $1.50 a night to live there we were a little horrified. That, we reflected, was what we used to pay ourself at the old Continental Hotel in Philly, the inn where the Prince of Wales (the old one) and Dickens and Lincoln and others stayed. We now look with greater and greater astonishment at all the cars we see in New York. How can any one afford to keep them?

We were dispatched to do some hasty marketing, in time for supper. We made off to our favourite shopping street—Amsterdam Avenue. Delightedly we gazed into those alluring windows. In a dairy, a young lady of dark and appealing loveliness made us welcome. When we ordered milk and laid in a stock of groceries, making it plain to her (by consulting a list) that we were speaking on behalf of the head of the house, she urged us to advise Titania to open an account. Money she seemed loath to accept: it could all be paid for at the end of the month, she said. It is well to shop referring perplexedly to a little list. This proves that you are an humble, honest paterfamilias, acting only under orders. To such credit is always lavish, and fair milkmaids generously tender.

Various tradesmen in that neighbourhood were surprised, in the tail end of a wet and depressing day, by unexpected increments of traffic. "Just nick the bone?" inquired the butcher, when, from our list, we read him the item about rib lamb chops. "Yes, just nick the bone," we assented, not being very definite on the subject. We were interested in admiring the thick sawdust on the floor, very pleasant to slide the foot upon. The laundryman was just closing when we arrived with our bundle. "Here's a new customer for you," we announced. Whatever private sorrows he has were erased from his manly forehead. He told us that he also does tailoring. Cleaning and pressing, he insisted. We had a private feeling, a little shameful, that he hasn't got as good a customer as he imagines. Next door to the tailor, by the way, and right opposite the apartment house, is a carpenter who advertises his skill at bookshelves.

How different it is from Salamis nights. Hanging out of the kitchen window (having gone to the rear of the apartment to see what the icebox is like: it's a beauty)—instead of Orion's Belt and the dry rustle of the trees, we see those steep walls of lighted windows, discreetly blinded, hear sudden shrills of music from above and below. Just through the wall, as we lie abed, we can hear the queer droning whine of the elevator; through the open window, the clang of trolleys on Broadway. Hunting through the books that belong in the furnished apartment, after startling ourself by reading Mr. D. H. Lawrence's poems called *Look! We Have Come Through!* we found an old Conan Doyle—always our favourite bedtime author. *The Adventures of Gerard*, indeed, and we are going to have a go at it immediately.

Yes, it's very different from Salamis; but Adventure is everywhere, and we like to take things as we find them. We have never been anywhere yet, whether in the steerage of the *Mauretania* or in a private lunchroom at the Bankers' Club, where there wasn't more amusement than we deserved.

[PS]

THE
THREE HOURS FOR LUNCH
CLUB

THREE HOURS FOR LUNCH

HUDSON STREET has a pleasant savour of food. It resounds with the dull rumble of cruising drays, which bear the names of well-known brands of groceries; it is faintly salted by an aroma of the docks. One sees great signs announcing cocoanut and whalebone or such unusual wares; there is a fine tang of coffee in the air round about the corner of Beach Street. Here is that vast, massy brick edifice, the New York Central freight station, built 1868, which gives an impression of being about to be torn down. From a dilapidated upper window hangs a faded banner of the Irish Republic. At noontime this region shows a mood of repose. Truckmen loll in sunny corners, puffing pipes, with their curved freight hooks hung round their necks. In a dark smithy half a dozen sit comfortably round a huge wheel which rests on an anvil, using it as a lunch table. Near Canal Street two men are loading ice into a yellow refrigerator car, and their practiced motions are pleasant to watch. One stands in the wagon and swings the big blocks upward with his tongs. The other, on the wagon roof, seizes the piece deftly and drops it through a trap on top of the car. The blocks of ice flash and shimmer as they pass through the sunshine. In Jim O'Dea's blacksmith shop, near Broome Street, fat white horses are waiting patiently to be shod, while a pink glow wavers outward from the forge.

At the corner of Hudson and Broome streets we fell in with our friend Endymion, it being our purpose to point out to him the house, one of that block of old red dwellings between Hudson and Varick, which Robert C. Holliday has described in *Broome Street Straws*, a book which we hope is known to all lovers of New York local colour. Books which have a strong sense of place, and are born out of particular streets—and especially streets of an odd, rich, and well-worn flavour—are not any too frequent. Mr. Holliday's Gissingesque appreciation of the humours of landladies and all the queer fish that shoal through the backwaters of New York lodging houses makes this Broome Street neighbourhood exceedingly pleasant for the pilgrim to examine. It was in Mr. Holliday's honour that we sallied into a Hudson Street haberdashery, just opposite the channel of Broome Street, and adorned ourself with a new soft collar, also having the pleasure of seeing Endymion regretfully wave away some gorgeous mauve and pink neckwear that the agreeable dealer laid before him with words of encouragement. We also stood tranced by a marvellous lithograph advertising a roach powder in a neighbouring window, and wondered whether Mr. Holliday himself could have drawn the original in the days when he and Walter Jack Duncan lived in garrets on Broome Street and were art students

together. Certainly this picture had the vigorous and spirited touch that one would expect from the draughting wrist of Mr. Holliday. It showed a very terrible scene, apparently a civil war among the roaches, for one army of these agile insects was treasonously squirting a house with the commended specific, and the horrified and stricken inmates were streaming forth and being carried away in roach ambulances, attended by roach nurses, to a neighbouring roach cemetery. All done on a large and telling scale, with every circumstance of dismay and reproach on the faces of the dying blattidæ. Not even our candour, which is immense, permits us to reprint the slogan the manufacturer has adopted for his poster: those who go prowling on Hudson Street may see it for themselves.

In the old oyster and chop house just below Canal Street we enjoyed a very agreeable lunch.

To this place the Broome Street garreteers (so Mr. Holliday has told us) used to come on days of high prosperity when some cheque arrived from a publisher. At that time the tavern kept an open fireplace, with a bright nest of coals in the chilly season; and there was a fine mahogany bar. But we are no laudator of acted time: the fireplace has been bricked up, it is true; but the sweet cider is admirable, and as for the cheesecake, we would back it against all the Times Square variety that Ben De Casseres rattles about. It is delightful and surprising to find on Hudson Street an ordinary so droll and Dickensish in atmosphere, and next door is a window bearing the sign WALTER PETER. We feel sure that Mr. Holliday, were he still living in those parts, would have cajoled the owner into changing that E to an A.

Our stroll led us north as far as Charlton Street, which the geographers of Greenwich Village claim as the lower outpost of their domain. Certainly it is a pleasing byway, running quietly through the afternoon, and one lays an envious eye upon the demure brick houses, with their old-fashioned doorways, pale blue shutters, and the studio windows on the southern side. At the corner of Varick Street is a large house showing the sign, "Christopher Columbus University of America." Macdougal Street gives one a distant blink of the thin greenery of Washington Square.

An unexpected impulse led us eastward on Grand Street, to revisit Max Maisel's interesting bookshop. We had never forgotten the thrill of finding this place by chance one night when prowling toward Seward Park. In bookshops of a liberal sort we always find it advisable to ask first of all for a copy of Frank Harris's *The Man Shakespeare*. It is hardly ever to be found (unfortunately), so the inquiry is comparatively safe for one in a frugal mood; and it is a tactful question, for the mention of this book shows the bookseller that you are an intelligent and understanding kind of person, and puts intercourse on good terms at once. However, we did find one book that we felt we simply had to have, as it is our favourite book for giving away to right-minded people—*The Invisible Playmate*, by William Canton. We fear that there are still lovers of children who do not know this book; but if so, it is not our fault.

Grand Street is a child at heart, and one may watch it making merry not only along the pavement but in the shop windows. Endymion's gallant spirit was strongly uplifted by this lively thoroughfare, and he strode like one whose heart was hitting on all six cylinders. Max Maisel's bookshop alone is enough to put one in a seemly humour. But then one sees the gorgeous pink and green allurements of the pastry cooks' windows, and who can resist those little lemon-flavoured, saffron-coloured cakes, which are so thirst-compelling and send one hastily to the nearest bar for another beaker of cider? And it seems natural to find here the oldest toyshop in New York, where Endymion dashed to the upper floor in search of juvenile baubles, and we both greatly admired the tall, dark, and beauteous damsel who waited on us with such patience and charity. Endymion by this time was convinced that he was living in the very heart and climax of a poem; he became more and more unreal as we walked along: we could see his physical outline (tenuous enough at best) shimmer and blur as he became increasingly alcaic.

Along the warm crowded pavement there suddenly piped a liquid, gurgling, chirring whistle, rising and dropping with just the musical trill that floats from clumps of creekside willows at this time of year. We had passed several birdshops on our walk, and supposed that another was near. A song sparrow, was our instant conclusion, and we halted to see where the cage could be hung. And then we saw our warbler. He was little and plump and red-faced, with a greasy hat and a drooping beer-gilded moustache, and he wore on his coat a bright blue peddler's license badge. He shuffled along, stooping over a pouch of tin whistles and gurgling in one as he went. There's your poem, we said to Endymion—"The Song-Sparrow on Grand Street."

We propose to compile a little handbook for

truants, which we shall call "How to Spend Three Hours at Lunch Time." This idea occurred to us on looking at our watch when we got back to our kennel.

[P]

ADVENTURES AT LUNCH TIME

THIS WINDOW by which we sit is really very trying to our spirit. On a clear fluid blue day the sunlight pours over the cliffs and craggy coves and angles of the great buildings round St. Paul's churchyard. We can see the temptation of being a cubist painter as we study all those intersecting planes of light and shadow. Across the way, on Fulton Street, above the girl in a green hat who is just now ingurgitating a phial of orangeade, there are six different roof levels, rising like steps toward the gold lightning bolts of the statue on top of the

Telephone and Telegraph Building. Each of these planes carries its own particular impact of light or shadow. The sunshine seems to flow like an impalpable cataract over the top of the Hudson Terminal, breaking and shining in a hundred splashes and pools of brightness among the stone channels below. Far down the course of Church Street we can see the top floors of the Whitehall Building. We think of the little gilt ball that darts and dances so merrily in the fountain jet in front of that building. We think of the merry mercators of the Whitehall Club sitting at lunch on the cool summit of that great edifice. We think of the view as seen from there, the olive-coloured gleam of the water, the ships and tugs speckled about the harbour. And, looking down, we can see a peaceful gentleman sitting on a bench in St. Paul's graveyard, reading a book. We think seriously of writing a note, "*What are you reading?*" and weighting it with an inkwell and hurling it down to him. This window continually draws our mind outward and sets us speculating, when we ought to be answering letters or making inquiries of coal dealers as to whether there is any chance of getting a supply for next winter.

On such a day, having in mind that we ought to write another chapter of our book "How to Spend Three Hours at Lunch Time," we issued forth with Endymion to seek refreshment. It was a noontide to stir even the most carefully fettered bourgeois to impulses of escapade and foray. What should we do? At first we had some thought of showing to Endymion the delightful subterranean passage that leads from the cathedral grottoes of the Woolworth Building to the City Hall subway station, but we decided we could not bear to leave the sunlight. So we chose a path at random and found ourselves at the corner of Beekman and Gold streets.

Now our intention was to make tracks toward Hanover Square and there to consider the world as viewed over the profile of a slab of cheesecake; but on viewing the agreeable old house at the corner of Gold Street—"The Old Beekman, Erected 1827," once called the Old Beekman Halfway House, but now the Old Beekman Luncheonette—no hungry man in his senses could pass without tarrying. A flavour of comely and respectable romance was apparent in this pleasant place, with its neat and tight-waisted white curtains in the upstairs windows and an outdoor stairway leading up to the second floor. Inside, at a table in a cool, dark corner, we dealt with hot dogs and cloudy cider in a manner beyond criticism. The name Luncheonette does this fine tavern serious injustice: there is nothing of the feminine or the soda fountain about it: it is robust, and we could see by the assured bearing of some well-satisfied habitués that it is an old landmark in that section.

But the brisk air and tempting serenity of the day made it seem emphatically an occasion for two lunches, and we passed on, along Pearl Street, in the bright checkerboard of sunbeams that slip through the trestles of the "L." It was cheerful to see that the same old Spanish cafés are still there, though we were a little disappointed to see that one of them has moved from its old-time quarters, where that fine brass-bound stairway led up from the street, to a new and gaudy palace on the other side. We also admired the famous and fascinating camp outfitting shop at 208 Pearl Street, which apparently calls itself WESTMINSTER ABBEY: but that is not the name of the shop but of the proprietor. We have been told that Mr. Abbey's father christened him so, intending him to enter the church. In the neighbourhood of Cliff and Pearl streets we browsed about enjoying the odd and savoury smells. There are all sorts of aromas in that part of the city, coffee and spices, drugs, leather, soap, and cigars. There was one very sweet, pervasive, and subtle smell, a caressing harmony for the nostril, which we pursued up and down various byways. Here it would quicken and grow almost strong enough for identification; then again it would become faint and hardly discernible. It had a rich, sweet oily tang, but we were at a loss to name it. We finally concluded that it was the bouquet of an "odourless disinfectant" that seemed to have its headquarters near by. In one place some bales of dried and withered roots were being loaded on a truck: they gave off a faint savour, which was familiar but baffling. On inquiry, these were sarsaparilla. Endymion was pleased with a sign on a doorway: "*Crude drugs and spices and essential oils.*" This, he said, was a perfect Miltonic line.

Hanover Square, however, was the apex of our pilgrimage. To come upon India House is like stepping back into the world of Charles Lamb. We had once lunched in the clubrooms upstairs with a charming member and we had never forgotten the old seafaring prints, the mustard pots of dark blue glass, the five-inch mutton chops, the Victorian contour of the waiter's waistcoat of green and yellow stripe. This time we fared toward the tavern in the basement, where even the outsider may penetrate, and were rejoiced by a snug table in the corner. Here we felt at once the true atmosphere of lunching, which is at its best when one can get in a corner, next to some old woodwork rubbed and shiny with age. Shandygaff, we found, was not unknown to the servitor; and the cider that we saw Endymion beaming upon was a blithe, clear yellow, as merry to look at as a fine white wine. Very well, very well indeed, we said to ourselves; let the world revolve; in the meantime, what is that printed in blackface type upon the menu? We have looked upon the faces of many men, we have endured travail and toil and perplexity, we have written much rot and suffered much inward shame to contemplate it; but in the meantime (we said, gazing earnestly upon the face of Endymion), in the meantime, we repeated, and before destiny administers that final and condign chastisement that we ripely merit, let us sit here in the corner of the India House and be of good cheer. And at this point, matters being so, and a second order of butter being already necessary, the waiter arrived with the Spanish omelet.

Homeward by the way of South Street, admiring the slender concave bows of fine ships—the *Mexico* and the *Santa Marta*, for instance—and privily wondering what were our chances of smelling blue water within the next quinquennium, we passed in mild and placid abandonment. On Burling Slip, just where in former times there used to hang a sign KIPLING BREW (which always interested us), we saw a great, ragged, burly rogue sitting on a doorstep. He had the beard of a buccaneer, the placid face of one at ease with fortune. He hitched up his shirt and shifted from one ham to another with supreme and sunkissed contentment. And Endymion, who sees all things as the beginnings of heavenly poems, said merrily: "As I was walking on Burling Slip, I saw a seaman without a ship."

[PP]

SECRET TRANSACTIONS OF THE THREE HOURS FOR LUNCH CLUB

THE DOCTOR having been elected a member of the club, a meeting was held to celebrate the event. Bowling Green, Esq., secretary, was instructed to prepare carefully confidential minutes. Weather: fair and tepid. Wind: N.N.E. Course laid: From starting line at a Church Street bookshop, where the doctor bought a copy of *Limbo*, by Aldous Huxley, to Pier 56, N. R. Course made good: the same.

The doctor was in excellent form. On the Fourteenth Street car a human being was arguing fiercely and loudly with the conductor about some controversial matter touching upon fares and destinations. The clamour was great. Said the doctor, adjusting his eyeglass and gazing with rebuke toward the disputants: "I will be gratified when this tumult subsides." The doctor has been added to the membership of the club in order to add social tone to the gathering. His charm is infinite; his manners are of a delicacy and an aplomb. His speech, when he is of waggish humour, carries a tincture of Queen Anne phraseology that is subtle and droll. A man, indeed! *L'extrême de charme*, as M. Djer-Kiss loves to say what time he woos the public in the theatre programmes.

The first thrill was when Bowling Green, Esq., secretary, cast an eye upward as the club descended from the Fourteenth Street sharabang, and saw, over the piers, the tall red funnels of the *Aquitania*. This is going to be great doings, said he to himself. O Cunard Line funnels! What is there that so moves the heart?

Bowling Green, Esq., confesses that it is hard to put these minutes into cold and calculated narrative. Among ships and seafaring concerns his heart is too violently stirred to be quite *maître de soi*.

The club moved forward. Welcomed by the suave commissionaire of the Cunard Line, it was invited to rise in the elevator. On the upper floor of the pier the members ran to the windows. There lay the *Aquitania* at her pier. The members' hearts were stirred. Even the doctor, himself a hardened man of the sea, showed a brilliant spark of emotion behind his monocular attic window. A ship in dock—and what a ship! A ship at a city pier, strange sight. It is like a lion in a circus cage. She, the beauty, the lovely living creature of open azure and great striding ranges of the sea, she that needs horizons and planets for her fitting perspective, she that asks the snow and silver at her irresistible stem, she that persecutes the sunset across the purple curves of the longitudes—tied up stiff and dead in the dull ditch of a dockway. The upward slope of that great bow, it was never made to stand still against a dusty pier-end.

The club proceeded and found itself in a little eddy of pure Scotland. The *Columbia* was just in from Glasgow—had docked only an hour before. The doctor became very Scots in a flash. "Aye, bonny!" was his reply to every question asked him by Mr. Green, the diligent secretary. The secretary was addressed as "lad." A hat now became a "bonnet." The fine stiff speech of Glasgow was heard on every side, for the passengers were streaming through the customs. Yon were twa bonny wee brithers, aiblins ten years old, that came marching off, with bare knees and ribbed woollen stockings and little tweed jackets. O Scotland, Scotland, said our hairt! The wund blaws snell frae and firth, whispered the secretary to himself, keeking about, but had not the courage to utter it.

Here the secretary pauses on a point of delicacy. It was the purpose of the club to visit Capt. David W. Bone of the *Columbia*, but the captain is a modest man, and one knows not just how much of our admiration of him and his ship he would care to see spread upon the minutes. Were Mr. Green such a man as the captain, would he be lowering himself to have any truck with journalists and such petty folk? Mr. Green would not. Mark you: Captain Bone is the master of an Atlantic liner, a veteran of the submarine-haunted lanes of sea, a writer of fine books (have you, lovers of sea tales, read *The Brassbounder* and *Broken Stowage*?), a collector of first editions, a man who stood on the bridge of the flagship at Harwich and watched the self-defiled U-boats slink in and come to a halt at the international code signal MN (Stop instantly!)— "Ha," said Mr. Green. "Were I such a man, I would pass by like shoddy such pitifuls as colyumists." But he was a glad man no less, for he knew the captain was bigger of heart. Besides, he counted on the exquisite tact of the doctor to see him through. Indeed, even the stern officials of the customs had marked the doctor as a man exceptional. And as the club stood patiently among the outward flux of authentic Glasgow, came the captain himself and welcomed them aboard.

Across immaculate decks, and in the immortal whiff, indefinable, of a fine ship just off the high seas, trod the beatified club. A ship, the last abiding place in a mannerless world of good old-fashioned caste, and respect paid upward with due etiquette and discipline through the grades of rank. The club, for a moment, were guests of the captain; deference was paid to them. They stood in the captain's cabin (sacred words). "Boy!" cried the captain, in tones of command. Not as one speaks to office boys in a newspaper kennel, in a voice of entreaty. The boy appeared: a curly-headed, respectful stripling. A look of respect: how well it sits upon youth. "Boy!" said the captain—but just what the captain said is not to be put upon vulgar minutes. Remember, pray, the club was upon British soil.

In the saloon sat the club, and their faces were the faces of men at peace, men harmonious and of delicate cheer. The doctor, a seafaring man, talked the lingo of imperial mariners: he knew the right things to say: he carried along the humble secretary, who gazed in melodious mood upon the jar of pickled onions. At sea Mr. Green is of lurking manners: he holds fast to his bunk lest worse befall; but a ship in port is his empire. Scotch broth was before them—pukka Scotch broth, the doctor called it; and also the captain and the doctor had some East Indian name for the chutney. The secretary resolved to travel and see the world. Curried chicken and rice was the word: and, not to exult too cruelly upon you (O excellent friends!), let us move swiftly over the gooseberry tart. There was the gooseberry tart, and again, a few minutes later, it was not there. All things have their appointed end. "Boy!" said the captain. (Must I remind you, we were on imperial soil.) Is it to be said that the club rose to the captain's cabin once more, and matters of admirable purport were tastefully discussed, as is the habit of us mariners?

"The drastic sanity of the sea"—it is a phrase from a review of one of the captain's own books, *Merchantmen-at-Arms*, which this club (so it runs upon the minutes), as lovers of sea literature, officially hope may soon be issued on this side also. It is a phrase, if these minutes are correct, from a review written by H. M. Tomlinson, another writer of the sea, of whom we have spoken before, and may, in God's providence, again. "The drastic sanity of the sea" was the phrase that lingered in our mind as we heard the captain talk of books and of discipline at sea and of the trials imposed upon shipmasters by the La Follette act. (What, the club wondered inwardly, does Mr. La Follette know of seafaring?) "The drastic sanity of the sea!" We thought of other sailors we had known, and how they had found happiness and simplicity in the ordered combat with their friendly enemy. A virtue goes out of a ship (Joseph Conrad said, in effect) when she touches her quay. Her beauty and purpose are, for the moment, dulled and dimmed. But even there, how much she brings us. How much, even though we do not put it into words, the faces and accents of our seafaring friends give us in the way of plain wisdom and idealism. And the secretary, as he stepped aboard the hubbub of a subway train, was still pondering "the drastic sanity of the sea."

[PP]

INITIATION

ALLURED BY the published transactions of the club, our friend Lawton presented himself at the headquarters toward lunch time and announced himself as a candidate for membership. An executive session was hastily convened. Endymion broke the news to the candidate that initiates in this select organization are expected to entertain the club at luncheon. To the surprise of the club, our genial visitor neither shrank nor quailed. His face was bland and his bearing ambitious in the extreme. Very well, he said; as long as it isn't the Beaux Arts café.

The itinerary of the club for this day had already been arranged by the secretary. The two charter members, plus the high-spirited acolyte, made their way along West Street toward the Cortlandt Street ferry. It was plain from the outset that fortune had favoured the organization with a new member of the most sparkling quality. Every few yards a gallant witticism fell from him. Some of these the two others were able to juggle and return, but many were too flashing for them to cope with. In front of the ferry house lay a deep and quaggish puddle of slime, crossable only by ginger-footed work upon sheets of tin. Endymion rafted his tenuous form across with a delicate straddle of spidery limbs. The secretary followed, with a more solid squashing technique. "Ha," cried the new member; "grace before meat!" Endymion and the secretary exchanged secret glances. Lawton, although he knew it not, was elected from that moment.

The ritual of the club, while stern toward initiates, is not brutal. Since you are bursar for the lunch, said the secretary, I will buy the ferry tickets, and he did so. On the boat these carefree men gazed blithely upon the shipping. "Little did I think," said Lawton, "that I was going for a sea voyage." "That," said the club, "is the kind of fellows we are. Whimsical. As soon as we think of a thing, we don't do it."

"Is that the *Leviathan* up there?" said one of the members, pointing toward a gray hull on the Hoboken horizon. No one knew, but the secretary was reminded of an adventure during the war. "One time I was crossing on this ferry," he said, "and the *Leviathan* passed right by us. It was just at dusk and her camouflage was wonderful. Her blotches and stripes were so arranged that from a little distance, in the twilight, she gave the impression of a much smaller vessel, going the other way. All her upper works seemed to fade out in the haze and she became a much smaller ship." "That would be a wonderful plan for some of these copious dowagers one sees," said the irreverent Lawton. "Yes," we said; "instead of a stout lady going in to dinner, you would see a slim flapper coming out."

Something was then said about a good friend of the club who had at one time worked for the Y. M. C. A. "What is he doing now?" asked one. "He's with Grace and Company," said the secretary. The candidate was unabashed. "Think," he said, "of a Y. M. C. A. man getting grace at last."

The club found the Jersey City terminal much as usual, and to our surprise the candidate kept up his courage nobly as he was steered toward the place of penance, being the station lunch counter. The club remembered this as a place of excellent food in days gone by, when trains from Philadelphia stopped here instead of at the Penn. Station. Placing the host carefully in the middle, the three sat down at the curving marble slab. The waiters immediately sensed that something unusual was toward. Two dashed up with courteous attentions. It was surmised by the club that the trio had happened to sit at a spot where the jurisdictions of two waiters met. Both the wings of the trio waved the waiters toward the blushing novice, making it plain that upon him lay all responsibility. "It is obvious," remarked the secretary, "that you, Lawton, are right on the boundary line where two waiters meet. You will have to tip them both."

The new member was game. "Well," he said, without a trace of nervousness; "what'll you have?" The choice fell upon breast of lamb. The secretary asked for ice tea. Endymion, more ruthless, ordered ginger ale. When the ginger ale came, Lawton, still waggish, observed the label, which was one of the many imitations of a well-known brand. "The man who invented the diamond-shaped label," said Lawton, "was certainly a pathfinder in the wilderness of the ginger ale business. This ginger ale," said Lawton, tasting it, "is carefully warmed, like old claret."

The club sought to keep their host's mind off the painful topic of viands. "Sitting here makes one feel as though he ought to be going to take a train somewhere," said one. "Yes, the express for Weehawken," said the vivacious host. From this it was only a step to speaking of Brooklyn. The secretary explained that the club had outlined a careful itinerary in that borough for proximate pursuit. Lawton told that he had at one time written an essay on the effect of Brooklyn on the dialogue of the American drama. "It is the butt end of Long Island," he cried, with cruel mirth. Lovers of Brooklyn in the club nearly blackballed him for this.

With ice cream and cottage pudding, the admirable menu proceeded. The waiters conferred secretly together. They carefully noted the cheerful carving of the host's brow. They will know him again. A man who bursts in suddenly upon a railroad lunch counter and pays for three such meals, here is an event in the grim routine! But perhaps the two charter members were feeling pangs of conscience. "Come," they said, "at least let us split the ginger ale checks." But Lawton was seeing it through. Not a drum was heard, not a funeral note, as our host to the cashier we hurried. The secretary bought a penny box of matches and lit the great man's cigarette for him. Endymion, equally stirred, ran to buy the ferry tickets for the return voyage. "This time," he said, "I will be the ferry godmother."

On the homeward passage, a little drowse fell upon the two charter members. They had lunched more richly than was their wont. "Oh, these distressing, heavy lunches!" as Aldous Huxley cries in one of his poems. But Lawton was still of bright vivacity. At that time the club was perturbed by the coming Harding–Cox election. "Which of the vice-presidents are you going to vote for?" he cried, and then said: "It looks to me like Debs or dubs."

Endymion and the secretary looked at each other solemnly. The time had come. "I, Endymion," said the chairman, "take thee, Lawton, to have and to hold, as a member of the club."

And the secretary tenderly pronounced the society's formula for such occasions: "There is no inanition in an initiation."

[PP]

CREED OF THE THREE HOURS FOR LUNCH CLUB

IT HAS BEEN SUGGESTED that the Three Hours for Lunch Club is an immoral institution; that it is founded upon an insufficient respect for the devotions of industry; that it runs counter to the form and pressure of the age; that it encourages a greedy and rambling humour in the young of both sexes; that it even punctures, in the bosoms of settled merchants and rotarians, that capsule of efficiency and determination by which Great Matters are Put Over. It has been said, in short, that the Three Hours for Lunch Club should be more clandestine and reticent about its truancies.

Accordingly, it seems good to us to testify concerning Lunches and the philosophy of Lunching.

There are Lunches of many kinds. The Club has been privileged to attend gatherings of considerable lustre; occasions when dishes of richness and curiosity were dissected; when the surroundings were not devoid of glamour and surreptitious pomp. The Club has been convened in many different places: in resorts of pride and in low-ceiled reeky taphouses; in hotels where those clear cubes of unprofitable ice knock tinklingly in the goblets; in the brightly tinted cellars of Greenwich Village; in the saloons of ships. But the Club would give a false impression of its mind and heart if it allowed any one to suppose that Food is the chief object of its quest. It is true that Man, bitterly examined, is merely a vehicle for units of nourishing combustion; but on those occasions when the Club feels most truly Itself it rises above such considerations.

The form and pressure of the time (to repeat Hamlet's phrase) is such that thoughtful men—and of such the Club is exclusively composed: men of great heart, men of nice susceptibility—are continually oppressed by the fumbling, hasty, and insignificant manner in which human contacts are accomplished. Let us even say, *masculine* contacts: for the first task of any philosopher being to simplify his problem so that he can examine it clearly and with less distraction, the Club makes a great and drastic purge by sweeping away altogether the enigmatic and frivolous sex and disregarding it, at any rate during the hours of convivial session. The Club is troubled to note that in the intolerable rabies and confusion of this business life men meet merely in a kind of convulsion or horrid passion of haste and perplexity. We see, ever and often, those in whose faces we discern delightful and considerable secrets, messages of just import, grotesque mirth, or improving sadness. In their bearing and gesture, even in hours of haste and irritation, the Club (with its trained and observant eye) notes the secret and rare sign of Thought. Such men are marked by an inexorable follow-up system. Sooner or later their telephones ring; secretaries and go-betweens are brushed aside; they are bidden to appear at such and such a time and place; no excuses are accepted. Then follow the Consolations of Intercourse. Conducted with "shattering candour" (as one has said who is in spirit a member of this Club, though not yet, alas, inducted), the meetings may sometimes resolve themselves into a ribaldry, sometimes into a truthful pursuit of Beauty, sometimes into a mere logomachy. But in these symposiums, unmarred by the crude claim of duty, the Club does with single-minded resolve pursue the only lasting satisfaction allowed to humanity, to wit, the sympathetic study of other men's minds.

This is clumsily said: but we have seen moments when eager and honourable faces round the board explained to us what we mean. There is but one indefeasible duty of man, to say out the truth that is in his heart. The way of life engendered by a great city and a modern civilization makes it hard to do so. It is the function of the Club to say to the City and to Life Itself: "Stand back! Fair play! We see a goodly matter inditing in our friend's spirit. We will take our ease and find out what it is."

For this life of ours (asserts the Club) is curiously compounded of Beauty and Dross. You ascend the Woolworth Building, let us say—one of man's noblest and most poetic achievements. And at the top, what do you find, just before going out upon that gallery to spread your eye upon man's reticulated concerns? Do you find a little temple or cloister for meditation, or any way of marking in your mind the beauty and significance of the place? No, a man in uniform will thrust into your hand a booklet of well-intentioned description (but of unapproachable typographic ugliness) and you will find before you a stall for the sale of cheap souvenirs, ash trays, and hideous postcards. In such ways do things of Beauty pass into the custody of those unequipped to understand them.

The Club thinks that the life of this city, brutally intense and bewildering, has yet a beauty and glamour and a secret word to the mind, so subtle that it cannot be closely phrased, but so important that to miss it is to miss life itself. And to forfeit an attempt to see, understand, and mutually communicate this loveliness is to forfeit that burning spark that makes men's spirits worth while. To such halting meditations the Club devotes its aspirations undistressed by humorous protest. If this be treason. . . !

[PP]

FULTON STREET, AND WALT WHITMAN

AT THE SUGGESTION of Mr. Christopher Clarke, the Three Hours for Lunch Club made pilgrimage to the old seafaring tavern at No. 2 Fulton Street, and found it to be a heavenly place, with listing brass-shod black walnut stairs and the equally black and delightful waiter called Oliver, who (said Mr. Clarke) has been there since 1878.

But the club reports that the swordfish steak, of which it partook as per Mr. Clarke's suggestion, did not appeal so strongly to its taste. Swordfish steak, we feel, is probably a taste acquired by long and diligent application. At the first trial it seemed to the club a bit too reptilian in flavour. The club will go there again, and will hope to arrive in time to grab one of those tables by the windows, looking out over the docks and the United Fruit Company steamer which is so appropriately named the *Banan*; but it is the sense of the meeting that swordfish steak is not in its line.

The club retorts to Mr. Clarke by asking him if he knows the downtown chophouse where one may climb sawdusted stairs and sit in a corner beside a framed copy of the *New-York Daily Gazette* of May 1, 1789, at a little table incised with the initials of former habitués, and hold up toward the light a glass of the clearest and most golden and amber-lucent cider known to mankind, and before attacking a platter of cold ham and Boston beans, may feel that smiling sensation of a man about to make gradual and decent advances toward a ripe and ruddy appetite.

Fulton Street has always been renowned for its taverns. The Old Shakespeare Tavern used to be there, as is shown by the tablet at No. 136 commemorating the foundation of the Seventh Regiment. The club has always intended to make more careful exploration of Dutch Street, the little alley that runs off Fulton Street on the south side, not far from Broadway. There is an eating place on this byway, and the organization plans to patronize it, in order to have an excuse for giving itself the sub-title of the Dutch Street Club. The more famous eating houses along Fulton Street are known to all: the name of at least one of them has a genial Queen Anne sound. And only lately a very seemly coffee house was established not far from Fulton and Nassau. We must confess our pleasure in the fact that this place uses as its motto a footnote from *The Spectator*—"Whoever wished to find a gentleman commonly asked not where he resided, but which coffee house he frequented."

Among the many things to admire along Fulton Street (not the least of which are Dewey's puzzling perpetually fluent grape-juice bottle, and the shop where the trained ferrets are kept, for chasing out rats, mice, and cockroaches from your house, the sign says) we vote for that view of the old houses along the south side of the street, where it widens out toward the East River. This vista of tall, leaning chimneys seems to us one of the most agreeable things in New York, and we wonder whether any artist has ever drawn it. As our colleague Endymion suggested, it would make a fine subject for Walter Jack Duncan. In the eastern end of this strip of fine old masonry resides the seafaring tavern we spoke of above; formerly known as Sweet's, and a great place of resort (we are told) for Brooklynites in the palmy days before the Bridge was opened, when they used to stop there for supper before taking the Fulton Ferry across the perilous tideway.

The Fulton Ferry—dingy and deserted now—is full of fine memories. The old waiting room, with its ornate carved ceiling and fine, massive gas brackets, peoples itself, in one's imagination, with the lively and busy throngs of fifty and sixty years ago. "My life then [1850–60] was curiously identified with

Fulton Ferry, already becoming the greatest in the world for general importance, volume, variety, rapidity, and picturesqueness." So said Walt Whitman. It is a curious experience to step aboard one of the boats in the drowsy heat of a summer afternoon and take the short voyage over to the Brooklyn slip, underneath one of the huge piers of the Bridge. A few heavy wagons and heat-oppressed horses are almost the only other passengers. Not far away from the ferry, on the Brooklyn side, are the three charmingly named streets—Cranberry, Orange, and Pineapple—which are also so lastingly associated with Walt Whitman's life. It strikes us as odd, incidentally, that Walt, who loved Brooklyn so much, should have written a phrase so capable of humorous interpretation as the following: "Human appearances and manners—endless humanity in all its phases—Brooklyn also." This you will find in Walt's Prose Works, which is (we suppose) one of the most neglected of American classics.

But Fulton Street, Manhattan—in spite of its two greatest triumphs: Evelyn Longman Batchelder's glorious figure of "Lightning," and the strictly legal "three grains of pepsin" which have been a comfort to so many stricken invalids—is a mere byway compared to Fulton Street, Brooklyn, whose long bustling channel may be followed right out into the Long Island pampas. At the corner of Fulton and Cranberry streets *Leaves of Grass* was set up and printed, Walt Whitman himself setting a good deal of the type. Ninety-eight Cranberry Street, we have always been told, was the address of Andrew and James Rome, the printers. The house at that corner is still numbered 98. The ground floor is occupied by a clothing store, a fruit stand, and a barber shop. The building looks as though it is probably the same one that Walt knew. Opposite it is a sign where the comparatively innocent legend BEN'S PURE LAGER has been deleted.

The pilgrim on Fulton Street will also want to have a look at the office of the Brooklyn *Eagle*, that famous paper which has numbered among its employees two such different journalists as Walt Whitman and Edward Bok. There are many interesting considerations to be drawn from the two volumes of Walt's writings for the *Eagle*, which were collected (under the odd title "The Gathering of the Forces") by Cleveland Rodgers and John Black. We have always been struck by the complacent naïveté of Walt's judgments on literature (written, perhaps, when he was in a hurry to go swimming down at the foot of Fulton Street). Such remarks as the following make us ponder a little sadly. Walt wrote:

> We are no admirer of such characters as Doctor Johnson. He was a sour, malicious, egotistical man. He was a sycophant of power and rank, withal; his biographer narrates that he "always spoke with rough contempt of popular liberty." His head was educated to the point of *plus*, but for his heart, might still more unquestionably stand the sign *minus*. He insulted his equals . . . and tyrannized over his inferiors. He fawned upon his superiors, and, of course, loved to be fawned upon himself. . . . Nor were the freaks of this man the mere "eccentricities of genius"; they were probably the faults of a vile, low nature. His soul was a bad one.

The only possible comment on all this is that it is absurd, and that evidently Walt knew very little about the great Doctor. One of the curious things about Walt—and there is no man living who admires him more than we do—is that he requires to be forgiven more generously than any other great writer. There is no one who has ever done more grotesquely unpardonable things than he—and yet, such is the virtue of his great, saline simplicity, one always pardons them. As a book reviewer, to judge from the specimens rescued from the *Eagle* files by his latest editors, he was uniquely childish.

Noting the date of Walt's blast on Doctor Johnson (December 7, 1846), it is doubtful whether we can attribute the irresponsibility of his remarks to a desire to go swimming.

The editors of this collection venture the suggestion that the lighter pieces included show Walt as "not devoid of humour." We fear that Walt's waggishness was rather heavily shod. Here is a sample of his light-hearted paragraphing (the italics are his):—

> Carelessly knocking a man's eye out with a broken axe, may be termed a *bad axe-i-dent.*

It was in Leon Bazalgette's *Walt Whitman* that we learned of Walt's only really humorous achievement; and even then the humour was unconscious. It seems that during the first days of his life as a journalist in New York, Walt essayed to compromise with Mannahatta by wearing a frock coat, a high hat, and a flower in his lapel. We regret greatly that no photo of Walt in this rig has been preserved, for we would like to have seen the gentle misery of his bearing.

[PP]

McSORLEY'S

THIS AFTERNOON we have been thinking how pleasant it would be to sit at one of those cool tables up at McSorley's and write our copy there. We have always been greatly allured by Dick Steele's habit of writing his Tatler at his favourite tavern. You remember his announcement, dated April 12, 1709:

> All accounts of gallantry, pleasure, and entertainment, shall be under the article of White's Chocolate-house; poetry, under that of Will's Coffee-house; learning, under the title of The Grecian; foreign and domestic news, you will have from Saint James's Coffee-house; and what else I have to offer on any other subject shall be dated from my own apartment.

Sir Dick—would one speak of him as the first colyumist?—continued by making what is, we suppose, one of the earliest references in literature to the newspaper man's "expense account." But the expenses of the reporter two centuries ago seem rather modest. Steele said:

> I once more desire my reader to consider that as I cannot keep an ingenious man to go daily to Will's under twopence each day, merely for his charges; to White's under sixpence; nor to The Grecian, without allowing him some plain Spanish, to be as able as others at the learned table; and that a good observer cannot speak with even Kidney* at Saint James's without clean linen: I say, these considerations will, I hope, make all persons willing to comply with my humble request of a penny-a-piece.

But what we started to say was that if, like Dick Steele, we were in the habit of dating our stuff from various inns around the town, our choice for a quiet place in which to compose items of "gallantry, pleasure, and entertainment" would be McSorley's —"The Old House at Home"—up on Seventh Street. We had feared that this famous old cabin of cheer might have gone west in the recent evaporation; but rambling round in the neighbourhood of the Cooper Union we saw its familiar doorway with a shock of glad surprise. After all, there is no reason why the old-established houses should not go on doing a good business on a Volstead basis. It has never been so much a question of what a man

* Evidently the bus boy.

drinks as the atmosphere in which he drinks it. Atrocious cleanliness and glitter and raw naked marble make the soda fountains a disheartening place to the average male. He likes a dark, low-ceilinged, and not too obtrusively sanitary place to take his ease. At McSorley's is everything that the innocent fugitive from the world requires. The great amiable cats that purr in the back room. The old pictures and playbills on the walls. The ancient clocks that hoarsely twang the hours. We cannot imagine a happier place to sit down with a pad of paper and a well-sharpened pencil than at that table in the corner by the window. Or the table just under that really lovely little portrait of Robert Burns—would there be any more propitious place in New York at which to fashion verses? There would be no interruptions, such as make versifying almost impossible in a newspaper office. The friendly bartenders in their lilac-coloured shirts are wise and gracious men. They would not break in upon one's broodings. Every now and then, while the hot sun smote the awnings outside, there would be another china mug of that one-half-of-1-per-cent. ale, which seems to us very good. We repeat: we don't care so much what we drink as the surroundings among which we drink it. We are not, if you will permit the phrase, sot in our ways. We like the spirit of McSorley's, which is decent, dignified, and refined. No club has an etiquette more properly self-respecting.

One does not go to McSorley's without a glimpse

at that curious old red pile Bible House. It happened this way: Our friend Endymion was back from his vacation and we were trying to celebrate it in modest fashion. We were telling him all the things that had happened since he went away—that Bob Holliday had had a fortieth birthday, and Frank Shay had published his bibliography of Walt Whitman, and all that sort of thing; and in our mutual excitement Endymion whisked too swiftly round a corner and caught his jacket on a sharp door-latch and tore it. Inquiring at Astor Place's biggest department store as to where we could get it mended, they told us to go to "Mr. Wright the weaver" on the sixth floor of Bible House, and we did so. On our way back, avoiding the ancient wire rope elevator (we know only one other lift so delightfully mid-Victorian, viz., one in Boston, that takes you upstairs to see Edwin Edgett, the gentle-hearted literary editor of the Boston *Transcript*), we walked down the stairs, peeping into doorways in great curiosity. The whole building breathed a dusky and serene quaintness that pricks the imagination. It is a bit like the shop in Edinburgh (on the corner of the Leith Walk and Antigua Street, if we remember) that R. L. S. described in "A Penny Plain and Twopence Coloured"—"it was dark and smelt of Bibles." We looked in at the entrance to the offices of the *Christian Herald*. The Bowling Green thought that what he saw was two young ladies in close and animated converse; but Endymion insisted that it was one young lady doing her hair in front of a large mirror. "Quite a pretty little picture," said Endymion. We argued about this as we went down the stairs. Finally we went back to make sure. Endymion was right. Even in the darkness of Bible House, we agreed, romance holds sway. And then we found a book shop on the ground floor of Bible House. One of our discoveries there was *Little Mr. Bouncer*, by Cuthbert Bede—a companion volume to *Mr. Verdant Green*.

But Dick Steele's idea of writing his column from different taverns round the city is rather gaining ground in our affections. There would be no more exciting way of spending a fortnight or so than in taking a walking tour through the forests of New York, camping for the night wherever we happened to find ourself at dark, Adam-and-Evesdropping as we went, and giving the nearest small boy fifty cents to take our copy down to the managing editor. Some of our enterprising clients, who are not habitual commuters and who live in a state of single cussedness, might try it some time.

The only thing we missed at McSorley's, we might add, was the old-time plate of onions. But then we were not there at lunch time, and the pungent fruit may have been hidden away in the famous tall ice box. Hutchins Hapgood once said, in an article about McSorley's in *Harper's Weekly*: "The wives of the men who frequent McSorley's always know where their husbands have been. There is no mistaking a McSorley onion." He was right. The McSorley onion—"rose among roots"—was *sui generis*. It had a reach and authenticity all its own.

We have said a good deal, now and then, about some of the taverns and chophouses we enjoy; but the one that tingles most strongly in our bosom is one that doesn't exist. That is the chophouse that might be put in the cellar of that glorious old round-towered building at 59 Ann Street.

As you go along Ann Street, you will come, between numbers 57 and 61, to an old passage-way running down to a curious courtyard, which is tenanted mostly by carpenters and iron-workers, and by a crowded store which seems to be a second-hand ship-chandlery, for old sea-boots, life preservers, fenders, ship's lanterns, and flags hang on the wall over the high stairway. In the cellars are smithies where you will see the bright glare of a forge and men with faces gleaming in tawny light pulling shining irons out of the fire. The whole place is too fascinating to be easily described. That round-tower house is just our idea of the right place for a quiet tavern or club, where one would go in at lunch time, walk over a sawdusted floor to a table bleached by many litres of slopovers, light a yard of clay, and call for a platter of beefsteak pie. The downtown region is greatly in need of the kind of place we have in mind, and if any one cares to start a chophouse in that heavenly courtyard, the Three Hours for Lunch Club pledges itself to attend regularly.

[PP]

THE CLUB IN HOBOKEN

THE ADVERTISEMENT ran as follows:

Schooner *Hauppauge*
FOR SALE
By U. S. Marshal,
April 26, 1 P.M.,
Pier G, Erie R. R.,
Weehawken, N. J.
Built at Wilmington, N. C., 1918; net tonnage 1,295; length 228; equipped with sails, tackle, etc.

This had taken the eye of the Three Hours for Lunch Club. The club's interest in nautical matters is well known and it is always looking forward to the day when it will be able to command a vessel of its own. Now it would be too much to say that the club expected to be able to buy the *Hauppauge* (the first thing it would have done, in that case, would have been to rename her). For it was in the slack and hollow of the week—shall we say, the bight of the week?—just midway between pay-days. But at any rate, thought the club, we can look her over, which will be an adventure in itself; and we can see just how people behave when they are buying a schooner, and how prices are running, so that when the time comes we will be more experienced. Besides, the club remembered the ship auction scene in *The Wrecker* and felt that the occasion might be one of most romantic excitement.

It is hard, it is very hard, to have to admit that the club was foiled. It had been told that at Cortlandt Street a ferry bound for Weehawken might be found; but when Endymion and the Secretary arrived there, at 12:20 o'clock, they learned that the traffic to Weehawken is somewhat sparse. Next boat at 2:40, said a sign. They hastened to the Lackawanna ferry at Barclay Street, thinking that by voyaging to Hoboken and then taking a car they might still be in time. But it was not to be. When the *Ithaca* docked, just south of the huge red-blotched profile of the rusty rotting *Leviathan*, it was already 1 o'clock. The *Hauppauge*, they said to themselves, is already on the block, and if we went up there now to study her, we would be regarded as impostors.

But the club is philosophic. One Adventure is very nearly as good as another, and they trod ashore at Hoboken with light hearts. It was a day of tender and untroubled sunshine. They had a queer sensation of being in foreign lands. Indeed, the tall tragic funnels of the *Leviathan* and her motionless derelict masts cast a curious shadow of feeling over that region. For the great ship, though blameless herself, seems a thing of shame, a remembrance of days and deeds that soiled the simple creed of the sea. Her great shape and her majestic hull, pitiably dingy and stark, are yet plainly conscious of sin. You see it in every line of her as she lies there, with the attitude of a great dog beaten and crouching. You wonder how she would behave if she were towed out on the open bright water of the river, under that clear sky, under the eyes of other ships going about their affairs with the self-conscious rectitude and pride that ships have. For ships are creatures of intense caste and self-conscious righteousness. They rarely forgive a fallen sister—even when she has fallen through no fault of her own. Observe the *Nieuw Amsterdam* as she lies, very solid and spick, a few piers above. Her funnel is gay with bright green stripes; her glazed promenade deck is white and immaculate. But, is there not just a faint suggestion of smugness in her mien? She seems thanking the good old Dutch Deity of cleanliness and respectability that she herself is not like this poor trolloping giantess, degraded from the embrace of ocean and the unblemished circle of the sea.

That section of Hoboken waterfront, along toward the green promontory crowned by Stevens Institute, still has a war-time flavour. The old Hamburg–American line piers are used by the Army Transport Service, and in the sunshine a number of soldiers, off duty, were happily drowsing on a row of two-tiered beds set outdoors in the April pleasantness. There was a racket of bugles, and a squad seemed to be drilling in the courtyard. Endymion and the Secretary, after sitting on a pier-end watching some barges, and airing their nautical views in a way they would never have done had any pukka seafaring men been along, were stricken with the very crisis of spring fever and lassitude. They considered the possibility of hiring one of the soldiers' two-tiered beds for the afternoon. Perhaps it is the first two syllables of Hoboken's name that make it so desperately debilitating to the wayfarer in an April noonshine. Perhaps it was a kind of old nostalgia, for the Secretary remembered that sailormen's street as it had been some years ago, when he had been along there in search of schooners of another sort.

But anatomizing their anguish, these creatures finally decided that it might not be spring fever, but merely hunger. They saw the statue of the late Mr. Sloan of the Lackawanna Railroad—Sam Sloan, the bronze calls him, with friendly familiarity. The aspiring forelock of that statue, and the upraised finger of Samuel Sullivan Cox ("The Letter Carriers' Friend") in Astor Place, the club considers two of the most striking things in New York statuary. Mr. Pappanicholas, who has a candy shop in the high-spirited building called Duke's House, near the ferry terminal, must be (Endymion thought) some relative of Santa Claus. Perhaps he *is* Santa Claus, and the club pondered on the quite new idea that Santa Claus has lived in Hoboken all these years and no one had guessed it. The club asked a friendly policeman if there were a second-hand bookstore anywhere near. "Not that I know of," he said. But they did find a stationery store where there were a number of popular reprints in the window, notably *The Innocence of Father Brown*, and Andrew Lang's *My Own Fairy Book*.

But lunch was still to be considered. The club is happy to add The American Hotel, Hoboken, to its private list of places where it has been serenely happy. Consider corned beef hash, with fried egg, excellent, for 25 cents. Consider rhubarb pie, quite adequate, for 10 cents. Consider the courteous and urbane waiter. In one corner of the dining room was the hotel office, with a large array of push buttons communicating with the bedrooms. The club, its imagination busy, conceived that these were for the purpose of awakening seafaring guests early in the morning, so as not to miss their ship. If we were, for instance, second mate of the *Hauppauge*, and came to port in Hoboken, The American Hotel would be just the place where we would want to put up.

That brings us back to the *Hauppauge*. We wonder who bought her, and how much he paid; and why she carries the odd name of that Long Island village? If he would only invite us over to see her—and tell us how to get there!

[PP]

THE CLUB AT ITS WORST

A BARBECUE and burgoo of the Three Hours for Lunch Club was held, the club's medical adviser acting as burgoomaster and Mr. Lawton Mackall, the managing director, as jest of honour. The news that Lawton was at large spread rapidly through the city, and the club was trailed for some distance by an infuriated agent of the Society for the Deracination of Puns. But Lawton managed to kick over his traces, and the club safely gained the quiet haven of a Cedar Street chophouse. Here, when the members were duly squeezed into a stall, the Doctor gazed cheerfully upon Endymion and the Secretary who held the inward places. "Now is my chance," he cried, "to kill two bards with one stone."

Lawton, says the stenographic report, was in excellent form, and committed a good deal of unforgivable syntax. He was somewhat apprehensive when he saw the bill of fare inscribed "Ye Olde Chop House," for he asserts that the use of the word "Ye" always involves extra overhead expense—and a quotation from Shakespeare on the back of the menu, he doubted, might mean a couvert charge. But he was distinctly cheered when the kidneys and bacon arrived—a long strip of bacon gloriously balanced on four very spherical and well-lubricated kidneys. Smiling demurely, even blandly, Lawton rolled his sheave of bacon to and fro upon its kidneys. "This is the first time I ever saw bacon with ball bearings," he ejaculated. He gazed with the eye of a connoisseur upon the rather candid works of art hanging over the club's corner. He said they reminded him of Mr. Coles Phillips's calf-tones. The Doctor was speaking of having read an interesting dispatch by Mr. Grasty in the *Times*. "I understand," said Lawton, "that he is going to collect some of his articles in a book, to be called 'Leaves of Grasty'."

Duly ambered with strict and cloudy cider, the meal progressed, served with humorous comments by the waitress whom the club calls the Venus of Mealo. The motto of the club is *Tres Horas Non Numero Nisi Serenas*, and as the afternoon was still juvenile the gathering was transferred to the water-front. Passing onto the pier, Lawton gazed about him with admirable naïveté. Among the piles of freight were some agricultural machines. "Ha," cried the managing director, "this, evidently, is where the Piers Plowman works!" The club's private yacht, white and lovely, lay at her berth, and in the Doctor's cabin the members proceeded to the serious discussion of literature. Lawton, however, seemed nervous. Cargo was being put aboard the ship, and ever and anon there rose a loud rumbling of donkey engines. The occasional hurrying roar of machinery seemed to make Lawton nervous, for he said apprehensively that he feared someone was rushing the growler. In the corridor outside the Doctor's quarters a group of stewardesses were violently altercating, and Lawton remarked that a wench can make almost as much noise as a winch. On the whole, however, he admired the ship greatly, and was taken with the club's plans for going cruising. He said he felt safer after noting that the lifeboats were guaranteed to hold forty persons with cubic feet.

By this time, all sense of verbal restraint had been lost, and the club (if we must be candid) concluded its session by chanting, not without enjoyment, its own sea chantey, which runs as follows:—

I shipped aboard a galleass
  In a brig whereof men brag,
But lying on my palliass
  My spirits began to sag.

I heard the starboard steward
  Singing abaft the poop;
He lewdly sang to looard
  And sleep fled from the sloop.

"The grog slops over the fiddles
  With the violins of the gale:
Two bitts are on the quarterdeck,
  The seamen grouse and quail.

"The anchor has been catted,
  The timid ratlines flee,
Careening and carousing
  She yaws upon the sea.

"The skipper lies in the scupper,
  The barque is lost in the bight;
The bosun calls for a basin—
  This is a terrible night.

"The wenches man the winches,
  The donkeymen all bray—"
  . . . I hankered to be anchored
  In safety in the bay!

[PP]

SUBURBAN LIFE IN ROSLYN

HOUSE-HUNTING

A CURIOUS VERTIGO afflicts the mind of the house-hunter. In the first place, it is sufficiently maddening to see the settled homes of other happier souls, all apparently so firmly rooted in a warm soil of contentment while he floats, an unhappy sea-urchin, in an ocean of indecision. Furthermore, how confusing (to one who likes to feel himself somewhat securely established in a familiar spot) the startling panorama of possible places in which he visualizes himself. One day it is Great Neck, the next it is Nutley; one day Hollis, the next Englewood; one day Bronxville, and then Garden City. As the telephone rings, or the suasive accents of friendly realtors expound the joys and glories of various regions, his uneasy imagination flits hoppingly about the compass, conceiving his now vanished household goods reassembled and implanted in these contrasting scenes.

Startling scenarios are filmed in his reeling mind while he listens, over the tinkling wire, to the enumeration of rooms, baths, pantries, mortgages, commuting schedules, commodious closets, open fireplaces, and what not. In the flash and coruscation of thought he has transported his helpless family to Yonkers, or to Manhasset, or to Forest Hills, or wherever it may be, and tries to focus and clarify his vision of what it would all be like. He sees himself (in a momentary close-up) commuting on the bland and persevering Erie, or hastening hotly for a Liberty Street ferry, or changing at Jamaica (that mystic ritual of the Long Island brotherhood). For an instant he is settled again, with a modest hearth to return to at dusk . . . and then the sorrowful compliment is paid him and he wonders how the impression got abroad that he is a millionaire.

There is one consoling aspect of his perplexity, however, and that is the friendly intercourse he has with high-spirited envoys who represent real estate firms and take him voyaging to see "properties" in the country. For these amiable souls he expresses his candid admiration. Just as when one contemplates the existence of the doctors one knows, one can never imagine them ill, so one cannot conceive of the friendly realtor as in any wise distressed or grieved by the problems of the home. There is something Olympian about them, happy creatures! They deal only in severely "restricted" tracts. They have a stalwart and serene optimism. Odd as it seems, one of these friends told us that some people are so malign as to waste the time of real estate men by going out to look at houses in the country without the slightest intention of "acting." As a kind of amusement, indeed! A harmless way of passing an afternoon, of getting perhaps a free motor ride and enjoying the novelty of seeing what other people's houses look like inside. But our friend was convinced of one humble inquirer's passionate sincerity when he saw him gayly tread the ice floes of rustic Long Island in these days of slush and slither.

How do these friends of ours, who see humanity in its most painful and distressing gesture (i.e., when it is making up its mind to part with some money), manage to retain their fine serenity and blitheness of spirit? They have to contemplate all the pathetic struggles of mortality, for what is more pathetic than the spectacle of a man trying to convince a real estate agent that he is not really a wealthy creature masking millions behind an eccentric pose of humility? Our genial adviser Grenville Kleiser, who has been showering his works upon us, has classified all possible mental defects as follows:

(*a*) *Too easy acquiescence*
(*b*) *A mental attitude of contradiction*

(*c*) *Undue skepticism*
(*d*) *A dogmatic spirit*
(*e*) *Lack of firmness of mind*
(*f*) *A tendency to take extreme views*
(*g*) *Love of novelty: that is, of what is foreign, ancient, unusual, or mysterious.*

All these serious weaknesses of judgment may be discerned, in rapid rotation, in the mind of the house-hunter. It would be only natural, we think, if the real estate man were to tell him to go away and study Mr. Kleiser's *How to Build Mental Power.* In the meantime, the vision of the home he had dreamed of becomes fainter and fainter in the seeker's mind—like the air of a popular song he has heard whistled about the streets, but does not know well enough to reproduce. How he envies the light-hearted robins, whose house-hunting consists merely in a gay flitting from twig to twig. Yet, even in his disturbance and nostalgia of spirit, he comforts himself with the common consolation of his cronies—"Oh, well, one always finds something"—and thus (in the words of good Sir Thomas Browne) teaches his haggard and unreclaimed reason to stoop unto the lure of Faith.

[P]

LONG ISLAND REVISITED

THE ANFRACTUOSITIES of legal procedure having caused us to wonder whether there really were any such place as the home we have just bought, we thought we would go out to Salamis, L. I., and have a look at it. Of course we knew it had been there a few weeks ago, but the title companies do confuse one so. We had been sitting for several days in the office of the most delightful lawyer in the world (and if we did not fear that all the other harassed and beset creatures in these parts would instantly rush to lay their troubles in his shrewd and friendly bosom we would mention his name right here and do a little metrical pirouette in his honour)—we had been sitting there, we say, watching the proceedings, without the slightest comprehension of what was happening. It is really quite surprising, let us add, to find how many people are suddenly interested in some quiet, innocent-looking shebang nestling off in a quiet dingle in the country, and how, when it is to be sold, they all bob up from their coverts in Flushing, Brooklyn, or Long Island City, and have to be "satisfied." What floods of papers go crackling across the table, drawn out from those mysterious brown cardboard wallets; what quaint little jests pass between the emissaries of the title company and the legal counsel of the seller, jests that seem to bear upon the infirmity of human affairs and cause the well-wishing adventurer to wonder whether he had ever sufficiently pondered the strange tissue of mortal uncertainties that hides behind every earthly venture . . . there was, for instance, occasional reference to a vanished gentleman who had once crossed the apparently innocent proscenium of our estate and had skipped, leaving someone six thousand dollars to the bad; this ingenious buccaneer was, apparently, the only one who did not have to be "satisfied." At any rate, we thought that we, who entered so modestly and obscurely into this whole affair, being only the purchaser, would finally satisfy ourself, too, by seeing if the property was still there.

Long Island and spring—the conjunction gives us a particular thrill. There are more beautiful places than the Long Island flats, but it was there that we earned our first pay envelope, and it was there that we first set up housekeeping; and as long as we live the station platform of Jamaica will move us strangely—not merely from one train to another, but also inwardly. There is no soil that receives a more brimming benison of sunshine than Long Island in late April. As the train moves across the plain it seems to swim in a golden tide of light. Billboards have been freshly painted and announce the glories of phonographs in screaming scarlets and purples, or the number of miles that divide you from a Brooklyn department store. Out at Hillside the stones that demarcate the territory of an old-fashioned house are new and snowily whitewashed. At Hollis the trees are a cloud of violent mustard-yellow (the colour of a safety-matchbox label). Magnolias (if that is what they are) are creamy pink. Moving vans are bustling along the road. Across the wide fields of Bellaire there is a view of the brown woods on the ridge, turning a faint olive as the leaves gain strength. Gus Wuest's road-house at Queens looks inviting as of old, and the red-brown of the copper beeches reminds one of the tall amber beakers. Here is the little park by the station in Queens, the flag on the staff, the forsythia bushes the colour of scrambled eggs.

Is it the influence of the Belmont Park race track? There seem to be, in the smoking cars, a number of men having the air of those accustomed to associate (in a not unprofitable way) with horses. Here is one, a handsome person, who holds our eye as a bright flower might. He wears a flowing over-coat of fleecy fawn colour and a derby of biscuit brown. He has a gray suit and joyful socks of heavy wool, yellow and black and green in patterned squares which are so vivid they seem cubes rather than squares. He has a close-cut dark moustache, his shaven cheeks are a magnificent sirloin tint, his chin splendidly blue by the ministration of the razor. His shirt is blue with a stripe of sunrise pink, and the collar to match. He talks briskly and humorously to two others, leaning over in the seat behind them. As he argues, we see his brown low shoe tapping on the floor. One can almost see his foot think. It pivots gently on the heel, the toe wagging in air, as he approaches the climax of each sentence. Every time he drives home a point in his talk down comes the whole foot, softly, but firmly. He relights his cigar in the professional manner, not by inhaling as he applies the match, but by holding the burned portion in the flame, away from his mouth, until it has caught. His gold watch has a hunting case; when he has examined it, it shuts again with a fine rich snap, which we can hear even above the noise of the car.

On this early morning train there are others voyaging for amusement. Here are two golfing zealots, puffing pipes and discussing with amazing persistence the minutiæ of their sport. Their remarks are addressed to a very fashionable-looking curate, whose manners are superb. Whether he is going to play golf we know not; at any rate, he smiles mildly and politely to all they say. Perhaps he is going round the course with them, in the hope of springing some ecclesiastical strategy while they are softened and chastened by the glee of the game. The name of their Maker, it is only fair to suspect, has more than once been mentioned on the putting green; and if it should slip out, the curate will seize the cue and develop it. In the meantime, one of the enthusiasts (while his companion is silenced in the act of lighting his pipe) is explaining to the cloth how his friend plays golf. "I'll tell you how he plays," he says. "Imagine him sitting down in a low chair and swinging a club. Then take the chair away and he still keeps the same position. That's what he looks like when he drives." The curate smiles at this and prepares his face to smile with equal gentleness when the other retorts.

After Floral Park the prospect becomes more plainly rural. The Mineola trolley zooms along, between wide fields of tilled brown earth. There is an occasional cow; here and there a really old barn and farmhouse standing, incongruously, among the settlements of modern kindling-wood cottages; and a mysterious agricultural engine at work with a spinning fly-wheel. Against the bright horizon stand the profiles of Garden City: the thin cathedral spire, the bulk of St. Paul's school, the white cupola of the hotel. The tree-lined vistas of Mineola are placidly simmering in the morning sun. A white dog with erect and curly tail trots very purposefully round the corner of the First National Bank. We think that we see the spreading leaves of some rhubarb plants in a garden; and there are some of those (to us very enigmatic, as we are no gardener) little glass window frames set in the soil, as though a whole house, shamed by the rent the owner wanted to charge, had sunk out of sight, leaving only a skylight.

As we leave East Williston we approach more

interesting country, with a semblance of hills, and wooded thickets still brownly tapestried with the dry funeral of last year's leaves. On the trees the new foliage sways in little clusters, catching the light like the wings of perching green butterflies. Some of the buds are a coppery green, some a burning red, but the prevailing colour is the characteristic sulphur yellow of early spring. And now we are set down at Salamis, where the first and most surprising impression is of the unexpected abundance of competitive taxicabs. Having reached the terminus of our space, we can only add that we found our estate still there—and there are a few stalks of rhubarb surviving from an earlier plantation.

[P]

A SUBURBAN SENTIMENTALIST

THAT WILD and engaging region known as the Salamis Estates has surprising enchantments for the wanderer. Strolling bushrangers, if they escape being pelleted with lead by the enthusiastic rabbit hunters who bang suddenly among thickets, will find many vistas of loveliness. All summer long we are imprisoned in foliage, locked up in a leafy embrace. But when the leaves have shredded away and the solid barriers of green stand revealed as only thin fringes of easily penetrable woodland, the eye moves with surprise over these wide reaches of colour and freedom. Beyond the old ruined farmhouse past the gnarled and rheumatic apple tree is that dimpled path that runs across fields, the short cut down to the harbour. The stiff frozen plumes of ghostly goldenrod stand up pale and powdery along the way. How many tints of brown and fawn and buff in the withered grasses—some as feathery and translucent as a gauze scarf, as nebulous as those veilings Robin Herrick was so fond of—his mention of them gives an odd connotation to a modern reader—

> So looks Anthea, when in bed she lyes,
> Orecome, or halfe betray'd by Tiffanies.

Our fields now have the rich, tawny colour of a panther's hide. Along the little path are scattered sumac leaves, dark scarlet. It is as though Summer had been wounded by the hunter Jack Frost, and had crept away down that secret track, leaving a trail of bloodstains behind her.

This tract of placid and enchanted woodland, field, brake, glen, and coppice, has always seemed to us so amazingly like the magical Forest of Arden that we believe Shakespeare must have written *As You Like It* somewhere near here. One visitor, who was here when the woods were whispering blackly in autumn moonlight, thought them akin to George Meredith's "The Woods of Westermain"—

> Enter these enchanted woods,
>   You who dare.
> Nothing harms beneath the leaves
> More than waves a swimmer cleaves.
> Toss your heart up with the lark,
> Foot at peace with mouse and worm.
>   Fair you fare.
> Only at a dread of dark
> Quaver, and they quit their form:

Thousand eyeballs under hoods
  Have you by the hair.
Enter these enchanted woods,
  You who dare.

But in winter, and in such a noonday of clear sunshine as the present, when all the naked grace of trunks and hillsides lies open to eyeshot, the woodland has less of that secrecy and brooding horror that Meredith found in "Westermain." It has the very breath of that golden-bathed magic that moved in Shakespeare's tenderest haunt of comedy. Momently, looking out toward the gray ruin on the hill (which was once, most likely, the very "sheepcote fenced about with olive trees" where Aliena dwelt and Ganymede found hose and doublet give such pleasing freedom to her limbs and her wit) one expects to hear the merry note of a horn; the moralizing Duke would come striding thoughtfully through the thicket down by the tiny pool (or shall we call it a mere?). He would sit under those two knotty old oaks and begin to pluck the burrs from his jerkin. Then would come his cheerful tanned followers, carrying the dappled burgher they had ambushed; and, last, the pensive Jacques (so very like Mr. Joseph Pennell in bearing and humour) distilling his meridian melancholy into pentameter paragraphs, like any colyumist. A bonfire is quickly kindled, and the hiss and fume of venison collops whiff to us across the blue air.

Against that stump—is it a real stump, or only a painted canvas affair from the property man's warehouse?—surely that is a demijohn of cider? And we can hear, presently, that most piercingly tremulous of all songs rising in rich chorus, with the plenitude of pathos that masculines best compass after a full meal—

Blow, blow, thou winter wind,
Thou art not so unkind
As man's ingratitude—

We hum the air over to ourself, and are stricken with the most perfect iridescent sorrow. We even ransack our memory to try to think of someone who has been ungrateful to us, so that we can throw a little vigorous bitterness into our tone.

Yes, the sunshine that gilds our Salamis thickets seems to us to have very much the amber glow of footlights.

In another part of this our "forest"—it is so truly a forest in the Shakespearean sense, as all Long Island forests are (e.g., Forest Hills), where even the lioness and the green and gilded snake have their suburban analogues, which we will not be laborious to explain—we see Time standing still while Ganymede and Aliena are out foraging with the burly Touchstone (so very like that well-loved sage Mr. Don Marquis, we protest!). And, to consider, what a place for a colyumist was the Forest of Arden. See how zealous contributors hung their poems round on trees so that he could not miss them. Is it not all the very core and heartbeat of what we call "romance," that endearing convention that submits the harsh realities and interruptions of life to a golden purge of fancy? How, we sometimes wonder, can any one grow old as long as he can still read *As You Like It*, and feel the magic of that best-loved and most magical of stage directions—*The Forest of Arden.*

And now, while we are still in the soft Shakespearean mood, comes "Twelfth Night"—traditionally devoted to dismantling the Christmas Tree; and indeed there is no task so replete with luxurious and gentle melancholy. For by that time the toys which erst were so splendid are battered and bashed; the cornucopias empty of candy (save one or two striped sticky shards of peppermint which elude the thrusting index, and will be found again next December); the dining-room floor is thick with fallen needles; the gay little candles are burnt down to a small gutter of wax in the tin holders. The floor sparkles here and there with the fragments of tinsel balls or popcorn chains that were injudiciously hung within leap of puppy or grasp of urchin. And so you see him, the diligent parent, brooding with a tended mournfulness and sniffing the faint whiff of that fine Christmas tree odour—balsam and burning candles and fist-warmed peppermint—as he undresses the prickly boughs. Here they go into the boxes, red, green, and golden balls, tinkling glass bells, stars, paper angels, cotton-wool Santa Claus, blue birds, celluloid goldfish, mosquito netting, counterfeit stockings, nickel-plated horns, and all the comical accumulation of oddities that gathers from year to year in the box labelled CHRISTMAS TREE THINGS, FRAGILE. The box goes up to the attic, and the parent blows a faint diminuendo, achingly prolonged, on a toy horn. Titania is almost reduced to tears as he explains it is the halloo of Santa Claus fading away into the distance.

[PP]

THE LITTLE HOUSE

AFTER MANY DAYS of damp, dull, and dolorous weather, we found ourself unexpectedly moving in a fresh, cool, pure air; an air which, although there was no sunlight, had the spirit and feeling of sunlight in it; an air which was purged and lively. And, so strangely do things happen, after days of various complexion and stratagem, we found ourself looking across that green field, still unchanged, at the little house.

Wasn't there—we faintly recall a saccharine tune sung by someone who strode stiffly to and fro in a glare of amber footlights—wasn't there a song about: "And I lo-ong to settle down, in that old Long Island town!" Wasn't there such a ditty? It came softly back, unbidden, to the sentimental attic of our memory as we passed along that fine avenue of trees and revisited, for the first time since we moved away, the wide space of those Long Island fields and the row of frame cottages. There was the little house, rather more spick and span than when we had known it, freshly painted in its brown and white, the privet hedge very handsomely shaven, and its present occupant busily engaged in trimming some tufts of grass along the pavement. We did not linger, and that cheerful-looking man little knew how many ghosts he was living among. All of us, we suppose, dwell amid ghosts we are not aware of, and this gentleman would be startled if he knew the tenacity and assurance of certain shades who moved across his small lawn that afternoon.

It was strange, we aver, to see how little the place had changed, for it seemed that we had passed round the curves and contours of a good many centuries in those four or five years. In the open meadow the cow was still grazing; perhaps the same cow that was once pestered by a volatile Irish terrier who used to swing merrily at the end of that cow's tail; a merry and irresponsible little creature, she was, and her phantom still scampers the road where the sharp scream of the Freeport trolley brings back her last fatal venture to our mind. It was strange to look at those windows, with their neat white sills, and to remember how we felt when for the first time we slept in a house of our own, with all those Long Island stars crowding up to the open window, and, waking in drowsy unbelief, put out a hand to touch the strong wall and see if it was still there. Perhaps one may be pardoned for being a little sentimental in thinking back about one's first house.

The air, on that surprising afternoon, carried us again into the very sensation and reality of those days, for there is an openness and breezy stir on those plains that is characteristic. In the tree-lined streets of the village, where old white clapboarded houses with green or pale blue shutters stand in a warm breath of box hedges, the feeling is quite different. Out on the Long Island prairie—which Walt Whitman, by the way, was one of the first to love and praise—you stand uncovered to all the skirmish of heaven, and the feathery grasses are rarely still. There was the chimney of the fireplace we had built for us, and we remembered how the woodsmoke used to pour gallantly from it like a blue pennon of defiance. The present owner, we fear, does not know how much impalpable and unforgotten gold leaped up the wide red throat of that chimney, or he would not dream of selling. Yes, the neighbours tell us that he wants to sell. In our day, the house was said to be worth $3,000. Nowadays, the price is $7,000. Even at that it is cheap, if you set any value on amiable and faithful ghosts.

Oh, little house on the plains, when our typewriter forgets thee, may this shift key lose its function!

[PP]

EVICTED BY AN OWL

I ABANDON the Knothole today. When I went out there I was startled to see sheets of MS on the floor, pictures fallen from the top of the high shelves, the 1855 Overholt bottle (long since empty, but noble souvenir of a certain Walt Whitman pilgrimage) toppled over (but undamaged). At first I supposed some human mischief, but picking up sheets of typescript, I saw on them—and on the big Webster's Unabridged—unmistakable proof that the intruder was a bird. Then, from a shadowy perch just under the roof, he swooped across and gave me a start. An owl, a handsome fellow with tall ears and speckled breast. He had come down the chimney, of course. Flattened warily in the triangle of the rafters, he watched me steadily. I whistled at him, tried to frighten him through the open door, but he only coasted from side to side—coming too near my head for comfort. I had no mind to sit there with him perched above me; so for the moment I've left him in charge, with the door open for exit.—It pleased me that the bird of wisdom should visit the place in person.

[CMB]

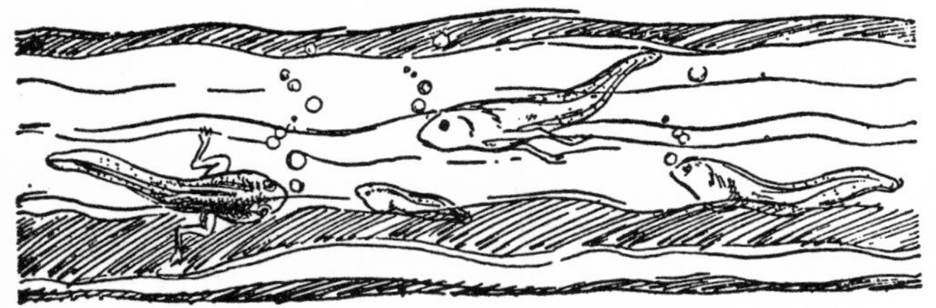

TADPOLES

NEAR OUR HOUSE, out in the sylvan Salamis Estates, there is a pond. We fear we cannot describe this pond to you in a way to carry conviction. You will think we exaggerate if we tell you, with honest warmth, how fair the prospect is. Therefore, in sketching the scene, we will be austere, churlish, a miser of adjectives. We will tell you naught of sun-sparkle by day where the green and gold of April linger in that small hollow landskip, where the light shines red through the faint bronze veins of young leaves—much as it shines red through the finger joinings of a child's hand held toward the sun. We will tell you naught of frog-song by night, of those reduplicated whistlings and peepings. We will tell you naught of. . . . No, we will be austere.

On one side, this pond reflects the white cloudy bravery of fruit trees in flower, veterans of an orchard surviving an old farmhouse that stood on the hilltop long ago. It burned, we believe: only a rectangle of low stone walls remains. Opposite, the hollow is overlooked by a bumpy hillock fringed with those excellent dark evergreen trees—shall we call them hemlocks?—whose flat fronds silhouette against the sky and contribute a feeling of mystery and wilderness. On this little hill are several japonica trees, in violent ruddy blossom; and clumps of tiger lily blades springing up; and bloodroots. The region prickles thickly with blackberry brambles, and mats of honeysuckle. Across the pond, looking from the waterside meadow where the first violets are, your gaze skips (like a flat stone deftly flung) from the level amber (dimpled with silver) of the water, through a convenient dip of country where the fields are folded down below the level of the pool. So the eye, skittering across the water, leaps promptly and cleanly to blue ranges by the Sound, a couple of miles away. All this, mere introduction to the real theme, which is Tadpoles.

We intended to write a poem about those tadpoles, but Endymion tells us that Louis Untermeyer has already smitten a lute on that topic. We are queasy of trailing such an able poet. Therefore we celebrate these tadpoles in prose. They deserve a prose as lucid, as limpid, as cool and embracing, as the water of their home.

Coming back to tadpoles, the friends of our youth, shows us that we have completed a biological cycle of much import. Back to tadpoles in one generation, as the adage might have said. Twenty-five years ago we ourself were making our first acquaintance with these friendly creatures, in the immortal (for us) waters of Cobb's Creek, Pennsylvania. (Who was Cobb, we wonder?) And now our urchins, with furious glee, applaud their sire who wades the still frosty quags of our pond, on Sunday mornings, to renew their supply of tads. It is considered fair and decent that each batch of tadpoles should live in their prison (a milk bottle) only one week. The following Sunday they go back to the pond, and a new generation take their places. There is some subtle kinship, we think, between children and tadpoles. No childhood is complete until it has watched their sloomy and impassive faces munching against the glass, and seen the gradual egress (as the encyclopædia pedantically puts it) of their tender limbs, the growing froggishness of their demeanour.

Some time when you are exploring in the Britannica, by the way, after you have read about Tactics and William Howard Taft, turn to the article on Tadpoles and see if you can recognize them as described by the learned G. A. B. An amusing game, we submit, would be to take a number of encyclopædia descriptions of familiar things, and see how many of our friends could identify them under their scientific nomenclature.

But it is very pleasant to dally about the pond on a mild April morning. While the Urchiness mutters among the violets, picking blue fistfuls of stalkless heads, the Urchin, on a plank at the waterside, studies these weedy shallows which are lively with all manner of mysterious excitement, and probes a waterlogged stump in hope to recapture Brer Tarry-pin, who once was ours for a short while. Gissing (the juvenile and too enthusiastic dog) has to be kept away from the pond by repeated sticks thrown as far as possible in another direction; otherwise he insists on joining the tadpole search, and, poking his snout under water, attempts to bark at the same time, with much coughing and smother.

The tadpoles, once caught, are taken home in a small yellow pail. They seem quite cheerful. They are kept, of course, in their native fluid, which is liberally thickened with the oozy emulsion of moss, mud, and busy animalculæ that were dredged up with them in clutches along the bottom of the pond. They lie, thoughtful, at the bottom of their milk bottle, occasionally flourishing furiously round their prison. But, since reading that article in the Britannica, we are more tender toward them. For the learned G. A. B. says: "A glandular streak extending from the nostril toward the eye is the lachrymal canal." Is it possible that tadpoles weep? We will look at them again when we go home to-night. We are, in the main, a kind-hearted host. If they show any signs of effusion. . . .

[PP]

MAGIC IN SALAMIS

WHY IS IT (we were wondering, as we walked to the station) that these nights of pearly wet Long Island fog makes the spiders so active? The sun was trying to break through the mist, and all the way down the road trees, bushes, and grass were spangled with cobwebs, shining with tiny pricks and gems of moisture. These damp, mildewy nights that irritate us and bring that queer soft grayish fur on the backs of our books seem to mean hilarity and big business to the spider. Along the hedge near the station there were wonderful great webs, as big as the shield of Achilles. What a surprising passion of engineering the spider must go through in the dark hours, to get his struts and cantilevers and his circling gossamer girders properly disposed on the foliage.* Darkness is no difficulty to him, evidently. If he lays his web on the grass, he builds it with a little tunnel leading down to earth, where he hides waiting his breakfast. But on such a morning, apparently, with thousands of webs ready, there can hardly have been enough flies to go round; for we saw all the appetent spiders had emerged from their tubes and were waiting impatiently on the web itself—as though the host should sit on the tablecloth waiting for his guest. Put a finger at the rim of the web and see how quickly he vanishes down his shaft. Most surprising of all it is to see the long threads that are flung horizontally through the air, from a low branch of a tree to the near-by hedge. They hang, elastic and perfect, sagged a little by a run of fog-drops almost invisible except where the wetness catches the light. Some were stretched at least six feet across space, with no supporting strands to hold them from above—and no branches from which the filament could be dropped. How is it done? Does our intrepid weaver hurl himself madly six feet into the dark, trusting to catch the leaf at the other end? Can he jump so far?

All this sort of thing is, quite plainly, magic. It is rather important to know, when you are dealing

* Perhaps the structural talent of our Salamis arachnids is exceptional. Perhaps it is due to the fact that the famous Engineers' Country Club is near by. Can the spiders have learned their technology by watching those cheerful scientists on the golf greens?

with magic, just where ordinary life ends and the mystery begins, so that you can adjust yourself to incantations and spells. As you make your green escape from town (which has magic of its own, but quite different) you must clearly mark the place where you pierce the veil. We showed it to Endymion lately. We will tell you about it.

There is a certain point, as you go out to Salamis on the railroad, when you begin to perceive a breath of enchantment in the landscape. For our own part, we become aware of a subtle spice of gramarye as soon as we see the station lamps at East Williston, which have tops like little green hats. Lamps of this sort have always had a fascination for us, and whenever we see them at a railway station we have a feeling that that would be a nice place to get off and explore.

And, of course, after you pass East Williston there is that little pond in which, if one went fishing, he could very likely pull up a fine fleecy cloud on his hook. Then the hills begin, or what we on Long Island consider hills. There are some fields on the left of the train that roll like great green waves of the sea; they surge up against the sky and seem about to spill over in a surf of daisies.

A quiet road runs up a hill, and as soon as you pass along its green channel, between rising thickets where rabbits come out to gape, you feel as though walking into a poem by Walter de la Mare. This road, if pursued, passes by a pleasing spot where four ways cross in an attenuated X. Off to one side is a field that is very theatrical in effect: it always reminds us of a stage set for "As You Like It," the Forest of Arden. There are some gigantic oak trees and even some very papier-maché-looking stumps, all ready for the duke, "and other Lords, like Foresters," to do their moralizing upon; and in place of the poor sequestered stag there is a very fine plushy cow, grazing, hard by a very agreeable morass. At the back (*L. U. E.*) is discovered a pleasing ruin, the carcass of an ancient farmstead, whose stony ribs are thickset with brambles; and the pleasant melancholy of an abandoned orchard rounds off the scene in the wings, giving a fine place for Rosalind and Celia and the leg-weary Touchstone to abide their cue.

Choosing the left-hand arm of the X, and moving past wild rose bushes toward the even richer rosegarden of the sunset, the fastidious truant is ushered (as was our friend Endymion the other evening) upon a gentle meadow where a solitary house of white stucco begs for a poet as occupant. This house, having been selected by Titania and ourself as a proper abode for Endymion and his family, we waited until sunset, frogsong, and all the other amenities of life in Salamis were suitable for the introduction of our guest to the scene. This dwelling, having long lain untenanted, has a back door that stands ajar and we piloted the awestruck lyrist inside. Now nothing rages so merrily in the blood as the instinct of picking out houses for other people, houses that you yourself do not have to live in; and those Realtors whom we have dismayed by our lack of enthusiasm would have been startled to hear the orotund accents in which we vouched for that property, sewage, messuage, and all. Here, we cried, is the front door (facing the sunset) where the postman will call with checks from your publishers; and here are the porcelain laundry tubs that will make glad the heart of the washerwoman (when you can get one).

Endymion's guileless heart was strongly uplifted. Not a question did he ask as to heating arrangements, save to show a mild spark in his eye when he saw the two fireplaces. Plumbing was to him, we saw, a matter to be taken on faith. His paternal heart was slightly perturbed by a railing that ran round the top of the stairs. This railing, he feared, was so built that small and impetuous children would assuredly fall headlong through it, and we discussed means of thwarting such catastrophe. But upstairs we found the room that caused our guest to glimmer with innocent cheer. It had tall casement windows looking out upon a quiet glimpse of trees. It had a raised recess, very apt for a bust of Pallas. It had space for bookcases. And then, on the windowsill, we found the dead and desiccated corpse of a swallow. It must have flown in through a broken pane on the ground floor long ago and swooped vainly about the empty house. It lay, pathetically, close against the shut pane. Like a forgotten and unuttered beauty in the mind of a poet, it lay there, stiffened and silent.

[PP]

N. S. N. S.

ONE OF THE pleasantest ways to pass an evening would be the composition of a prospectus for the N. S. N. S. The N. S. N. S. is an old and favorite project of my own, which recurs to me with great force just now because only this afternoon I discovered that an old farmhouse, on one of Long Island's handsomest and least known harbors, might be available for the purpose. Of the charms of that old grange, with its huge red barn and its lonely purview over grassy tidal estuary and sandy cliffs, I shall not speak. It has a rich Biblical aroma in the name of its harbor; it throbs with crickets in these warm evenings. But all that is irrelevant, and anyhow I should want it to remain uneasy of access.

But there can be no ill in mentioning the notion of the N. S. N. S., which means the North Shore Night School. It is my dearest and perhaps most selfish dream.

If my own case is any criterion, I find that from about the age of 35 onward people supposedly grownup begin to have a real hankering to go to school. By that time they have begun to be aware of their dangerous ignorance in most of the things that really matter; and also, if they are the right sort of people, they have had a good many of their prejudices knocked out of them. They have learned enough of the decencies of social intercourse to make them agreeable companions; and they know that Time is on the march. And in their own particular line of work, whatever it may be, they have learned enough to have useful experience to impart.

The idea, then, is to gather together, for a definite and concerted attack upon the secrets of life, a community of those aspiring and mutually entertaining ignoramuses. None, unless singularly precocious, should be younger than 30; none, unless preternaturally virid, should be older than 60. For it is within the gamut of those thirty years, one may rationally maintain, that most human animals reach their widest range of mirth and possibility.

I am sorry to have to add that the membership of this academy would be admitted only on somewhat stringent principles. In the first place it would be my idea that the fees must be pretty stiff, for the regime and exquisite simplicity of the establishment would come high. And a strenuous oath would have to be sworn that all classroom procedures would be entirely confidential outside the school campus. For the prime requisite of success would be a complete candor. It would be necessary for the scholars to lay aside those agreeable hypocrisies that make social life possible, and speak with full honesty of their own experiences and opinions. Only so would it be possible to reach any conclusions as to the motives that really govern men and women in their careers and metaphysics.

The attempt of a group of intelligent and personable citizens to discover among themselves what they really do think about it all, under guarantee that anything said would never be used against them, surely would deserve encouragement.

But this sounds a bit sombre. (In fact, of course, it would be incredibly entertaining. Nothing Boswell or Casanova ever wrote could conceivably be more amusing.) The core of the matter is that it seems a pity there is such ineffective intercommunication among human beings during that period of their lives when they are most active and still have some chance of improving their ideas. Under present conditions men and women are so incredibly immersed in the job of earning a living and raising a family (or, in wealthier circles, in the job of trying to avert boredom) that they rarely exchange any sincere and leisurely speculations on the things that most genuinely concern them.

And another thing: the lamentable fact is that only the smallest percentage of people have really any idea of Fun. They have forgotten, or never knew, how to have a Good Time. The almost inconceivable overplus of tippling caused by Prohibition is an odd evidence of this.

Now in the North Shore Night School it would not be necessary, except for very special seminar courses, to employ high-priced experts on the faculty. The whole point of the thing would be that every member would undertake to conduct courses in the subjects he (or she) understood best. If you ask me what kind of studies we would undertake let me set down some of the topics in which I myself should desire instruction. I should enroll at once in any available courses dealing with Small Boat Sailing, Folk Dancing, Elementary Piano Playing, Comparative Religions, Algebra, Domestic Mechanics (including the principles of Plumbing and the Internal Combustion Engine), Electricity, Gardening, French Vintages, and Municipal Politics.

Perhaps you will remark that many of these subjects are offered in extension courses, summer schools, etc.; but under the cheerful conditions of the N. S. N. S. they would be ensued in the true Socratic spirit of inquisitive frolic. Life at its best should be almost a continuous picnic or Platonic supper party. It is indeed a kind of beach party, on the edge of a very large ocean indeed. At the North Shore School spiritual improvement would proceed not so much by formal instruction as by swapping of anecdotes. There would be much inordinate hilarity, but also there would be a remarkable infusion of loveliness. The motives and impulses that actuate people are often much finer than is commonly imagined; almost everyone wants to live life beautifully and generously; and the ambition of the school would be to encourage an opportunity of discovering how much of Milton and Shelley and John Donne and Thomas Edison there is in almost everybody if given a fair chance to express themselves.

The deep desire in everyone to find out about things is too little cherished. For most of us, our schooling is in large measure wasted because it came when we were not ripe for it. The N. S. N. S. would try to remind people that the analytical geometry and French grammar we neglected in youth are really thrilling and fascinating, and are an integral part of life. Think what larks a group of grown people could have in studying Chaucer together, and taking up Latin. It is the oldest dream on earth, the vision of an ideal community. To make it really successful it would have to be undertaken not as a grave affair but as a huge junket; and it shouldn't meet too often. I suppose it won't happen; but anyhow some day I shall sit down and write out that Prospectus.

One of the most interesting courses would be devoted to helping Rich People spend their surplus in really imaginative and creative ways. Have you ever thought how much could be accomplished by an Association for the Improvement of the Condition of the Rich?

The N. S. N. S. would be an art school, for investigation of the art of living.

[IR]

CONSIDER THE COMMUTER

WHEN THEY tell us the world is getting worse and worse, and the follies and peevishness of men will soon bring us all to some damnable perdition, we are consoled by contemplating the steadfast virtue of commuters. The planet grows harder and harder to live on, it is true; every new invention makes things more complicated and perplexing. These new automatic telephones, which are said to make the business of getting a number so easy, will mean (we suppose) that we will be called up fifty times a day—instead of (as now) a mere twenty or thirty, while we are swooning and swinking over a sonnet. But more and more people are taking to commuting and we look to that to save things.

Because commuting is a tough and gruelling discipline. It educes all the latent strength and virtue in a man (although it is hard on those at home, for when he wins back at supper time there is left in him very little of what the ladies so quaintly call "soul"). If you study the demeanour of fellow-passengers on the 8:04 and the 5:27 you will see a quiet and well-drilled acceptiveness, a pious non-resistance, which is not unworthy of the antique Chinese sages.

Is there any ritual (we cry, warming to our theme) so apt to imbue the spirit with patience, stolidity, endurance, all the ripe and seasoned qualities of manhood? It is well known that the fiercest and most terrible fighters in the late war were those who had been commuters. It was a Division composed chiefly of commuters that stormed the Hindenburg Stellung and purged the Argonne thickets with flame and steel. Their commanding officers were wont to remark these men's carelessness of life. It seemed as though they hardly heeded whether they got home again or not.

See them as they stand mobbed at the train gate, waiting for admission to the homeward cars. A certain disingenuous casualness appears on those hardened brows; but beneath burn stubborn fires. These are engaged in battle, and they know it—

a battle that never ends. And while a warfare that goes on without truce necessarily develops its own jokes, informalities, callousnesses, disregard of wounds and gruesome sights, yet deep in their souls the units never forget that they are drilled and regimented for struggle. We stood the other evening with a Freeport man in the baggage compartment at the front of a train leaving Brooklyn. We two had gained the bull's-eye window at the nose of the train and sombrely watched the sparkling panorama of lights along the track. Something had gone wrong with the schedule that evening, and the passengers of the 5:27 had been shunted to the 5:30. As fellow mariners will, we discussed famous breakdowns of old and the uncertainties of the commuter's life. "Yes," said our companion, "once you leave home you never know when you'll get back." And he smiled the passive, placable smile of the experienced commuter.

It is this reasonable and moderate temper that makes the commuter the seed wherewith a new generation shall be disseminated. He faces troubles manifold without embittered grumbling. His is a new kind of Puritanism, which endures hardship without dourness. When, on Christmas Eve, the train out of Jamaica was so packed that the aisle was one long mass of unwillingly embraced passengers, and even the car platforms were crowded with shivering wights, and the conductor buffeted his way as best he could over our toes and our parcels of tinsel balls, what was the general cry? Was it a yell against the railroad for not adding an extra brace of cars? No, it was good-natured banter of the perspiring little officer as he struggled to disentangle himself from forests of wedged legs. "You've got a fine, big family in here," they told him: "you ought to be proud of us." And there was a sorrowing Italian who had with him a string of seven children who had tunnelled and burrowed their way down the packed aisle of the smoking car and had got irretrievably scattered. The father was distracted. Here and there, down the length of the car, someone would discover an urchin and hold him up for inspection. "Is this one of them?" he would cry, and Italy would give assent. "Right!" And the children were agglomerated and piled in a heap in the middle of the car until such time as a thinning of the crowd permitted the anxious and blushing sire to reassemble them and reprove their truancy with Adriatic lightnings from his dark glowing eyes.

How pleasing is our commuter's simplicity! A cage of white mice, or a crated goat (such are to be seen now and then on the Jamaica platform) will engage his eye and give him keen amusement. Then there is that game always known (in the smoking car) as "peaknuckle." The sight of four men playing will afford contemplative and apparently intense satisfaction to all near. They will lean diligently over seat-backs to watch every play of the cards. They will stand in the aisle to follow the game, with apparent comprehension. Then there are distinguished figures that move through the observant commuter's peep-show. There is the tall young man with the beaky nose, which (as Herrick said)

> Is the grace
> And proscenium of his face.

He is one of several light-hearted and carefree gentry who always sit together and are full of superb cheer. Those who travel sometimes with twinges of perplexity or skepticism are healed when they see the magnificent assurance of this creature. Every day we hear him making dates for his cronies to meet him at lunch time, and in the evening we see him towering above the throng at the gate. We like his confident air toward life, though he is still a little too jocular to be a typical commuter.

But the commuter, though simple and anxious to be pleased, is shrewdly alert. Every now and then they shuffle the trains at Jamaica just to keep him guessing and sharpen his faculty of judging whether this train goes to Brooklyn or Penn Station. His decisions have to be made rapidly. We are speaking now of Long Island commuters, whom we know best; but commuters are the same wherever you find them. The Jersey commuter has had his own celebrant in Joyce Kilmer, and we hope that he knows Joyce's pleasant essay on the subject which was published in that little book, *The Circus and Other Essays*. But we gainsay the right of Staten Islanders to be classed as commuters. These are a proud and active sort who are really seafarers, not commuters. Fogs and ice floes make them blench a little; but the less romantic troubles of broken brake-shoes leave them unscotched.

Of Long Island commuters there are two classes: those who travel to Penn Station, those who travel to Brooklyn. Let it not be denied, there is a certain air of aristocracy about the Penn Station clique that we cannot waive. Their tastes are more delicate. The train-boy from Penn Station cries aloud "Choice, delicious apples," which seems to us almost an affectation compared to the hoarse yell of our Brooklyn news-agents imploring "Have a comic cartoon book, 'Mutt and Jeff,' 'Bringing Up Father,' choclut-covered cherries!" The club cars all go to Penn Station: there would be a general apoplexy in the lowly terminal at Atlantic Avenue if one of those vehicles were seen there. People are often seen (on the Penn Station branch) who look exactly like the advertisements in *Vanity Fair*. Yet we, for our humility, have treasures of our own, such as the brightly lighted little shops along Atlantic Avenue and a station with the poetic name of Autumn Avenue. The Brooklyn commuter points with pride to his monthly ticket, which is distinguished from that of the Penn Station nobility by a red badge of courage—a bright red stripe. On the Penn Station branch they often punch the tickets with little diamond-shaped holes; but on our line the punch is in the form of a heart.

When the humble commuter who is accustomed to travelling via Brooklyn is diverted from his accustomed orbit, and goes by way of the Pennsylvania Station, what surprising excitements are his. The enormousness of the crowd at Penn Station around 5 P.M. causes him to realize that what he had thought, in his innocent Brooklyn fashion, was a considerable mob, was nothing more than a trifling scuffle. But he notes with pleasure the Penn Station habit of letting people through the gate before the train comes in, so that one may stand in comparative comfort and coolness downstairs on the train platform. Here a vision of luxury greets his eyes that could not possibly be imagined at the Brooklyn terminal—the Lehigh Valley dining car that stands on a neighbouring track, the pink candles lit on the tables, the shining water carafes, the white-coated stewards at attention. At the car's kitchen window lolls a young coloured boy in a chef's hat, surveying the files of proletarian commuters with a glorious calmness of scorn and superiority. His mood of sanguine assurance and self-esteem is so complete, so unruffled, and so composed that we cannot help loving him. Lucky youth, devoid of cares, responsibilities, and chagrins! Does he not belong to the conquering class that has us all under its thumb?

What does it matter that he (probably) knows less about cooking than you or I? He gazes with glorious cheer upon the wretched middle class, and as our train rolls away we see him still gazing across the darkling cellars of the station with that untroubled gleam of condescension, his eyes seeming (as we look back at them) as large and white and unspeculative as billiard balls.

In the eye of one commuter, the 12:50 SATURDAY ONLY is the most exciting train of all. What a gay, heavily-bundled, and loquacious crowd it is that gathers by the gate at the Atlantic Avenue terminal. There is a holiday spirit among the throng, which pants a little after the battle down and up those steps leading from the subway. (What a fine sight, incidentally, is the stag-like stout man who always leaps from the train first and speeds scuddingly along the platform, to reach the stairs before any one else.) Here is the man who always carries a blue cardboard box full of chicks. Their plaintive chirpings sound shrill and disconsolate. There is such a piercing sorrow and perplexity in their persistent query that one knows they have the true souls of minor poets. Here are two cheerful stenographers off to Rockaway for the week-end. They are rather sarcastic about another young woman of their party who always insists on sleeping under sixteen blankets when at the shore.

But the high point of the trip comes when one changes at Jamaica, there boarding the 1:15 for

Salamis. This is the train that on Saturdays takes back the two famous club cars, known to all travellers on the Oyster Bay route. Behind partly drawn blinds the luncheon tables are spread; one gets narrow glimpses of the great ones of the Island at their tiffin. This is a militant moment for the white-jacketed steward of the club car. On Saturdays there are always some strangers, unaccustomed to the ways of this train, who regard the two wagons of luxury as a personal affront. When they find all the seats in the other cars filled they sternly desire to storm the door of the club car, where the proud steward stands on guard. "What's the matter with this car?" they say. "Nothing's the matter with it," he replies. Other more humble commuters stand in the vestibule, enjoying these little arguments. It is always quite delightful to see the indignation of these gallant creatures, their faces seamed with irritation to think that there should be a holy of holies into which they may not tread.

A proud man, and a high-spirited, is the conductor of the 4:27 on weekdays. This train, after leaving Jamaica, does not stop until Salamis is reached. It attains such magnificent speed that it always gets to Salamis a couple of minutes ahead of time. Then stands the conductor on the platform, watch in hand, receiving the plaudits of those who get off. The Salamites have to stand patiently beside the train—it is a level crossing—until it moves on. This is the daily glory of this conductor, as he stands, watch in one hand, the other hand on the signal cord, waiting for Time to catch up with him. "*Some* train," we cry up at him; he tries not to look pleased, but he is a happy man. Then he pulls the cord and glides away.

Among other articulations in the anatomy of commuting, we mention the fact that no good trainman ever speaks of a train *going* or *stopping* anywhere. He says, "This train *makes* Sea Cliff and Glen Cove; it don't make Salamis." To be more purist still, one should refer to the train as "he" (as a kind of extension of the engineer's personality, we suppose). If you want to speak with the tongue of a veteran, you will say, "He makes Sea Cliff and Glen Cove."

The commuter has a chance to observe all manner of types among his brethren. On our line we all know by sight the two fanatical checker players, bent happily over their homemade board all the way to town. At Jamaica they are so absorbed in play that the conductor—this is the conductor who is so nervous about missing a fare and asks everyone three times if his ticket has been punched—has to rout them out to change to the Brooklyn train. "How's the game this morning?" says someone. "Oh, I was just trimming him, but they made us change." However thick the throng, these two always manage to find seats together. They are still hard at it when Atlantic Avenue is reached, furiously playing the last moves as the rest file out.

Then there is the humorous news-agent who takes charge of the smoking car between Jamaica and Oyster Bay. There is some mysterious little game that he conducts with his clients. Very solemnly he passes down the aisle distributing rolled-up strips of paper among the card players. By and by it transpires that some one has won a box of candy. Just how this is done we know not. Speaking of card players, observe the gaze of anguish on the outpost. He dashes ahead, grabs two facing seats and sits in one with a face contorted with anxiety for fear that the others will be too late to join him. As soon as a card game is started there are always a half dozen other men who watch it, following every play with painful scrutiny. It seems that watching other people play cards is the most absorbing amusement known to the commuter.

Then there is the man who carries a heavy bag packed with books. A queer creature, this. Day by day he lugs that bag with him yet spends all his time reading the papers and rarely using the books he carries. His pipe always goes out just as he reaches his station; frantically he tries to fill and light it before the train stops. Sometimes he digs deeply into the bag and brings out a large slab of chocolate, which he eats with an air of being slightly ashamed of himself. The oddities of this person do not amuse us any the less because he happens to be ourself.

So fares the commuter: a figure as international

as the teddy bear. He has his own consolations—of a morning when he climbs briskly upward from his dark tunnel and sees the sunlight upon the spread wings of the Telephone and Telegraph Building's statue, and moves again into the stirring pearl and blue of New York's lucid air. And at night, though drooping a little in the heat and dimness of those Oyster Bay smoking cars, he is dumped down and set free. As he climbs the long hill and tunes his thoughts in order, the sky is a froth of stars.

[PP]

LETTING OUT THE FURNACE

THE PRUDENT COMMUTER (and all commuters are prudent, for the others are soon weeded out by the rigours of that way of life) keeps the furnace going until early May in these latitudes—assuming that there are small children in the house. None of those April hot waves can fool him; he knows that, with cunning management, two or three shovelfuls of coal a day will nurse the fire along, and there it is in case of a sudden chilly squall. But when at last he lets the fire die, and after its six months of constant and honourable service the old boiler grows cold, the kindly glow fades and sinks downward out of sight under a crust of gray clinkers, our friend muses tenderly in his cellar, sitting on a packing case.

He thinks, first, how odd it is that when he said to himself, "We might as well let the fire go out," it kept on sturdily burning, without attention or fuel, for a day and a half; whereas if he had, earlier in the season, neglected it even for a few hours, all would have been cold and silent. He remembers, for instance, the tragic evening with the mercury around zero, when, having (after supper) arranged everything at full blast and all radiators comfortably sizzling, he lay down on his couch to read Leonard Merrick, intending to give all hands a warm house for the night. Very well; but when he woke up around 2 A.M. and heard the tenor winds singing through the woodland, how anxiously he stumbled down the cellar stairs, fearing the worst. His fears were justified. There, on top of the thick bed of silvery ashes, lay the last pallid rose of fire. For as every pyrophil has noted, when the draught is left on, the fire flees upward, leaving its final glow at the top; but when all draughts are shut off, it sinks downward, shyly hiding in the heart of the mass.

So he stood, still drowsily aghast, while Gissing (the synthetic dog) frolicked merrily about his unresponsive shins, deeming this just one more of those surprising entertainments arranged for his delight.

Now, on such an occasion the experienced commuter makes the best of a bad job, knowing there is little to be gained by trying to cherish and succour a feeble remnant of fire. He will manfully jettison the whole business, filling the cellar with the crash of shunting ashes and the clatter of splitting kindling. But this pitiable creature still thought that mayhap he could, by sedulous care and coaxing, revive the dying spark. With such black arts as were available he wrestled with the despondent glim. During this period of guilty and furtive strife he went quietly upstairs, and a voice spoke up from slumber. "Isn't the house very cold?" it said.

"Is it?" said this wretched creature, with great simulation of surprise. "Seems very comfortable to me."

"Well, I think you'd better send up some more heat," said this voice, in the tone of one accustomed to command.

"Right away," said the panic-stricken combustion engineer, and returned to his cellar, wondering whether he was suspected. How is it, he wondered, that ladies know instinctively, even when vested in several layers of blankets, if anything is wrong with the furnace? Another of the mysteries, said he, grimly, to the synthetic dog. By this time he knew full well (it was 3 A.M.) that there was naught for it but to decant the grateful of cinders and set to work on a new fire.

Such memories throng in the mind of the commuter as he surveys the dark form of his furnace, standing cold and dusty in the warm spring weather, and he cleans and drains it for the summer vacation. He remembers the lusty shout of winter winds, the clean and silver nakedness of January weather, the shining glow of the golden coals, the comfortable rustling and chuckle of the boiler when alive with a strong urgency of steam, the soft thud and click of the pipes when the pressure was rising before breakfast. And he meditates that these matters, though often the cause of grumbles at the time, were a part of that satisfying reality that makes life in the outposts a more honest thing than the artificial convenience of great apartment houses. The commuter, no less than the seaman, has fidelities of his own; and faithful, strict obedience to hard necessary formulæ favours the combined humility and self-respect that makes human virtue. The commuter is often a figure both tragic and absurd; but he has a rubric and discipline of his own. And when you see him grotesquely hasting for the 5:27 train, his inner impulse may be no less honourable than that of the ship's officer ascending the bridge for his watch under a dark speckle of open sky.

[PP]

MADONNA OF THE TAXIS

SPEAKING OF COMMUTING, the Long Island Railroad owes us $7, and we are wondering how long it will take us to collect it.

The incident, tragic as it was, will prove a lesson to us never again to be unfaithful to our beloved Brooklyn.

On Wednesday evening we had to decide whether we would take the train for Salamis from Penn. Station or from Brooklyn. We decided we would take it from Penn. Station, because we were without reading matter, and knew that at Penn. Station we could stop in at the bookshop in the Arcade and get something to amuse us en route. All began merrily. We got to the station at 9 o'clock, bought an Everyman edition of Kit Marlowe's plays, and, well supplied with tobacco, we set sail on the 9:10 vehicle. How excellent are the resources of civilization, said we to ourself, as we retraced the sorrows of Dr. Faustus. Here we are, we cried, sitting at ease in a brilliantly lighted smoker reading "Cut is the branch that might have grown full straight," and in fifty minutes we will greet again the shabby but well-loved station at Salamis. We even meditated on writing a little verse in Marlowe's own vein, to be called "The Passionate Long Islander to His Love."

> Come live with me and be my love
> And we will all the pleasures prove
> That Patchogue, Speonk, Hempstead fields,
> Ronkonkoma or Yaphank yields.

At this moment, which was 9:15, and just issuing from the tunnel, the train stopped, all lights went out, and we sat gazing at the dreary dormitory of Pullman cars in Long Island City.

For thirty-six minutes we sat so. Occasionally there would be the sound of a heavy sigh, a long-drawn suspiration of some mentally troubled commuter whose feels (in the language of Opal Whiteley) were not satisfaction feels; but commuters are a tested and toughened lot. The time lagged heavily and darkly by, but there was no shrill outcry, no futile beating of the breast. One shining thought there was to console, and the conductor ratified it (we asked him ourself). "Oh, yes," he said, "the Oyster Bay connection waits for this train at Jamaica." We envisaged the picture of that battered and faithful old Oyster Bay loco, waiting patiently for its lovers along the windy platform, and we were heartened.

But when we got to Jamaica, the old harridan steam train had gone.

Then, indeed, hearts were broken. Then there was scudding to and fro, and voices raised in menace and imprecation. The next train to Oyster Bay, said the officials, leaves at 12:10. The mourners gathered in little groups, drawn by their several affinities. Those who yearned for Garden City formed one posse. Those who yearned for Babylon and Bayshore, another. But, let it proudly be said, the Oyster Bay group were the loudest in outcry, the angriest in mood. We have a pride of our own on the Oyster Bay branch. ("Cut was the branch that might have gone full straight.") In Salamis alone, Gen. Pershing is living there, and Dorothy Gish visits sometimes. Are we to be trifled with? Off went the Oyster Bay contingent, some twenty angry, to see the Station Master. Words were passed, without avail.

We ourself are a realist at such moments. We saw that the Station Master held no balm for the sufferers. We fled from the brutal scene. Downstairs one taxi, the only one, was just embarking a passenger and wheeling off. For an instant (we confess it) our nerve was shaken. We screamed, and there was in that scream the dreadful keening note of a lioness balked of her whelps or a commuter ravished of his train. Ha! the taxi halted. It was, strangely enough, a lady chauffeur, and tender of heart. No man chauffeur would have halted at such a time, but this madonna of taxi drivers had a bosom of pity. Her fare, already in situ, was bound for Garden City. They agreed to take us along, and after Garden City had been made she would steer for Salamis.

O Lady Taxi Driver of Jamaica, a benison befall thee. The wind roared stiffly across the plains, and the small henry made leeway. The small henry scuttled like a dog, half sideways, nosing several points upward into the gale in order to pursue a straight course. The other passenger was plainly a Man of Large Affairs, sunk in a generous melancholy. There was little talk. We sat, or, when the roadway required it, leaped aloft like striking trout. Garden City was duly reached, and then, by and by, the woody glens of Salamis Heights. The fare we paid our saviour was $7. We did not grudge it her. She has a seven-year-old boy, and all day she keeps house, all night she runs her taxi. But, in candour, we think the railroad owes us that $7. It has ever been held a point of honour that the Oyster Bay train shall wait for its children. When there are only two after-dinner trains, that seems not much to ask.

If we had gone from Brooklyn, all would have been well.

[PS]

MIDSUMMER IN SALAMIS

IN MIDSUMMER the morning walk to the station is one long snuff of green and gold. On the winding stony lane through the Estates, before you reach the straight highway to the railroad, it is a continual sharp intake through the nostrils, an attempt to savour and identify the rich, moist smells of early day. That tangle of woodland we would like to call by the good old English word *spinney*, if only to haul in an equally ancient pun. It is in the spinney that you get the top of the morning. Dew is on the darkening blackberries. Little gauzy cobwebs are spread everywhere on grass and bushes, suggesting handkerchiefs dropped by revelling midnight dryads. The little handkerchiefs are all very soppy—do the dryads suffer from hay fever? As you emerge onto the straight station road, it is comforting if you see, not far away, some commuter whose time-sense is reliable trudging not too far ahead. When that long perspective is empty anxiety fills the breast. Across the level Long Island plain come occasional musical whistles from trains on the other line—the Westbury branch. But the practiced commuter knows his own whistle and alarms not at alien shrillings.

In midsummer the subaltern life around us is grown lusty. The spider is in his heyday and cannot be denied. Even indoors he shrewdly penetrates. Looking for a book along the shelves, our eye was caught by the hasty climb of one small spinner, who had been hanging on his airy cord apparently also scanning the titles. To the top of the case he retired, beyond reach. We wish him luck and hope no domestic besom may find him. The young lumpish robins that used to flutter heavily across the road, easily within grasp, fat paunches of feathers upon incapable wings—these are now strong of flight and cat-safe. The young rabbits with whom our woods are crowded no longer stand curiously in the roadway almost until our foot is on them. They too are maturing and have learned wise suspicion. The mole nightly increases his meandering subway, which looks like a zigzagging varicose vein on the surface of the lawn. And Gissing, untaught by menace or thrashing, every night buffets down more of the phlox plants so carefully set out by Titania, in his caperings with a roving Airedale from no one knows where. Only the pond noises seem to have lessened in vitality. The frogs are growing cynical, perhaps. In the sylvester midnight—thanks to Mr. C. E. Montague for that pretty phrase—they utter only an occasional disillusioned twangle, like the pluck of a loose bass string.

But there are signs that the Salamis Estates, so long a rustic Nirvana, are going to fall under the hand of civilization. Which will, one doubts not, have its advantages. It will be helpful to have gas to cook with; and sidewalks are enjoyable for baby carriages and velocipedes. But we shall never forget the happy Salamis Estates as they still are—the lonely roads through virgin woods; the little hidden lakes; the old abandoned orchard buried in overgrowth of vines and forest; solitude and sanctuary. It is our darling old horror of a Salamis railway station that has spared us the evils of "development." The casual passenger looking out on that gruesome pagoda of claret-coloured brick and the huddle of wooden shacks around it, can only think of Salamis as a place damned and forgotten. When some of our neighbours grunt about that station we think inwardly of it with affection. It has spared us much. There are some people, of course, who really like to live in an artificed toy park like Nassau Boulevard or Garden City. We were raised on the books of Mayne Reid and Du Chaillu; we are for the jungle.

Yet we would not admit impediments to progress, if it does not rob our rustic Eden of all its wilderness charm. And anyhow progress is coming willy-nil. Actually, in the past six months, we have seen several houses built on the outskirts of our region. The new Methodist kirk, though apparently halted temporarily while our good dominy raises some more funds, is already shoulder-high. Another church, years ago foundered to the status of a saloon, now does brisking business as garage. The little empty lodge at the entrance to the Estates, where we vote on election days, will some day be a tea-room, we suspect. It is ideal for that purpose, with its big open fireplace. In fact, we have heard influential Salamites say that it could be had almost rent-free by some really refined lady as a pekoe-saloon. Those who move the destinies of the Estates, think that a nice tea-room there would help the tone of the neighbourhood. We pass this information on to ambitious ladies, on condition we are allowed to have three lumps and an extra pat of butter.

It is all very interesting, because we are going to have a unique opportunity to see exactly how civilization works. We have watched new signboards go up at the front and back entrances to the Estates. Not long ago a hundred thousand people might have gone by and never known our little world was there. We study the new board of a Mortgage Company announcing Desirable Plots. Yes, we can see a plot. Civilization is plotting to take us under its wing. We are going to have a good look at this thing they call civilization and see how it goes about it. Five years from now will we be able to see cows being driven home from their daily pasture near our Green Escape? We are not blind to omens. Just as lightning glimmers even through eyelids closed in bed, so behind the leafy screen of our still scatheless sanctum we can see the bright eyes of Real Estate men blazing in the sky. Well . . . there are compensations. Our title is clean and clear, and our second mortgage sticks to us closer than a shin-plaster. Wait till they try to buy us out; we'll get some of our own back.

So we meditate, partly as poet and partly as Man of Affairs, as we walk homeward up the hill. The singing peanut-wagon of George Vlachos, steaming its thin, pensive tune, comes clopping wearily down the road, the white horse shambling a bit after a long day on the highways. FRESH ROSTED PEANUTS, CANDY, ICE CREAM, says the legend. We note the pile of fresh shingles beside the little house going up near the station; we sniff the tang of mortar where our good friend Mr. Corliss will next year be preaching the word of God in his new steeple-house (as George Fox would have called it). We wonder where the Salamis Heights movie will be, when it comes? That, and an occasional street-lamp up in our tangled knolls, will make it easier to keep servants, very likely. And think of having gas to cook with instead of those oil stoves. . . . Yes, perhaps civilization will have merits.

[PS]

EPITAPH FOR ANY NEW YORKER

I, who all my life had hurried,
   Came to Peter's crowded gate;
And, as usual, was worried,
   Fearing that I might be late.
So, when I began to jostle
   (I forgot that I was dead),
Patient smiled the old Apostle:
   "Take your Eternity," he said.

Parsons' Pleasure